The History of Barrel Racing in Professional Rodeo

By Gail Hughbanks Woerner

EAKIN PRESS Fort Worth, Texas
www.EakinPress.com

Copyright © 2024
By Gail Hughbanks Woerner
Published By Eakin Press
An Imprint of Wild Horse Media Group
P.O. Box 331779
Fort Worth, Texas 76163
1-817-344-7036
www.EakinPress.com
ALL RIGHTS RESERVED

Paperback ISBN 978-1-68179-359-7
Hardback ISBN 978-1-68179-360-3
eBook ISBN 978-1-68179-361-0

ALL RIGHTS RESERVED. No part of this book may be reproduced in any form without written permission from the publisher, except for brief passages included in a review appearing in a newspaper or magazine.

Table of Contents

Intro: The History of Barrel Racing..v
Preface viii
Chapter One: The Very First Barrel Races 1
Chapter Two: Circling the Barrels Spreads 5
Chapter Three: All-Girl Rodeos 11
Chapter Four: The Girls Rodeo Association 17
Chapter Five: Barrel Racing Added at RCA Rodeos 22
Chapter Six: GRA All-Girl Rodeos & More 29
Chapter Seven: College Competition Finally Includes Women 38
Chapter Eight: Magazines Help Barrel Racing Spread Even Farther 43
Chapter Nine: Things Aren't What They Appear to Be 48
Chapter Ten: Canadian Barrel Racing 51
Chapter Eleven: States Begin to Form GRA Chapters 57
Chapter Twelve: Barrel Racing at the National Finals Rodeo 66
Chapter Thirteen: Roll Out the Barrels 72
Chapter Fourteen: Barrel Horses: Find — Train — Win 83
Chapter Fifteen: Dirt 94
Chapter Sixteen: Girls Rodeo Assn. Becomes Women's Professional Rodeo Assn. 101
Chapter Seventeen: Equal Monies — Or We Don't Compete! 105
Chapter Eighteen: Barrel Racing Sponsors 111
Chapter Nineteen: The Last Decade of the Twentieth Century 114
Chapter Twenty: Barrel Racing in the Twenty-First Century 119
Chapter Twenty-One: Tragedies — In the Barrel Racing World 129
Chapter Twenty-Two: ProRodeo Hall of Fame Inducts Barrel Racers & Horses 136
Chapter Twenty-Three: Barrel Racing for Fun, Exercise & Peace of Mind ...141
Chapter Twenty-Four: 2018 Wrangler National Finals Rodeo 147
Chapter Twenty-Five: 2019 Wrangler National Finals Rodeo 152
Chapter Twenty-Six: 2020 — A Year Like No Other 158
Chapter Twenty-Seven: 2021 — Rodeo World Improving Slowly From Pandemic 164
Chapter Twenty-Eight: 2022 — The World Of Rodeo Is Back!! Better Than Ever!!.....167
Chapter Twenty-Nine: 2023 — It Keeps Getting More Exciting, Year After Year........170
Some Outstanding Barrel Racing Horses to Remember 175
Some of the Important Women in Barrel Racing 186
Appendix 1: GRA-WPRA World Champion Barrel Racers 216
Appendix 2: Year-End & Finals 218
Appendix 3: Barrel Racing Rookies of the Year 248
Appendix 4: AQHA Horse of the Year 249
Appendix 5: Barrel Racing World Records 250
Appendix 6: *Scoti Flit Bar Rising Star Award* 251
Appendix 7: ProRodeo Hall of Fame Inductee 252
Appendix 8: Additional Barrel Racing Records 254
Appendix 9: College Barrel Racing National Champions 255
Appendix 10: Girls Rodeo Association Founding Members 257
Appendix 11: GRA and WPRA Presidents 258
Endnotes 261
Index 273
Author Bio 288

Intro
The History of Barrel Racing

Women have been competing in rodeo and performing in Wild West shows since the mid-1880s. Buffalo Bill Cody hired Annie Oakley, the best-known woman sharpshooter of the day. But men, producing these events, were always the ones deciding to include women in their programs. The women who chose to compete or perform at that early time became lady bronc riders, relay race riders, Roman riders, trick and fancy riders, trick ropers, and an occasional roper or bulldogger. Certain rodeos held events for women, such as cowgirl bronc riding, cowgirl trick riding, or cowgirl trick roping, plus various races, such as cowgirl Roman riding and cowgirl relay races. Some rodeo producers, men, of course, seemed to strictly forbid women from competing. In the world of roundups, rodeos, frontier days, and anything else they called a cowboy/cowgirl gathering in the late 1800s and early 1900s, events for women were held spasmodically. By the end of the 1920s, however, some rodeos that held women's events started to eliminate the various competitions for women.

It has often been said that when bronc-rider Bonnie McCarroll died at Pendleton, in 1929, a few days after she was bucked off a bronc at the Round-Up — that was what ended the era of women competitions. McCarroll was riding with hobbled stirrups (stirrups tied together under the bronc's belly). The bronc fell on her and because her foot was caught in the hobbled stirrup she was dragged around the arena. She was rushed to the hospital and died a few days later. The Pendleton Round-Up, however, did make a decision to discontinue cowgirl roughstock events after that year, due to McCarroll's tragic death. In 1915 a photograph of McCarroll, getting bucked off a bronc and landing on her neck, upside down with legs flailing in the air, was reprinted in 1929, making people think it was a photograph of the bronc accident that caused her death. The sensational photo, fourteen years after it was taken, spread across the country and more rodeos decided to stop bronc riding for women.

The facts are that few cowgirls ever got killed riding broncs. During 1929 many of the women bronc riders were well known for their abilities atop a bronc, and were aging and beginning to retire from the tough sport. In fact, Bonnie McCarroll had told her husband, that her bronc ride at Pendleton was her last ride, and she would retire from the sport. Some of the other women's events were also cancelled about this same time, such as Roman riding and relay races. It became a time of change in rodeo for cowgirls. Later riding Roman-style often became part of a rodeo performer's act. Competitions for trick riders and trick roping for both men and women were also being phased out as competitions during this same time period. Fortunately, cowboys and cowgirls with these amazing talents were later hired by rodeo producers as performers, not as competitors.

Through the years rodeo has experienced many changes, and those cowgirls that loved the rodeo world and became skilled at their crafts often had to adjust their expertise to fit the rodeo format. In most cases they went from being contestants to paid contract acts. Rodeo changed their competition format from one era to the next to fit the times. But it was decided by men, and the cowgirls never had a say in the decisions that were made.

But cowgirls never gave up! Whether it was a competition, a performance, or an event strictly for cowboys, they continued to do what they did best. There were times women competed against cowboys in a 'cowboy's only event' and were allowed to try their hand at it. But if they ever outdid the men, it was generally not well received.

Pee Wee Burge, a young girl from Switzerland, told of entering a jackpot roping in California, and a man friend offered her a horse she could use when roping. That was until she beat him and the other male competitors. Suddenly the use of her friend's horse was no longer available to her. But she didn't give up, she got her own horse, and continued to rope. But she also became a good trick rider and lady bronc rider and performed at many rodeos until she retired.

It took cowgirls much determination, patience and persistence to stay in the rodeo world but they persevered until they finally got what they deserved — equality.

Preface

Barrel racing is one of the most exciting events in rodeo today and in seconds displays speed, beautiful horses, and handsomely dressed women. It takes a great deal of practice to excel in this event where riders are required to run a clover-leaf pattern around three pre-set barrels and have the option of starting their run on either side of the arena. At most events an electric eye starts and stops the time as they enter and exit the arena. Times can range from thirteen to eighteen seconds, depending on the size of the arena, length of the pattern. That has not always been the case and why it is important to know the history of the event.

I came from the plains area of northeastern Colorado, and when I was young and wanted to compete in events involving horses, there was no barrel racing in my area. This was the late 1940s and early 1950s. Burwell, Neb., started having barrel racing in 1949. Cheyenne Frontier Days didn't hold their first barrel race until 1971. The Logan County Fair & Rodeo held in Sterling, Colo., had barrel racing for the first time in 1958. The National Western Stock Show & Rodeo in Denver held their first barrel race in 1960.

The only event I could enter, as a youngster, was a "fourteen years and under" pleasure class for boys and girls. The judge would ask the competitors to "walk, trot and canter your horse." He might have you turn and go the opposite direction, to make sure your horse had the right lead, and then line up. He might ask you to back your horse, but he might not. The competition was quite elementary, and other than making sure you could get your mount to follow the judge's instructions, the only other requirement was to make sure your horse led with the proper foot. Then the judge picked youngsters for first, second, third and fourth place. Sometimes depending on how many were in the contest they might even have a fifth and sixth place.

I competed against boys and girls of all ages, fourteen years old and younger. Often I competed on horses I had never seen before. You see, I spent a great deal of my youth with my paternal grandpa, Jess Hughbanks, and if we ended up at a horse competition, he would enter me, whether we had a horse there or not.

It didn't matter to me. I had such respect for my grandpa I would ride any horse he told me to ride. I always seemed to be quite compatible with each one. Today I realize, my grandpa had probably questioned the owners of the horses he picked for me to compete on and knew they were well trained and gentle. I am so blessed to have had this upbringing. Life was so simple then.

The relationship between a girl and a horse is hard to define. It can serve in so many ways to fulfill a need. It can be a calming influence to both. Riding alone through the pastures witnessing the actions of the birds and critters around you can be an education in itself. Moving a herd from one pasture to the next is such satisfaction when you and your horse do your part.

I was an only child, living on a ranch with my parents and my paternal grandparents. My horses were my main pals. Even when my grandpa was not available I could be found at the barn or on the back of one of our horses. I rode bareback if I was alone because I wasn't big enough to lift a saddle onto a horse. Bareback was my preferred way to ride anyway after my saddle turned on me and I scraped all the skin off one side of my face. My grandpa would always say, "Anyone can ride a horse. Just put one leg on each side and your mind in the middle."

I regret that barrel racing had not arrived in Logan County, Colo., during my youth. Who knows, I might have excelled at it, or it might have been a fleeting experience for me. So many gals have been challenged by barrel racing and practiced . . . practiced and practiced. A few have gone on to become the best in the world and named world champions. Just a few have even worn the coveted #1 back number at the Professional Rodeo Cowboys Association's National Finals Rodeo. This means they earned more money for the year than any other professional rodeo competitor, man or woman. Wearing the coveted #1 at the PRCA National Finals Rodeo is an amazing accomplishment for a cowgirl! Barrel Racing has long been the only event for cowgirls, versus seven events for cowboys, although breakaway roping is starting to give women a second event in the sport.

Women have been in rodeos, Wild West shows, and all kinds of equine endeavors for well over 100 plus years. Women have been recognized by those producing rodeos as having the abilities to attract numerous spectators with their barrel racing, bronc riding, Roman riding, trick riding, and roping talents. Their creative western wear, often designed and created by themselves, and their curls and make-up have always been a colorful addition next to the clothing worn by cowboys. Many changes and styles have occurred during the past century. Some changes worked while others were tried then discarded. But in the rodeo arena today the barrel racing event is the favorite event for many spectators as well as for the women who compete, and one of the most challenging. Here is their history.

Chapter One
The Very First Barrel Races

Barrel racing, as we know it today, had a beginning far different than what it is now. It didn't begin as a competition, and it wasn't created for speed. It was strictly to parade young ladies representing their communities in front of the rodeo audience in their best western finery. The primary emphasis was placed on beauty, personality, and the clothes they chose to wear. It wasn't only horseback riding attire but fancy formal wear, too. These gowns were selected for the dances held in the evenings. It was also not called barrel racing. Here is how it began . . .

Stamford, Texas, lies in the heart of ranch country. It is north of Abilene, with Lubbock 137 miles to the northwest and Fort Worth 143 miles to the east. Stamford was a small town of 4,095, according to the 1930 census. That year the folks in and around the town decided to hold a gathering they called the Texas Cowboy Reunion, with the purpose being to follow and preserve the traditions of the western ranch country.

They included a rodeo with a special calf roping contest for old-timers. Cowboys who entered this special event for old-timers had to have worked on ranches doing cowboy chores before 1895 and be at least fifty-five-years of age. Ninety-eight cowboys contested in that calf roping event and additional events included wild cow milking, steer riding, and bronc riding. Pioneer cattlemen of the state were honored guests and 335 cowboys who worked on ranches for a minimum of thirty-five years signed up for membership in the Texas Cowboy Reunion Old-Timers Association. In addition to the rodeo, they held a parade with fifty Comanche Indians providing the evening entertainment, followed by an old-fashioned cowboy dance.[1]

The Texas Cowboy Reunion was such a success that the following year, 1931, 198 contestants competed, and cash prizes were awarded. Texas Ranger Tom Hickman was the primary judge and he bragged that the Stamford rodeo outdid other rodeos he had judged in Chicago, New York City, and London.

But the second year, Stamford made a change that would alter rodeo forever. They began inviting sponsors and other chambers of commerce from surrounding towns to designate a young lady, sixteen years or older, to represent the cattlemen in their area and act as their sponsor during the Reunion. The primary purpose for including these young girls was to add a little charm and glamour to this otherwise completely masculine event. It was also important to have young ladies available to dance with the cowboys at the dances scheduled in the evenings. The young ladies (called sponsors) were to ride in the parade, attend the Sponsors Ball held at the country club, participate in dances the next two nights, and be present at a special breakfast at Stamford Inn.[2]

The addition of these young ladies was such a success it was a part of the Texas Cowboy Reunion from then on. Prizes were added in 1932 and given to the two sponsors having the most attractive riding outfits, the best mounts, and showing the best horsemanship. The horsemanship judging included the women

Sponsor girls at the Stamford Cowboy Reunion represented their communities in the 1930s. *Photo Courtesy of Cowboy Country Museum, Stamford, Texas.*

riding a figure-eight pattern around the barrels placed in a row. The prizes awarded were riding boots for first place and silver-mounted spurs for second place. In 1933, three prizes were offered in the "sponsors" contest. The prizes were handmade riding boots and two pairs of silver-mounted spurs. In 1935 they changed the configuration of the barrels from a figure eight to a cloverleaf pattern.

The Texas Cowboy Reunion grew in numbers of spectators and competitors year by year, with more permanent construction of grandstands for spectators and additional competitions outside the rodeo arena. Fiddle contests, chuckwagons, a Quarter Horse show, a cutting horse contest, the Hardin-Simmons Cowboy Band performed, and much more. In 1940 a girls' calf roping was held but was not included the following year. In 1943, due to World War II, no rodeo was held due to most of the men on the committee, and many of the contestants had gone off to war. However, the following year the Reunion returned.

It was not until 1949 that the biggest change in the sponsor contest was made at the Texas Cowboy Reunion. The sponsors were judged strictly on their barrel racing speed for the first time. In 1956 the Reunion changed the spacing of the barrels in the arena, to meet the specifications of the the American Quarter Horse Association. Although by this time, barrel racing was being held at numerous rodeos across the state and beyond. By 1949 at all other rodeos, the shortest time around the barrels was the winning factor and had been for years. Stamford held to their earlier sponsor rules.

Stamford always had a local sponsor, but she never competed. She was the one to set the pattern for the barrel race, rode in the parade and grand entries, and assisted the local hostess who saw that the visiting sponsors felt welcome in Stamford. Other local women also assisted in finding housing, registering the girls, and helping with any of their needs. The book entitled *50 Years of A Living Legend – Texas Cowboy Reunion and Old Timers Association* listed sponsors from nearby communities that were judged as winners beginning in 1932. Miss Curley Seale, of Baird, Texas, was the winner that first year. Some of the winners throughout the years went on to be well-known in barrel racing and later the Girls Rodeo Association, including; Thena Mae Farr, Faye Oglesby, Sherry Price (Combs Johnson), Florence Price (Youree), and Mildred Cotton (Farris).[3]

Sherry Price (Combs Johnson) of Addington, Okla., recalled that in the 1950s, her mother drove her to the sponsor barrel race in Stamford. She was only fourteen, but she had lied about her age because she wanted to compete. She remembered at Stamford the clothing required was as vital as her riding ability. She thought this was highly unusual as she was a young girl more interested in barrel racing. She won the barrel race there in 1953 when she was only fifteen. Her sister Florence Price (Youree) won it in 1954. For years at many of the barrel races in other towns, because the riding of horses around the barrels had begun at the Stamford Cowboy Reunion as part of the sponsor program, these other towns also called their event the sponsor event instead of barrel racing.[4] It took a long time before the word 'sponsor' was dropped from barrel racing competition.

Chapter Two
Circling the Barrel Spreads

After the earlier era of lady bronc riders, Roman riders, relay race riders, and an occasional lady bulldogger (1880-1930), the rodeo world had fewer events for women. Colonel W.T. Johnson, the primary producer of rodeos in the early 1930s, still held events for women, including trick riding, bronc riding, and Roman racing. He realized that the public would come to his rodeos to see a woman engage in dangerous events.

Johnson was a showman and added much to his rodeos. He also originated the horseback quadrille, which was the first event after the grand entry in his rodeos. Couples performed to music, on horseback, putting their mounts through the motions while cantering in the arena, criss-crossing in front of other couples. But when Johnson sold his World Championship Rodeo and left the sport in 1937, these events started to disappear. By 1942 the cowgirl bronc riding had been eliminated, and the cowboy and cowgirl trick riding had become an exhibition, not a competition.

The 1930s changed significantly for women in rodeo. The introduction of the sponsor program in rodeo at Stamford definitely promoted women for their beauty, femininity, and choice of exquisite clothing, formally and on horseback. This is not to say those ranch gals that worked alongside cowboys in ranch work changed. Many of the young women from the country still maintained their 'tom-boy' actions and their attitude that they could do anything a cowboy could do. But regardless of the ranch-raised women's opinions many of the earlier dangerous competitions for women began to be phased out at most rodeos.

The first barrel racing competitions spread in open, or amateur, rodeos across the state of Texas, and beyond, by the mid-thirties. But the competitions from rodeo to rodeo varied in how it was presented, the rules that were used, and how winners were compensated. Speed with which a person rode their mount around the barrels, however, was the only way to win a barrel race. Some rodeos used a straight line of two or three barrels (sometimes called a figure eight) while other rodeos used the cloverleaf pattern. Some rodeos paid off with money, but more often it was with feminine gifts, such as nylons, make-up boxes, or beauty and hair products.

Billie Hinson McBride, a youngster in that era, recalled in addition to barrel racing there were also girls' flag race events at some rodeos. A woman raced her horse from one end of the arena to the other end, picked up a small flag in a barrel, and raced back to the other end of the arena with it. McBride said the rodeo at Coleman, Texas, gave prizes to the winners of the flag race which were quite nice. They included a saddle, boots, a watch, bridle, and always some money.

"I won twice at Coleman and got a watch each time. One time I got second and was awarded a pair of boots," McBride recalled.[1]

The 1930s were unusual years in that many things happened that were 'new' to those living in that time. The Depression took a tremendous toll on many. In some ways rural life didn't change as much as it did for those living in urban areas. But Mother Nature had something to do with weather changes such as the Dust Bowl that hit mid-America, during the Depression. It ravaged the land blowing the top soil to who knows where, and did change the rural areas of Colorado, Kansas, Oklahoma, Texas and New Mexico.

Farming was greatly diminished in those areas. It is said that too many people turned pasture land into fields so they could grow wheat, which was selling at a great price, for the times. When the Dust Bowl arrived it caused the top soil to blow away when the winds came and no crops were able to be grown. At the same time, many of the workers in factories throughout the country began forming organizations they called unions in an attempt to improve wages for their skills. Also the rumblings of the upcoming war in Europe were being heard throughout the

United States.

In the midst of the 1930s the rodeo cowboys that had been complaining for more than twenty years about the small amount of prize money they won at rodeos were no further ahead in their attempt to raise prize money than they were twenty years before. Competitors were also critical of some of the judges that were picked to decide who the winners would be. The cowboys had absolutely no say in the rules, money or judging of rodeos.

After years of trying to convince the rodeo committees and producers that it was unfair to the competitor not to include the cowboys' entry fees in the prize money and nothing had changed. Prize money was so meager at times they could hardly afford to get down the road to the next rodeo even if they did win some at the previous rodeo. Many threats had been made, but to no avail.

However, in 1935 when the cowboys and cowgirls threatened they would not participate in the annual parade that kicked off the Fort Worth Stock Show and Rodeo, unless their entry fees were added to the prize money, they finally got some attention.

The officials responded, "Absolutely not, we can not do that." But the cowboys and cowgirls held tight to their threat. Forty-five minutes after the parade was supposed to start and the streets lined with spectators, and of course, lots of children waiting for the annual parade, the officials finally gave in. They added the exact amount of the cowboys' and cowgirls' entry fees to the purse, $4,030. Once that had been confirmed the contestants mounted their horses, rode in the parade, competed in the rodeo and it all went off without a hitch.[2]

Throughout the rest of 1935 and 1936 the rodeo cowboys and cowgirls discussed what they should do to get all rodeos to include entry fees. They knew they couldn't challenge each rodeo they went to that they wouldn't compete, as they did in Fort Worth. With many secret hours of planning, especially during the annual Madison Square Garden rodeo in October 1936, they finalized what they had to do.

Colonel W.T. Johnson, of San Antonio, Texas, owned World Championship Rodeo, and was the biggest rodeo producer in the country. He put on the largest and best rodeos, including the Madison Square Garden rodeo in New York City, and the Boston Garden rodeo which followed the New York event. But, he would never include the entry fees in the purse, although the cowboys had begged him for years.

The cowboys secretly prepared a petition and had sixty-one signatures of the best cowboys in the business, indicating if Colonel Johnson did not include their entry fees in the purse, at the Boston Garden rodeo, they would not compete. The cowboys had argued with Johnson for years about adding their entry fees to the purse, but he totally ignored their requests. He thought that rodeo cowboys would continue to compete even if he didn't add their entry fees to the purse. Regardless, it wasn't fair to the cowboys.

The petition was presented to Colonel Johnson the afternoon before the first performance at Boston Garden. He looked at it, refused to agree to the requests, and walked away. The cowboys also left Boston Garden after they presented the petition.

Secretly, tickets for that night's performance had been bought for all the petition-signers. The Colonel, meanwhile, tried rustling up anyone he could find to take the cowboys' places in the competition. Some were grooms that merely 'mucked' the stalls. Others were very amateurish and had no cowboy experience. No broncs were ridden, and no calves roped during the first performance. The cowboys sat together in the grandstands, cat-calling and booing the poor talent giving their best effort in the arena. Before long, the rest of the audience began to join in the booing, unhappy with the lack of ability being displayed.

Finally, the manager of Boston Garden told Colonel Johnson if he didn't accept the cowboys request to include entry fees, Johnson would never put on another rodeo in the Garden. Reluctantly, Johnson stopped the rodeo, spectators got their money back, and the actual first performance was held the following night. Just as happened in Fort Worth, the next night cowboys all mounted up, and the rodeo went off without a hitch.

The cowboys realized by this time they couldn't protest and

get a petition signed at every rodeo they entered. They needed more strength. On November 6, just a few days after their protest, the cowboys formed the very first cowboy-run organization for rodeo called the Cowboys' Turtle Association (CTA). Once those cowboys formed the 'Turtle' organization they knew rodeos would improve for the contestants. The main thrust of the Turtles was to insist that entry fees be added to the prize money, better-qualified judges be used, and at least $100 prize money for each event. Soon it became a reality. However, in the beginning women were not allowed to join the Cowboys' Turtle Association.[3]

The ruling for women to join the CTA was changed in 1938 on March 16 after a meeting with Peggy Long, representing the cowgirl bronc riders, at the Fort Worth rodeo. The cowgirls won their demands and Peggy Long signed for the cowgirl bronc riders. This commitment also included cowgirls that were trick riders, trick ropers, as well as other performers, such as the quadrille riders. The Turtles realized that cowgirls in rodeo were also important and necessary for a good, well-rounded event.[4]

Colonel Johnson sold his World Championship Rodeo as well as his stock, parade horses and tack the following year. He honored all his upcoming contracts, but by 1937 it was sold. His right-hand man, Everett Colborn, continued to be the ramrod of the World Championship Rodeo for the new owners. By 1939 the Madison Square Garden Rodeo still held the horseback quadrille, cowgirls' bronc riding contest, and the cowboys' and cowgirls' trick and fancy riding exhibitions. But something new was added that year. Taken from the 1939 Madison Square Garden Rodeo program;

> *From Texas ranch society eight pretty girls, daughters of wealthy cattle Barons are attending as 'Sponsor Girls' who represent their various local Texas districts in the big rodeos where they compete against one another in horsemanship, but never appear in the regular prize money rodeo contests with the older cowboy and cowgirl competitors. These youthful beautifies are called 'Sponsor Girls' because they are sponsored socially and otherwise by the localities they represent. The eight Sponsor Girls are; Miss Sydna Yokley*

from Canadian; Miss Mary Nell Edwards and Miss Anna Belle Edwards from Big Spring; Miss Elizabeth Miller at Fluvanna; Miss Walter Fay Cowden from Midland; Miss Fern Sawyer of Brownfield; Miss Peggy Minnick of Crowell, and Miss Fay Marburger of Abilene."[5]

Much emphasis in the program was put on their family prominence and their ranching status. Event No. 6 in the 1939 program was 'Exhibition of Calf Roping by Sydna Yokley, Canadian, Texas.' Event No. 12 was 'Exhibition of Horsemanship by the Texas Ranch 'Sponsor Girls.' The girls' participation consisted of skilled horsemanship and point riding each night and at matinees each Saturday and Sunday. They rode around obstacles, mounted and dismounted and put their horses through various paces. Prizes were fancy saddles. Winners were selected on a basis of 25% for personal appearance, 25% for the appearance of their mounts and 50% for horsemanship."[6]

The following year at the Madison Square Garden Rodeo six young ladies were invited but their title changed to "Ranch Girls." They were from six different locales in five states, Oregon, Arizona, Texas, New Mexico, and northern and southern California. Instead of the competition held the year before they were to ride into the arena among a herd of Texas Longhorns and six of the steers had the color assigned to each girl, and she had to cut that steer out of the herd and drive it from the ring as quick as possible. It was also mentioned in the program that each would receive trophies and there is a special prize for fastest time in the contest. Event No. 9 in the 1940 Madison Square Garden Rodeo Program was 'Home on the Range' Starring Gene Autry with the Ranch Girls.'[7]

By 1943 The Rodeo Ranch Girls were invited to attend the Madison Square Garden Rodeo in New York to provide beauty, glamour and experienced horsemanship, but there was no competition mentioned. They attended and were expected to promote the rodeo at various places chosen for publicity purposes in New York City.[8]

Chapter Three
All-Girl Rodeos
When World War II started, eligible men hurried off to war in the early 1940s. Some locales halted their annual rodeos due to the lack of cowboys and not enough men to form a rodeo committee. A flurry of all-girl rodeos cropped up during this time. Several in Texas were staged to entertain the troops at nearby bases and the women were able to continue to compete.[1]

One of the first all-girl rodeos was organized by Fay Kirkwood, a Fort Worth horsewoman and society figure who earlier had traveled around the state to help promote the Fort Worth Livestock Show and Rodeo. She met Tad Lucas on a publicity trip and they became friends.

Bonham, Texas, was the site for Kirkwood's first all-girl rodeo, June 26 to 29, 1942. Although Kirkwood organized, she realized her main abilities were in promoting and getting publicity for the rodeo. She hired Fred Alvord, long-time rodeo man, to handle the production work. Pete and Alice Adams served as announcer and arena secretary.

Many of the veteran cowgirls that had been in rodeo for some time attended including Tad Lucas, Vaughn Krieg, Alice Adams, Vivian White and Claire Thompson. The women roped calves, rode broncs and even bulldogged. Sponsor contests (barrel races) were held for the local amateur cowgirls.

Kirkwood's rodeo was a major success with huge crowds attending and the event received a great deal of positive coverage. But some of the area women came expecting to be able to compete against the 'seasoned' contestants such as Tad Lucas and Vaughn Kreig. When they discovered these contests were closed to them they were extremely disappointed. They didn't hesitate to express

Faye Kirkwood produced one of the first all-girl rodeos. *Photo courtesy of Dr. Charles "Bud" Townsend.*

their disappointment to Kirkwood, after the rodeo.[2]

Kirkwood changed her format for the next all-girl rodeo, which was held in Wichita Falls, Texas, July 31 to August 2. The rodeo had more contests and the professional events were open to any who wished to compete. There were twenty events on the program and the sponsor girls had the following events: No. 7 Review and Introduction of Sponsor Girls; No. 9 Sponsor Girls Musical Chair Race; No. 13 Sponsor Girls Flag Race; No. 17 Sponsor Girls Reining Contest. There was no barrel race listed.[3]

Another former Madison Square Garden bronc riding champion, Vaughn Krieg and her husband, Lynn Huskey, built an arena on their ranch in Oklahoma and held rodeos there starting in 1937 called the Flying V Rodeos and plenty of cowboys came to compete.

Six years later, in 1942 Vaughn put together Vaughn Krieg's Flying V All Cow-Girl Rodeo Company. All the rodeos had patriotic themes because it was her plan to entertain at military bases. Her first rodeo opened at Paris, Texas, in September. She featured six events for professional cowgirls, three contract acts, and a sponsor contest. The cowgirls competed in calf roping, bronc riding, bulldogging, a cutting contest, steer riding and wild cow milking. Her event got attention, but did not get as much coverage as Kirkwood did for her earlier all-girl rodeos.

It is not known if Vaughn had a second rodeo, but likely she did not. During these days the increased rationing of tires and gasoline slowed any traveling down and most small rodeos were also cancelled due to World War II.[4]

All-girl rodeos then disappeared for a time. The war and it's ravaging of so much of Europe's countryside was the main topic and so was the concern for the men that had gone to fight in the war. Gene Autry also bought into Colonel Johnson's World Championship Rodeo and this created another major change concerning the role women played in rodeo.

Autry had his own rodeo company earlier and produced rodeos mostly held in indoor arenas in cities east of the Mississippi River. Autry's position on women in rodeo was quite different than many of the other rodeo producers. He wanted women to use their beauty and dress in outstanding western clothing. He did not want them to participate in any male-oriented events such as bronc riding, bulldogging and such.

However, that wasn't the opinion of all rodeos being held. The West of the Pecos Rodeo committee decided to 'pretty-up' their rodeo in 1945 and voted to invite 'lady sponsors' to compete for prizes. It was reported they would be judged on their horsemanship abilities but they were informed they were expected to wear 'flashy western wear.'

The girls went all out with eighteen invited girls entered in the event. Lillian Cowan was hostess to the visiting girls, as well as being a competing contestant. Cowan competed through 1954 in the barrel racing contest at the Pecos rodeo. Jo Ramsey (later marrying Tater Decker) came the longest distance — from McAlester, Oklahoma. Two girls came from Hobbs and Lovington, N. Mex., and the rest were from various Texas towns. Margaret Montgomery from Sheffield won the two day contest.[5]

The sponsor event was a major hit in Pecos, and was repeated in 1946. It was still by invitation only and prizes ranged from a custom-made saddle to nylon stockings. In 1947 the West of the Pecos Rodeo barrel race was changed and was open to anyone wanting to enter. Prizes were awarded and three barrels were placed twenty steps apart in a cloverleaf pattern. Blanche Altizer, Snookie Griffith and Margaret Owens were in charge of the correct placement of barrels.[6] The event was still called 'Sponsor Contest' and the winners were: Powers, Greene and McGilvary (no first names were given in the 50th Anniversary West of the Pecos Rodeo program).[7]

In the Teague, Texas, newspaper headline was "Teague Rodeo Is Grand Success." This was held on July 4, 1947. In addition to the regular events such as bareback bronc riding, calf roping, bull dogging, bull riding and wild cow milking that listed their winners was written;

> *Near the end of the performance was the ladies barrel race, with dainty little eleven year old, Barbara Jo McSpadden, of Houston, riding like a veteran and placing in the finals." Winners in the barrel races were: First Night: - Nelda Wills (Patton), First Overall: Sue Williams, Corsicana, Second – Nelda Wills (Patton), Teague; Third – Rita Jo Ward, Coolidge, Fourth – Barbara Jo McSpadden, Houston.*

In a letter to the author in April 2016, Nelda Patton said "When I was at Teague in '47 we ran straight barrels."[8]

Frances Crane Smith wrote, in part, about her life, "Started running barrels long before the cloverleaf was ever thought of. It was three barrels in a row, you made two 360 degree turns and one 180 degree turn and straight back to the finish line and you never heard of buying a barrel horse, you made one out of whatever you had. "[9]

Dr. Charles "Bud" Townsend became a college history professor, but also spent every summer announcing rodeos for a number of rodeo producers remembered his first barrel race: "It was in the late 1940s but it wasn't a cloverleaf, it was straight-away."

He also could recall that his home community of Nocona, Texas, got one of the local young ladies prepared to go to a similar event like Stamford, in Midland, Texas. The girls were chosen more for beauty, and the clothes they wore, than their horsemanship.[10]

Barbara Smith remembered seeing her very first barrel race in Ponder, Texas, in 1950, and it was also straight barrels.[11] This was still a time that the producers or rodeo committees were not all committed to using cloverleaf barrel racing. Some places still preferred putting the barrels in a straight row.

Wilma Standard, a horsewoman, was co-producer of several all-girl rodeos held in southern California starting in 1947. Standard entered cowgirl calf roping contests in her area of California and chalked up sixteen wins. She was quite versatile in her abilities and worked for a stock contractor, but in her spare-time made colorful cowboy shirts for well-known cowboys, such as Casey Tibbs, of that era.

The first all-girl rodeo was held on the Sawtelle Government Hospital grounds and put on as entertainment for hospitalized veterans. The boys in the hospital practically tore down the stands in enthusiasm over the cowgirls competing in the arena. Unfortunately her plan to take these all-girl rodeos to other veteran hospitals was cut short when her financial backers failed to provide her with the funds they had promised.[12]

Nancy Binford and Thena Mae Farr, were both West Texas ranch-raised women who were gifted athletes and had won many sponsor contests (barrel racing), as well as other rodeo competitions. They often talked of helping women have more competitive events in traditional rodeo contests such as roping and roughstock, as well as barrel racing. After talking about it for several years they decided to produce their own all-girl rodeo.

Their rodeo was held in Amarillo, Texas, September 23 through the 26, 1947. The girls had much success promoting their Tri-State All-Girl Rodeo and had seventy-five contestants to enter. They boasted $1,260 in prizes and mount money, with entry fees ranging from $5 to $15. The all-around champion was given a horse trailer. The contests were; bareback bronc riding, calf roping, barrel racing, cutting contest and team tying. Mount money was paid for saddle bronc riders and steer riders, and no entry fees were charged.

Dude Barton, from Matador, Texas, won the barrel racing, which was still being called the 'sponsor contest.' Dude, a very competent cowgirl also won the calf roping. Fern Sawyer, from New Mexico, won the all-around title. Sawyer won the team tying, second in the cutting contest, third in both calf roping and the 'sponsor contest.'[13]

The sponsor contest that originated at the Stamford, Texas, Cowboy Reunion was to add beauty and femininity to the event. Girls from prominent ranches were chosen to attend, but their horsemanship and athletic ability was not high in qualifications. Some of the young ladies did have it all, but the Stamford Reunion did not care as much about their expertise in maneuvering their steed around the barrels at breakneck speed. When speed became important, it happened at other rodeos around Texas and beyond.

Other rodeos changed the rules and required the shortest time around the three barrels was the winner. The original name, sponsor, lasted as long as twenty years after it began in Stamford, and at some other rodeos, too. Although the need for speed changed the original contest, some places didn't change the name from sponsor event to barrel racing until much later.[14]

Chapter Four
The Girls Rodeo Association

The Amarillo Tri-State All Girl Rodeo was determined to be such a success the same group of women made plans to form a permanent organization of rodeo cowgirls to be sure future rodeos would be held for them. On February 28, 1948, thirty-eight women gathered at the San Angelus Hotel in San Angelo, Texas, and formed The Girls Rodeo Association (GRA). *Please note: this was the first women's organization created soley for women, by women.*[1]

Margaret Owens Montgomery was elected president; Dude Barton, vice president; and Mrs. Sid Pearson, secretary. The first board of directors included; Dixie Reger, Jackie Worthington, Blanche Altizer, and Vivian White.[2]

That first year the board members actively met with rodeo committees and producers, persuading them to include women's events using GRA rules. They were very successful, and although the committees could choose from various events for girls, barrel racing was the most often chosen. West of the Pecos Rodeo had previously been holding barrel racing and giving gift items to the winners. The GRA directors requested Pecos pay money instead of gifts for prizes. They complied with $100 in prize money to be added to the cowgirls' entry fees, and four places would be paid.

The first GRA book of articles of association, by-laws, and rules was 1949.

The officers were: Margaret Montgomery, Ozona, Texas, president; Dixie Lee Reger, Woodward, Okla., vice president; Mrs. Katherine Pearson, Bray, Texas, secretary-treasurer; Sug Owens, Big Lake, Texas, publicity agent.

Directors were: Jackie Worthington, Jacksboro, Texas, all riding events; Nancy Binford, Wildorado, Texas; all roping events; Fern Sawyer, Crossroads, N.M., cutting horses; Janette Campbell, Claude, Texas, sponsor events (barrel racing); Tad Lucas, Fort

Worth, Texas, contract performers.

The GRA book was very thorough and included, in addition to the above-mentioned articles of association, by-laws, and rules and officers and directors; it defined; penalties for infraction of rules, policy, the rules, and general rules, GRA point awards, duties of the representatives; and rules for each event.

Flag and Barrel Race Rules for Rodeo Producers to Observe.

1. It is suggested that the calf roping score line be used as a starting and finish line for the girl's flag and barrel races. If this is impossible because of arena conditions, the starting and finish line must be marked with ropes buried in the ground. The horse's nose will be flagged as he passes between these ropes.

2. All barrels and flag stands must be twenty yards or farther apart. Nothing under twenty yards. The arena conditions will enable you to decide the distance over twenty yards that you wish to place the flag stands or barrels.

3. The following method of marking the flag stands and the barrels has proved satisfactory to all concerned:

Take a three-foot piece of one-inch rope and tie several large knots to the end of it. Dig a hole approximately one-and-one-half feet deep, depending on the ground that you are working on. Place the end of the rope that has the knot in it in the hole. Tamp the dirt in securely around it, leaving about one foot of rope out of the ground. If desired a one-pound coffee can may be cemented to the end of the rope instead of the knot being tied in it. This will not leave a soft place in the arena nor will the stock trip over the ropes. The above measurments are approximate.

One of these ropes should be buried at the location of each flag stand or barrel. By using this method the flag stand or barrels will be in the same place during the entire show.

The official rodeo secretary will take the entry fees and handle the pay-off for the girls events.

(Next came a drawing for flag race rules which will not be displayed, and rules for two stand flag race)

Barrel Race Rules
Straight Barrel Race

May be run to left or right of first barrel.

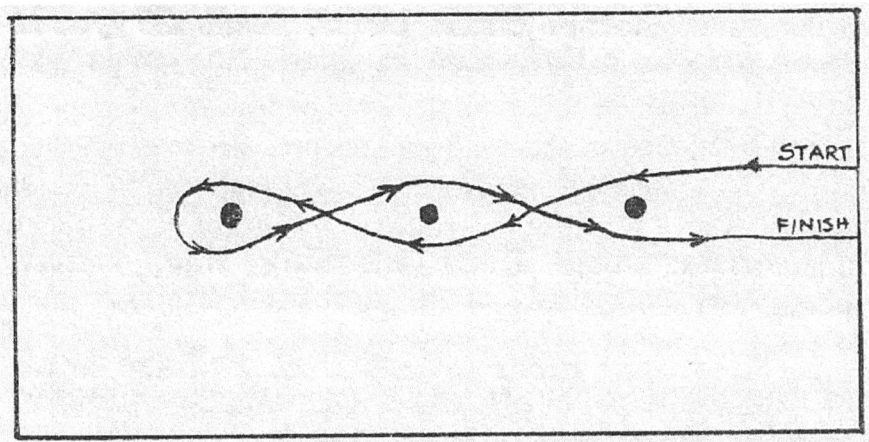

Clover Leaf Barrel Race

May go to either right or left barrel first but must make two left turns and one right turn or two right turns and

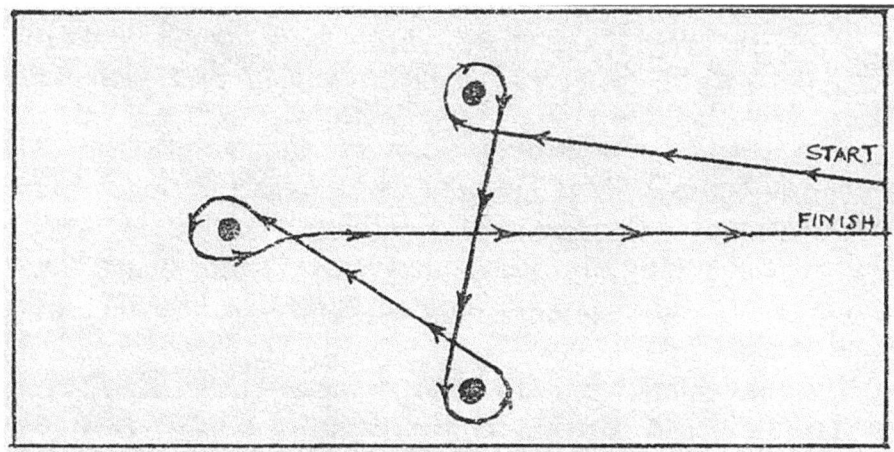

one left turn.

1. Any type barrel race.
2. Knocking over barrel, or not following the pattern set by the rodeo, disqualifies contestants for that go-round and for finals.
3. The starting line and barrels must be marked permanently for entire show.
4. First barrel must be at least 20 yards from starting line, and at least 20 yards between barrels.[3]

The Girls Rodeo Association rules stated each dollar won in a sanctioned rodeo event was a point for the contestant. At the end of the year, each contestant with the most points in each event was the champion for that year. If GRA members were competing in GRA-sanctioned events held in Rodeo Cowboys Association (RCA) rodeos, the rules required the cowgirls to ride in parades and always be dressed in colorful cowgirl attire. RCA also had a strict dress code which required cowboys to wear jeans, boots, hats, and long-sleeved cowboy shirts in the arena and in publicity and program photos.[4]

The October 4 through 7, 1948 Tri-State All-Girl Rodeo sponsored by Tri-State Fair, Amarillo, Texas, had four performances. The total purse was $2,500 plus $10 entry fees for each event. There were seven events, plus the mad scramble ($80 in prizes). The events receiving prize money were bareback bronc riding, calf roping, sponsor contest (barrel racing), cutting horse contest, ribbon roping, bull riding, and saddle bronc riding. All the events had a purse of $250 plus entry fees, except the saddle bronc riding, which paid mount money. Entries closed on October 3 at 9 p.m.[5]

The first Girls Rodeo Association world champions in 1948 were: all-around – Margaret Owens; bareback riding – Jackie Worthington; bull riding – Jackie Worthington; calf roping – Betty Dusek; team roping – Blanche Altizer Smith; barrel racing – Margaret Owens; cutting horse – Margaret Owens; and ribbon roping – Judy Hays.[6]

During the first few years of GRA, they adjusted their events somewhat. In 1949 ribbon roping and cutting horse events were not listed, but saddle bronc riding was added to events receiving prize money. However, in 1950 the two events eliminated from the year before were back on, and the saddle bronc event was absent. New organizations and members often need to adjust their basics to meet the members' needs. A trial and error time is important to determine what the members want to compete in or what needs to be eliminated. Also, do the rules fit the event?[7]

In the first year of the GRA, 1948, there were seventy-four members, and they held sixty events across the country. Two years later, in 1950, they boasted one hundred members.[8]

Chapter Five
Barrel Racing Added at RCA Rodeos

Burwell, Neb., an early rodeo town, held a one-day rodeo in 1921. It grew quickly; years later, that rodeo was called *Nebraska's Big Rodeo*, and later, it was designated *The Outdoor Rodeo Capital of Nebraska*.

Barrel racing was first included in 1949. It was the only event in which women competed for prize money. Other events for men by that time had two go-rounds as it became a four-day rodeo. The barrel racing, however, was four go-rounds so that each competitor could compete for all four days of the rodeo.

Amy McGilvray won with a score of 78.7 seconds (in four rounds). Jeanelle McGilvray was second; third was Mrs. Ted Powers, and fourth was June Probst. The fastest time was a 19.4-second run and was made by both of the McGilvray girls.

The following year Mrs. I.W. Young won the barrel race. However, the next year, 1951, the barrel race was replaced by the ladies flag race. But in 1952, barrel racing was back and continued from then on. LaTonne Sewalt won the average in barrel racing at Burwell in 1952, '53, '54, '56 & '57.[1]

Sidney, Iowa, had their first rodeo in 1923 and was sponsored by the American Legion. Their first GRA cloverleaf barrel race was held in 1949.[2]

The GRA world champion barrel racer in 1949 was Amy McGilvray, and LaTonne Sewalt won it in 1950 when she was only eleven-years-old.[3] LaTonne won it again in 1954.

In January 1950, a small magazine entitled *Powder Puffs & Spurs* was launched with James Cathey, who created it and was the editor. Cathey was a photographer that took photographs at various rodeos in and around Fort Worth, his home. But he eventually committed to being the official photographer at their all-girl rodeo in Fort Smith, Ark., and their first GRA National

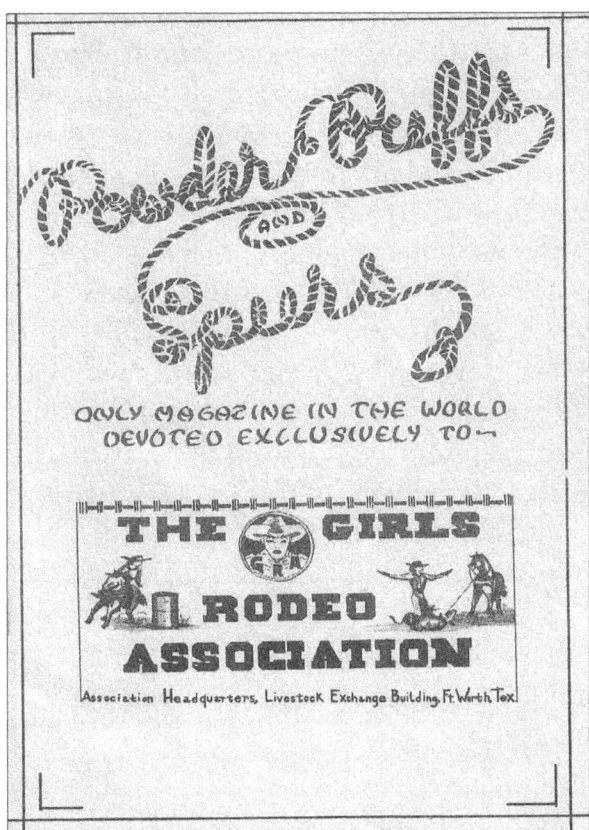
Powder Puffs and Spurs was the first print publication devoted entirely to women's rodeo.

Finals rodeo in 1949.

Cathey was impressed with their determination to grow the organization. He worked along with the board and officers of GRA to promote it. Eventually, he was asked by GRA to be their publicity director. *Powder Puff & Spurs* was the only magazine exclusively for the GRA. The February 1950 issue held the results of the Houston Rodeo barrel racing. LaTonne Sewalt was the winner and celebrated her eleventh birthday during the rodeo. She took the lead in the sponsor standings in six trips around the cloverleaf on her bay pony. Houston was the first time a barrel race competition had been held in an indoor arena.[4]

In 1950 Frances Crane, a barrel racer, married Dude Smith, a rough stock cowboy. She made only amateur rodeos until she married. Once she held a GRA card, she also had an RCA card because she timed and kept books, making her eligible to work RCA rodeos.

Dude worked four events in rodeo, and Frances barrel raced. She joined both organizations in 1967 and went to rodeos in the summer. Because she had two boys in school, she was unable to rodeo much when school was in session. However, she was in the top-fifteen and qualified for the RCA National Finals in her rookie year. She placed in five of the nine performances and finished eighth but won the average with 155.0 in nine go-rounds. She got $745 at the finals and made $3,477 for the year. She also went to the National Finals in 1969, finishing ninth.[5]

Other 1950 GRA sanctioned rodeos were listed in the *Powder Puff and Spurs* magazine: Lake Charles, LA., Feb. 24-26, with a purse of $120 plus entry fees; Baton Rouge, LA., March 4-10, $700 purse plus $20 entry fee; Fort Stockton, TX, May 12-14, an All Girl Rodeo, each event purse $250 plus entry fees; Pecos, TX., July 1-4, $300 with $20 entry fee; Burwell, NE., Aug. 9 – 12, with $700 prize money with $20 entry fee; Sidney, IA., on August 15-19, $250 prize money with $20 entry fee; Abilene, KS., Aug 22-25, with $250 purse and $15 entry fee; and Woodward, OK., Sept. 1-4, flag and barrel races, $400 purse with $20 entry fee.

Powder Puff & Spurs' advice for competitors was given in that same issue:

> 1. Be sure to thank their sponsors when winning prizes.
> 2. Be aware of their appearance and behavior in public. Colorful clothes were suggested.
> 3. Smoking and drinking were considered taboo.[6]

The March issue added an All-Girl Rodeo at Belton, and cloverleaf barrel racing at Burnet, Bay City, San Saba, Junction, and Kerrville, all Texas towns, April through July. The GRA members were hustling rodeos and totally committed to their new organization.[7]

Publicity agent for GRA, Margaret Montgomery, had a statement in the April issue of *Powder Puffs & Spurs*;

> *While I was in Colorado in January, I did a little inquiring concerning the GRA. As Director of Publicity, I considered it pretty important that I find out why there wasn't as much activity on the part of girls away from Oklahoma, Texas, and New Mexico. Conversations proved that many from the northern, Northwestern, and west coast areas had no idea what a barrel race was, especially how it was carried on by the GRA. That's all right because very few people in*

the southwest know about steer decorating, either. But, the answer to the question of why there aren't enough girls who are interested in girl events. The conclusion was that there were enough girls, but no unified effort was made to have a smooth running contest event. Also, few girls could own and maintain a good running or roping horse without a chance to contest him.[8]

Jerry Armstrong wrote a column in Western Horseman called 'Picked Up In The Rodeo Arena.' In the August 1950 issue, in part, he wrote;

One long-ago night (25 years ago) in the Salinas, CA, rodeo headquarters Joe Cassidy, a roper and old outlaw, brought up the subject of all-girl rodeos. He had the revolutionary idea of producing such shows. Everyone in the room guffawed loudly over his crazy scheme. But one individual said to him, "Shush up if you or anyone else ever produces all-girl rodeos, Salinas and half of the shows in the country will fold up." - - - - Some 25 years later, all-girl rodeos are a reality – heretofore, GRA contests have been held mainly in Texas, but they are now branching out to other Western states and, in time, will be seen east of the Mississippi. Many western impresarios are now including an event or two for the girls in their programs. For example, the Pikes Peak or Bust Rodeo at Colorado Springs."[9]

Armstrong went on to tell about the Coleman, Texas, May all-girl rodeo that had the largest crowd to yet witness an all-girl rodeo for this two-day three performance events. Dub Spence, Triangle Bell rodeo ranch, Belton, Texas, furnished the stock. Tad Lucas and Dixie Reger clowned the show. In the fast barrel racing contest, Margaret Montgomery was the winner."[10]

Some of the rodeos where GRA barrel races were included:

Killeen, Texas, winner Wanda Harper, $32.00 and a silver buckle, Donna Faye Hinson was second, Fannie Mae Cox was third, and Dorothy Epperson was fourth.

Fort Stockton, Texas, LaTonne Sewalt won first and received

$82.50, Amy McGilvray second, Margaret Montgomery third and Janelle McGilvray fourth.[11]

Coleman, Texas, winner Margaret Montgomery $69.00, Amy McGilvray second, Janelle McGilvray & Jackie Worthington tied for fourth.

Carrollton, Texas, Yvonne Lewis won first & received $154.00, Jackie Worthington and Wynona Barnett tied for second & third and tied for fourth, fifth, & sixth were Beulah Brown, Wanda Harper, Alleen Hines, Thena Mae Farr.[12]

Llano, Texas, Margaret Montgomery won first with $38.00 plus a trophy saddle, second was Amy McGilvray, third Wanda Harper, fourth Janelle McGilvray.

Bastrop, Texas, First won by Dixie Toalson for $19.20 plus a gold and silver belt buckle, second was Jean Steeper, third Virginia Reger.[13]

Brownfield, Texas, won by June Probst $26.00, second was Sissy Allen, third Fannie Mae Cox, fourth Donna Faye Hinson.

Belton, Texas, Mary Black won $55.30 for first place, second was Wanda Harper $41.50, third & fourth tied were Pat McClain and Wynona Barnett, each receiving $20.75.[14]

Corpus Christi, Texas, Nancy Bragg won first and $70.00.

Leo Cremer, one of the top rodeo producers from Montana, had the Pikes Peak or Bust Rodeo at Colorado Springs, Colo., contract from 1937 until his death in 1953. He encouraged the committee to add barrel racing and ladies' calf roping in 1950. The Pikes Peak or Bust Rodeo and the Burwell, Neb., rodeos were held at the same time. There was some concern about two major rodeos having the event simultaneously. A notice in the *Powder Puffs and Spurs* May issue mentioned that it would give some of the girls that were hesitant to enter against some of the top-level barrel racers a better opportunity of getting 'in the money,' as the top-level gals couldn't be at both rodeos.[15]

In the book *Pikes Peak or Bust Rodeo: The First Fifty Years*, there is

Leo Cremer, stock contractor and rodeo producer, riding Murphy, at the Colorado State Fair in Pueblo. *Photo by John A. Stryker, courtesy of Stan Searle.*

no mention of barrel racing or ladies' calf roping in 1950. The first mention of women's barrel racing in the book was in 1959. Jane Mayo of Okemah, Okla., was the winner that year and was the GRA barrel racing champion in 1959, 1960, and 1961. Pikes Peak or Bust rodeo held the barrel racing again in 1960. It was not listed as an event in 1961 but did appear again in 1962 through 1968. In 1969 it was absent again. However, it was added in 1970 and has continued there from then on.[16]

Faye Blackstone, a trick rider from Nebraska, started her career in the arena in the 1930s. She married Vic Blackstone, a saddle bronc rider, and they made their home in Florida. When rodeos began phasing out trick riding, Faye found it harder to find work as a trick rider. While in Texas, she witnessed the barrel races and merely turned her great horsemanship to this new event. She took the barrel racing concept back home to Florida and introduced it to the cowgirls there. It didn't take long before it was a part of many of the Florida rodeos. Faye became the 1953 and 1956 Florida Barrel Racing Champion.[17]

Deadwood, S.D., had its first barrel race in 1957, and Bonnie Titus won. The Friday, August 2, first day program had the seventeenth event titled "Girls Barrel Race." Six women were entered, and all were from nearby towns – Spearfish, Sturgis, Rapid City, and Belle Fourche, S.D. The following year the program listed eleven entries with three from out-of-state – Colorado and Wyoming; however, in their *Days of 76, A Deadwood Tradition* book on the history of the rodeo, no mention was made of the 1958 race. The only barrel racing year in the book for the 1960s was 1968, with Jane Geigle as the winner. The book only indicated barrel racing in 1971 with Vickie Selman winner and 1975 with Connie Combs as the winner. Jon Mattson, long-time rodeo committee man and instrumental in the Deadwood Rodeo Museum being erected, wrote, "I couldn't find a program with barrel racing listed from 1959 to 1973. I believe our first GRA barrel race was 1974 through 1980, and then it became a WPRA event in 1981."[18]

The Overland Trail Rodeo, held in Sterling, Colo., in 1958, dedicated the new rodeo grounds and had barrel racing for "Girls 15 Years and older" and "Boys 15 Years and older." Entry fees were $10, and the purse was $25 for each event. Robert Montgomery was manager, announcer was Harrison Fell of Lamar, Colo., Hoss Inman, also of Lamar, provided the stock, and Buddy Heaton was the rodeo clown. Vern Hastings, Jr. was in charge of the barrel race, according to their program.[19]

By 1958 it was reported there were GRA sanctioned barrel races in twenty-one states and Havana, Cuba. Most of the members were single women at first, but as time went on, many of the barrel racers married rodeo cowboys and were more interested in competing at RCA rodeos (where their husbands were competing) than at GRA all-girl rodeos. For awhile, the rules were that only monies won at GRA-sanctioned rodeos would count toward the GRA all-around title.[20]

Chapter Six

GRA All-Girl Rodeos & More

The All-Girl rodeo in Amarillo, Texas, on October 4 through 7, 1948 held the following events; bareback riding, cutting horse contest, brahma bull riding, ribbon roping, sponsor contest and calf roping. First day money winners in the sponsor contest were: first Blanche Altizer, second Dude Barton, third Jackie Worthington, fourth split between Mrs. Russel Allen and Faye Marburger. Second day money won by: first Margaret Montgomery, second Amy McGilvary, third and fourth split between Betty Barron and Jewell Lutich. The average winners were: first Dude Barton, second Blanche Altizer, third Jackie Worthington, fourth Margaret Montgomery.[1]

LaTonne Sewalt won the world championship barrel race title for 1950 in Tulsa, Okla., at the World's Championship All-Girl Rodeo. It was stated that the barrel race was the most contested-for title. LaTonne was only eleven and quite small for her age. Just three years earlier her father, Royce, was named world champion calf roper. In less than two years she had accomplished more than one could expect from an eleven-year-old girl "who is just a might cute in her tight-fitting Western clothing, with her long platinum-blonde curls swirling down to her shoulders," said James Cathey in the magazine *Back in the Saddle*. During the Houston rodeo in 1950 she was proclaimed the first cowgirl champion ever awarded the honor at that rodeo. Besides receiving $695 cash, a beautiful buckle, and increased personal pride, she was kissed by Roy Rogers, the cowboy movie star. She just kept winning and for the year she won $3,665.82. Her favorite horse, *Little Joe* was her mount.[2]

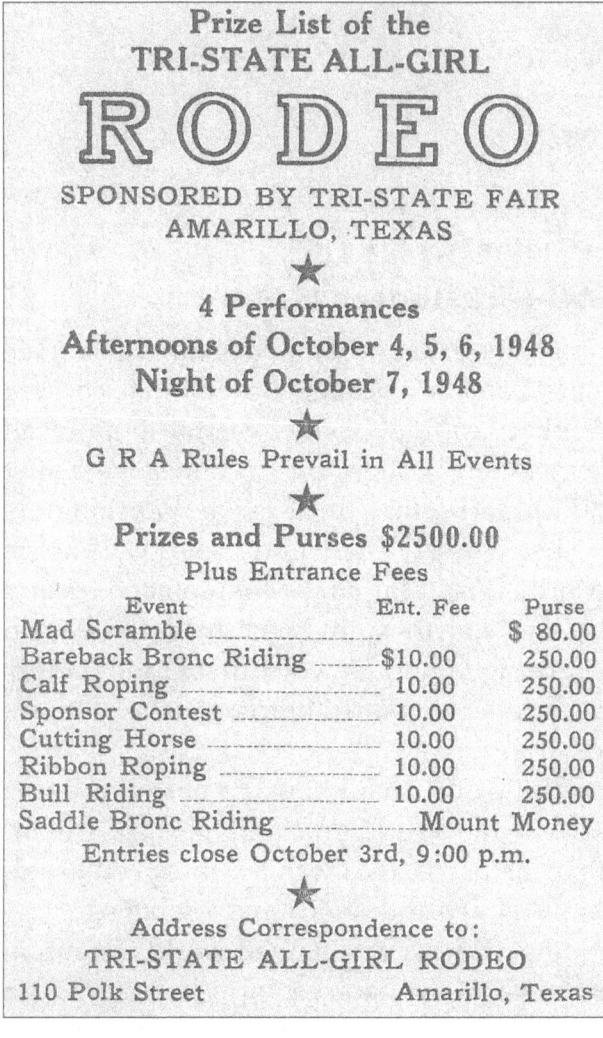

In 1950 the Tulsa Finals for the Girls Rodeo Association was produced by Jerry Rippeteau, who also produced the July, 1950, rodeo in Corpus Christi. The Tulsa All-Girl Rodeo Finals was held indoors in the pavilion in Tulsa, Okla., and was considered a total success. Approximately 20,000 people attended and the most 'hotly' contested event was the sponsor contest (barrel race). Throughout the season Margaret Montgomery (Owens) and LaTonne Sewalt kept switching leads in the standings. With LaTonne's win in Tulsa she ended the year with 316 points more than Margaret. The final totals for those in the event were:

LaTonne Sewalt	$3665.82
Margaret Montgomery	3349.65
June Probst	1965.15
Wanda Harper	1268.32[3]

In the 1951 January issue of *Hoofs and Horns* the Girls Rodeo Association column listed the 1950 champion cowgirls. It also reported:

> *In the most contested-for cowgirl event — the barrel race — top honors were won by tiny eleven-year-old LaTonne Sewalt of Brownwood, Texas. She won $3,665 at over two dozen approved rodeos throughout the year. LaTonne rides 'Little Joe', a five year old bay Quarter gelding which she trained herself. Horsemanship was taught her by her father, Royce Sewalt, 1947 RCA World's Champion Calf Roper.*

Later on in the same column a report was made on the All-Girl Rodeo in Tulsa, Okla., in October of 1950. Also said about LaTonne was the fact that . . . "some Champions were all ready known, but some races were very much in doubt. LaTonne settled it in fine order by making a clean sweep of all day monies and the average."[4]

In 1951 All-Girl rodeos were held in Corpus Christi, Texas; Natchez, Miss.; West Monroe, La.; Fort Stockton, Texas; Oklahoma City, Okla.; Seymour, Texas; and Tulsa, Okla. Barrel racing was held at all but the Natchez rodeo.[5]

A full page ad ran in the May/June, 1951 *Powder Puff & Spurs* magazine announcing "TWO BIG ALL GIRL RODEOS." One was to be held in Colorado Springs, June 22 through the 24, and the second to be held at Seymour, Texas, July 18 through 21. Nancy Binford was in charge of the Colorado Springs event, and Thena Mae Farr was handling the Seymour event. The ad indicated each had a purse of $3,600. Entry fees were $20 for each event — bareback bronc riding, calf roping, barrel race, cutting horse, ribbon roping and bull riding, with purses of $600 for each event and a buckle to each champion cowgirl.[6] There was also an All-Girl rodeo in Oklahoma City during the summer of '51.

The first San Antonio All-Girl Rodeo was held in September, 1951, sponsored by the San Antonio Police Welfare Fund. In *This Month in San Antonio the Official Hotel Greeters Guide* was the following article — in part:

> *Coming out of the chutes at the Bexar County Coliseum astride some of the wildest stock that ever churned the arena in any rodeo will be some of the most amazing cowgirl riders*

in the nation from September 25th through the 29th. The event will be the first world's championship all-cowgirl rodeo ever witnessed in San Antonio. More than 150 contestants, members of the Girls Rodeo Association, will compete for $7,500 in prize money and for gold and silver championship belt buckles. The producer is Jerry Rippiteau, born and reared in Oklahoma's sprawling Osage nation who now makes his home in Corpus Christi. Rippiteau himself was for many years one of the nation's top cowhands and rodeo performers and he carries the scars of both with him now. Asking no special consideration because they are members of the so-called 'weaker' sex, the cowgirls competing in the all-girl rodeo will work the same stock as used by the men in the nation's biggest rodeos. They will compete in bareback bronc, calf roping, saddle bronc and wild Brahma bull riding contests. Other events will include barrel racing, cutting horse contest and ribbon roping.[7]

A follow-up report on the Colorado Springs event informed everyone "Farr and Binford advised that the cowgirl turnout at Colorado Springs set a new record, not only in entries, but in states represented. Girls were there from nine states. The public reception was not what was expected or needed, but they are not disenheartened over the future of other shows there." Some of the participants from the mountain states were; Mary Ann Harms from

Belmont, Mont.; Ramona Merritt of Federal, Wyo.; Vicky Lynn Ferrell, Lamar, Neb.; Edna Thate and Mary Lee Coughlin, Denver, Colo.; Sandra and Julia Casement, West Plains, Colo.; and Della and Frances Simon, from Limon, Colo.[8]

Powder Puff & Spurs, the only magazine in the world devoted exclusively to cowgirls — striving toward a broader cowgirl participation in equestrian sports and toward the advancement of the Girls Rodeo Association, had a column 'In the Editor's Mail Box,' July, 1951, had a letter printed anonymously that said, in part:

> *I am an ex-GRA member, but I can't seem to see fit to go along with some of the stuff that's taking place. I love the GRA and think it has great possibilities when it is run for the cowgirls and not just for the benefit of a few. There are too many good shows that everyone knows wants a girl's event, but if the directors can't be there, they don't care about the other girls. And too, there are lots of barrel races that are held that just a few girls know about. Just look at the approved shows for last year and then compare them with those which sent in results to be counted. There are enough cowgirls to have barrel races at six rodeos in Texas at one time. Also, we girls need more different kinds of sponsor events. If I was just starting to ride, I wouldn't enter an event where I had to ride against a world champion. Give the youngsters a chance, especially at the girls rodeos. - - - Something else bothers me. It is how the old members treat new riders and prospective members. They should give these girls a big rush and woo them like a sorority does. Instead they act like they don't like it because the new girls try to talk to them. If you ask me, they don't want any competition.*[9]

A letter to the editor, James Cathey, with another point of view was included in the Sept-Oct. 1951 issue by Frances Weeg. Here is what she had to say in the matter:

> *Since reading the girl's letter in the July issue of PP&S and talking to you about it, I am writing this letter to express*

1951 G.R.A Champions: (left to rigt) Lucyle Cowey, Saddle Bronc-Rae Beach, Bareback-Ruby Gobble, Team Tying-Rose Garrett Brown, Bull Riding-Jackie Worthington, All-Around and Cutting Horse-Wanda Harper, Calf Roping and Ribbon Roping-Margaret Owens, Sponsor Contest-Sally Taylor, *Powder Puffs and Spurs* Sportsmanship Award.

my opinion about the letter. I also, think the GRA has great possibilities. But when I say that, I am thinking of the past as well as the future. Every girl knows what the GRA has done for the cowgirls. It has made possible all the girl rodeos and with them came many more girl's events at other rodeos. The money added is more than doubled. If a girl is interested in only barrel races there are plenty to make. The girls that work only that event should make it a point to know about every one of the barrel races.

When I started to rodeo I rode against world champions. I was young in experience as well as age. I knew I had no chance against them until I was in their class. I was determined to practice and become as good as they were. Although I have never held any of the titles, I hope I never win one until I have earned it. No one deserves one until they have earned it. No one is favored at the girl's shows.

> *The old members will not associate with a girl that is new to them until they know something about her. When they learn something about her they will accept her as one of them. If a girl really wants to rodeo, that minor factor won't stop her. Being nice to someone and accepting them are two different things.*
>
> *The GRA has and will continue to benefit every girl who wants to rodeo where there is plenty of competition. Every girl who has been President has done her very best I'm sure. Thena Mae has already done her part. She has gotten more shows and a lot more money at the all-girl shows. In all due respect I hope I haven't hurt anyone's feelings by writing this letter. I am not criticizing the GRA and never will. To me it is more than an association, it is the chance to go to all-girl rodeos and not just to $50 barrel races.*

The 'anonymous' letter-writer who wrote the first letter, followed up with a second letter in the same issue of Ms. Weeg's comments, and said, in part:

> *- - - I got a letter from a friend who was at the San Antonio All-Girl Rodeo and she said she never saw the girls any friendlier and they sure tried to help the new girls and the girls seem to have a more considerate attitude. I sure hope the girls will continue to try to help all the fine people who are trying to help them. I will always have a good word to say about the GRA as a whole.*[10]

There will always be two sides to every situation, and actually it never hurts to have someone play 'the devil's advocate.' When concerns are brought to the attention of those involved there is often more understanding, thoughtfulness and consideration used than before. But it generally takes someone willing to be outspoken and critical to get things changed and be better.

The results from the barrel racing rodeo finals for 1952 were: first place, Wanda Harper; second was LaTonne Sewalt; third was Mary Black, and fourth went to Jackie Worthington. Billie Gamblin, of Fort Worth, was president, Jackie Worthington, of

Jacksboro, Texas, was vice president and Blanche Altizer, from Dryden, Texas, was secretary-treasurer at the time. Wanda Harper also won the all-around, by winning the barrel racing and the calf roping, too. Runner up was Jackie Worthington.[11]

By 1953 the North Platte, Neb., rodeo introduced for the first time, the ladies cloverleaf barrel race. Margaret Chamberlin, of North Platte, won all three days and received $150.[12] Also in 1953 the GRA held their very first finals in Dallas, Texas, but received very little publicity.[13]

On January 30, 1955, Rodeo Cowboys Association (RCA) president, Bill Linderman, and GRA president, Jackie Worthington signed an agreement that the RCA would strongly urge their rodeo committees to have a GRA approved barrel race. They also agreed that RCA would not complete a contract or agreement with any barrel racing association other than the GRA.[14]

The Texas Barrel Racing Association (TBRA) was formed in Fort Worth in 1955. Whether this organization was started because of the amateur status of the Fort Worth barrel racing event, or it was just time to form the TBRA so their members could be seriously considered professional barrel racers.

The 'Glamour Girl' emphasis, in some rodeos, with beauty, fashion and personal appearances disgusted many women competitors who put their ability to compete first. They wanted to emphasize their abilities as horsewomen and competitors. The charter was signed and dated February 11, 1955. Those present were Donna Harrison, Peggy Ligon, Hilda Davis, Peggy Sanders, Opal Hendrick, Hay Oglesby (Jr), Loraine Adams, NaDell Lacy, Bettye Sargent, Yvonne Walker, Velda Smith, Barbara Cummings and NaRay McHood.[15]

The TBRA grew to 125 members from Texas, Oklahoma, New Mexico, Arizona, and Louisiana in a very short time. Velda Smith was the first president, with Faye Oglesby as vice president and NaRay McHood as secretary. This was the first all-woman strictly barrel racing association in the United States. The last year TBRA filed a tax report as an active association was 1985.[16]

The San Angelo Stock Show and Rodeo did not start barrel rac-

First Meeting of the Texas Barrel Racing Association in 1955.

ing until 1957. That year it was won by local contestant, Billie McBride. The following year the Stock Show and Roping Fiesta was held but no rodeo. Apparently the new coliseum being built was the reason the rodeo was eliminated.

In 1959 Wanda Bush won the barrel racing and in 1960 Mildred Farris won with top winnings of $83.50. No winner was announced for 1961, but a photo of Sammy Fancher barrel racing that year, was in their *Fifty Years at the San Angelo Stock Show & Rodeo Also Featuring 27 Years of Roping Fiesta History* book. In 1962 Wanda Bush and Sissy Thurman tied for the win.[17]

Prescott Frontier Days in Arizona had their first barrel race in 1959. The 1958 daily program for that event listed barrel racing, but for some unknown reason it did not take place. It was presumed it was cancelled to accommodate pari-mutual horse racing that afternoon and not enough time was left to prepare the arena dirt. The 1959 winner was Phyllis Turnage of Seligman, Ariz.[18]

Also in 1959 Prunty Brothers Diamond A Rodeo Company held an All-Amateur Rodeo in Elko, Nev., which continued through 1973. The first barrel race at Elko was held at the first rodeo and was won by Shirley Jensen of Fallon, Nev. An earlier rodeo held in Elko started in 1912 and continued until 1918. Elko's rodeo was sometimes amateur, other years a semi-professional event and some years a professional rodeo. Then there were times it wasn't held at all. However, according to records barrel racing has been held there every year since it began in 1959.[19]

Chapter Seven
College Competition Finally Includes Women

For the early part of the twentieth century, very few rural young people went to college. It was still a vision of parents that their offspring would stay on the ranch or farm and take over the family business. A smattering of youth from the country attended business schools but rarely did they go to a college or university. When they did start attending, it was primarily to agricultural and mechanical schools, and in that number, there were very few women students. The first college rodeo, held at Texas A&M, was held in 1920 as a fundraiser.[1] No events were held for women at that rodeo as it was an all-male college, primarily military. Women were not admitted to Texas A&M until 1963.

In 1938 a California college rodeo was held with several colleges competing against one another. In 1948 at the first collegiate rodeo held at Sul Ross State Teachers College (Texas). Those in attendance formed the National Intercollegiate Rodeo Association (NIRA). It happened with encouragement from Hank Finger, president of the Sul Ross Rodeo Association, with Jim Watts and Buster Lindley in agreement. "A few cowgirls, along with a drove of cowboys, sent in their membership fees to the NIRA the first year. The cowgirls created their own events and tried to convince the administrators and the outside world that they had a legitimate right to rodeo with the cowboys."[2]

The NIRA held its first convention in Denver, Colo., April 15 and 16, 1949, with Charlie Rankin presiding. They adopted a constitution, bylaws, rules, etc., and elected officers. Rankin of Texas A&M was president, vice president was Joe Forney of Colorado A&M, and Evelyn Bruce Kingsbery of Sul Ross State was chosen as publicity director. She was the only elected woman for some time and did an excellent job of getting publicity for college rodeos in western-related magazines for NIRA.[3]

This was a time that did not encourage the idea of women doing men's jobs. Rodeo was reaching the time when it was trying desperately to be considered a 'sporting event.' In earlier times, rodeo producers often called a rodeo a "show," which was a holdover term from the era of Wild West shows. Inexperienced fans didn't understand that rodeo events were always competitions. Whereas Wild West shows were exhibitions of the old West. On rare occasions, a Wild West show might hold a competition in bronc riding or roping, but it was not the norm. Often posters advertising a rodeo would even call it a 'show.' It took rodeo many years to get rid of that term and make the general public think of rodeo as a sport. The term "show" in rodeo, continued longer than it should have, which was exactly the same thing barrel racing faced since its beginning when it was called a 'sponsor' event.

The first women's championship in the NIRA was in 1951, when the finals were held in Fort Worth, Texas. Seven women from six colleges competed in two events — barrel racing and the flag race. Jo Gregory Knox of Sul Ross College won the national all-around championship. She won the flag race and placed third in the barrel race. There was no listing of the individual events for women at the end of that year's finals, only the women's all-around.

It wasn't until 1955, at the NIRA Finals in Lake Charles, La., that barrel racing and goat tying were listed as well. Kathlyn Younger Knox of McNeese State won the barrel racing, and Becky Jo Smith Doom of Hardin-Simmons University, won the goat tying as well as the women's all-around.[4]

Betty Sims Solt began her barrel racing career in high school in 1950. She grew up in New Mexico and found that at most rodeos in those days, when winning girls would get a watch or some feminine item while the men received saddles and such. It was very unequal, and she resented it. She grew up with five brothers on the family ranch and did the same work they did. She realized women deserved more attention and appreciation, and from then on, she worked to achieve it. She attended college at New Mexico A&M,

Betty Sims Solt from New Mexico, was the 1957 National Intercollegiate Rodeo Association (NIRA) all-around cowgirl and the 1957 and 1958 barrel racing national champion. *Courtesy of the Rodeo News*.

and in 1957 at the NIRA finals she won the women's all-around and the barrel racing. She repeated her barrel racing win again the following year. She joined Sylvia Mahoney in 1992 to help form the NIRA Alumni Association and after a career in teaching, she retired and ranched. Betty was inducted into the National Cowgirl Hall of Fame in 1990.[5]

In a 1967 December issue of *Hoofs and Horns*, an interesting article entitled "Racing Through College" by Jimmie Hurley told of two sisters and how they spent their time away from class and studying. Beth and Alice Williams from Caldwell, Idaho, were both in college with Beth at Baylor University and Alice attending Rice University on a full-tuition scholarship. Both girls competed in barrel racing, but Alice, who was chosen to be Miss Rodeo Texas at the Miss Rodeo America contest, was first runner-up.

So while Beth was winning barrel races, Alice won rodeo queen and sweetheart contests. The girls give ninety-percent of the credit to their parents for what they accomplished because their parents always provided the very best horses. Beth rode a thirteen-year-old sorrel mare named *Garbe's Inde*, sired by *Tommy Star*, out of a Thoroughbred mare. Beth said, "She has lots and lots of speed and is extremely willing."

During the summer between semesters, Beth won $2,850 at Oregon and Idaho barrel races. She placed in twenty-four rodeos that she entered and won all but eight of them. Alice reported $1,000 in winnings. "I didn't have my usual horse because she was being bred to *Hobby Horse*," Alice said.

Their mom traveled with the girls during the summer, putting her personal interests aside, and as the girls' pointed out — their dad was understanding, too. He had to fix his own meals.[6]

Martha Tompkins, daughter of Harry Tompkins, all-around and bull riding world champion, and Rosemary Colborn Tompkins, was attending Tarleton State University in Stephenville, Texas, where she was on the woman's rodeo team and ran barrels. In 1971 at the NIRA finals, the Tarleton woman's team won the national championship, and Martha also won the barrel racing championship.[7]

Reg Kesler Rodeo put on that year's NIRA finals in Bozeman, Mont. Liz, Reg's wife and partner, could recall she was up in the

Martha Tompkins was the 1971 NIRA barrel racing champion. *Courtesy of Martha Tompkins.*

announcer's stand working when she realized Martha had won. Liz knew Martha's parents weren't there due to rodeo commitments elsewhere and hurried down to the arena to congratulate her. Later that same year, Martha made quite a name for herself in competition as she also qualified for the National Finals Rodeo.[8]

In 1985 Merrill Adams Angermiller was elected national faculty president of the NIRA board, the very first female faculty-elected board president. She was instructor of journalism and coach at Southwest Texas Junior College and had competed as a student for Eastern New Mexico University. The NIRA board also elected their first female student president in 1989, Molly McAuliffe Hepper. She was raised on a ranch near Fort Klamath, Ore., and attended two years at Blue Mountain Community College, and graduated from Montana State University in 1990. She won the 1986 NIRA women's all-around title.[9]

A unique situation happened in 2001 when the Oklahoma State University women's rodeo team consisted of only four barrel racers. Going to the college finals that were held at Casper, Wyo., the four women won the women's championship and Janae Ward, granddaughter of Florence Youree, GRA president, won the barrel racing title, with Julie Warner coming in second. The four barrel racers were: Shannon Herrmann, Julie Warner, Gretchen Benbenek, and Janae Ward. Sylvia Mahoney, author of the book, *College Rodeo, From Show to Sport*, included a photo of the four women holding a huge check for $7,000 for Oklahoma State University. According to Sylvia, this win had never happened before in college finals competition where all four on the team were competing only in one event and would probably never happen again.[10]

As time moves forward, so many things change in the way people think. Respect is so important in many ways. The women who enjoyed rodeo competition worked hard to show the world how good they were at their sport. It took a long time for the women in rodeo to gain the respect of other competitors, but they were determined. Those women who attended colleges and universities and were studying to keep their grades up while also competing, found that respect and proved they deserved it.

Chapter Eight
Magazines Help Barrel Racing Spread Even Farther

In 1952 both the Girls Rodeo Association and the National Intercollegiate Rodeo Association had columns in *Hoofs and Horns* magazine reporting activities of their organizations. The column for the Girls Rodeo Association was written by Ted and Betty Lamb, trick riders and horse trainers of the era. They wrote mainly about where rodeos for women were being held. With reports from the arenas such as "An RCA rodeo in Killeen, Texas, held a barrel race and Wanda Harper of Mason, Texas, made the fastest time and was awarded a fine pair of boots by the committee."[1]

This indicated that the women were still being given prizes, instead of money, which the cowboys were receiving at rodeos approved by the Rodeo Cowboys Association. The Lambs' referred to cloverleaf barrel races in communities scattered throughout Texas.[2]

But in the October issue, they reported, "I have received a number of letters from girls all over the United States inquiring about the GRA. I am sincerely happy to see that my (GRA) column is read by so many girls who are interested in barrel racing and in joining our Association."[3]

Hoofs and Horns magazine started being published in the early 1930s as a magazine for dude ranches in Arizona and the west. However, when 'Ma' Hopkins took over as editor in 1932 and the format shifted to concentrate on rodeo, including the Cowboys' Turtle Association (CTA) formed in 1936, and the Rodeo Association of America (RAA) formed in 1929. The RAA was run by businessmen and rodeo committeemen, while the CTA was an association of rodeo cowboys. By 1937 the magazine became the 'Bible' for rodeo, spreading the news of rodeo to those interested.

During World War II, many cowboys joined and fought overseas or handled military responsibilities in the states. Harry Rowell of Rowell Rodeo in California paid for subscriptions to *Hoofs and Horns* for many of the servicemen, both in the states and overseas. The magazine was the only thread they had to their beloved rodeo while fighting half a world away.

Ma Hopkins' readership was vast among rodeo people across the country, and to be able to have a column in the magazine would only spread the word about GRA and barrel racing that much quicker. A list of RCA rodeos holding cloverleaf barrel racing with $20 entry fees were listed. Although the prize monies varied, Baton Rouge, La., had a $900 purse. Burwell, Neb., had a $650 purse, while Sidney, Iowa, had $1,500, and McAlester, Okla., purse was $450.[4]

First cover of Hoof & Horns magazine to use a barrel racing photograph. The photograph is of D'Ann Young at Sidney, Iowa, in 1958. *Photographer O.J. Hebrank.*

By 1953 the North Platte, Neb., rodeo introduced, for the first time, the ladies cloverleaf barrel race. Margaret Chamberlin of North Platte won all three days and received $150.[34] Also, in 1953, the GRA held their first finals in Dallas but received very little publicity.[5]

The cover of the *Hoofs and Horns* February issue in 1954 was a photograph of D'Ann Young barrel racing in Sidney, Iowa. "Ma" Hopkins wrote, "We have not meant to neglect the girls in their rodeo achievements, but most of the pictures of them that we have received have been too poor to reproduce.[6]

Other popular magazines, such as *Western Horseman*, also began including articles about barrel racing. James Cathey wrote an interesting account of the horses used for the event 1952:

There is today a competitive event in horsemanship that is so keen that less than half a dozen contenders are capable of taking championship honors. In rodeo, this fired-up event is the cowgirls' barrel race. Little has been written or said about the highly trained and skilled horses that speed over a prescribed course and negotiate precision right and left turns. But, the truth is undeniable that the requirements are so many and so fine that few horses are considered as outstanding. The barrel racer is called upon to do practically all the things any other performing horse must do and then more. The girls who own and ride these highly trained performers are a very particular group about matters pertaining to their horses. In gathering and simulating material, it was found that requirements of a barrel racer are numerous. Many things enter into the picture, such as the type of horse, his temperament to handling and hauling, how he is trained, and the temperament and skill of the rider. In many sections of the country, barrel racing is judged as a performance class at horse shows. But, in the south- west, almost every rodeo has this fast and furious event because of public demand, brought about by the speed and color. In trying to determine why the winners were continually the same, many interviews and surveys were made to determine just what makes a good barrel racer.

No two observations were the same, but by consolidating notes and comparing them, certain conclusions were much in evidence. To be a good barrel racer, a horse 1. must have a heart to want to run, 2. must have speed. 3. must have ability to handle himself with speed, and 4. his performance at the barrel must be to perfection. Performance on the barrel is very important in that the horse must 1. suddenly reduce his speed, 2. make the turn in the proper lead, 3. turn with his hind feet under him, and 4. break and score for another straightaway run. A horse that can't change his leads on the other two barrels is lost. Many horses can run "a hole in the the wind" but lose out on performance at the barrel. Many top reining and performing horses haven't the speed. Combining speed and performance eliminates would-be's by the hundreds. The better horses turn with their heads low

> and their eyes on the ground and barrel. In comparing the roping, dogging, cutting, reining, racing, and barrel racing horses, we find that the barrel racer must very nearly meet the total requirements of the others — and then some. Roping, dogging, and race horses must be able to break and score well and must have speed. Cutting and reining horses must be collected at all times and must be able to turn in the proper lead and with their hind feet under them. Like the others, the barrel horse must know what's to be done and how to do it.[7]

Jan Youren, a GRA world champion bareback rider from Emmett, Idaho, and I were talking recently, and she admitted she was not a barrel racer, but she did share this experience in her early days of competition:

> I began competing when I was eleven-years-old. The first all-girl rodeo in Idaho was in 1955, and my dad, Sterling Alley, entered me in every event. My sister, who was a barrel racer, had broken her leg, so we took her barrel racing horse 'Doc' with us for me to ride in the barrel racing event. I had never ridden a bareback horse or seen a barrel race. Before the barrel race, I had drawn a bareback horse that slammed me into the ground, and I hit the ground so hard I had a concussion but didn't know it. I was still off in 'lala land' by the time the barrel racing started, but I got on Doc and went around the barrels. Doc won it for me; I was so out of it I knew I hadn't had anything to do with the win.

Youren admitted she never barrel raced again, but she did win lots of bronc and bull ridings. She is a five-time bareback world champion. She also had fifteen children, and competed for fifty-one years until she was sixty-three.[8]

In the 1956 *Rodeo Sports News Annual*, the official publication of the Rodeo Cowboys Association, an article appeared entitled: "The Girls Rodeo Association" by B. Kalland. The article told the history of the organization and indicated that the RCA was supportive in every way and agreed to use the GRA events in many of their sactioned rodeos. It went on to give requirements of an all-girl rodeo, how much prize money was required to enter each event, etc. It also stated GRA by-laws and rules, similar to the

RCA by-laws and rules:

> *The GRA roughstock events must be ridden for six seconds. Saddle bronc riders are allowed two reins and may use hobbles (stirrups tied together under the horse's belly) if desired. In bareback riding, the rider can use one hand or two on the rigging but must decide which hand before leaving the chute. Spurs must be in the horse's shoulders on leaving the chute or be fined 10 points. In calf roping, the rope may either be dallied or tied hard and fast. Two throws are permitted, with a 10-second penalty for beating the barrier. The calf cannot be busted and must be thrown by hand. In team roping, four loops are allowed, two at the head and two at the heels, and hobbled below the hocks. The steer must be headed around the horns, over the head or around the neck, and loop may include one front foot."* The only mention of barrel racing in this article was: *"For the All-Girl Rodeos, there must be at least five events, which usually consist of bareback riding, calf roping, barrel races, ribbon roping, cutting horses, and/or bull riding. Team tying may also be added or substituted.*

No references to the rules for barrel racing were included.[9]

In the early days of barrel racing, being a part of a rodeo, the rider never knew what the pattern would be. Someone on the committee would set the pattern, and the racers were expected to follow. Ardith Bruce and her horse *Red* were the first to win a title going to the left barrel first.

Ardith Bruce at the Houston Astrodome in 1969.
Photograph by Ferrell Butler - Courtesy of Rodeo News.

Chapter Nine
Things Aren't What They Appear to Be

Mary Lou LeCompte wrote in *Cowgirls of the Rodeo* — "In 1954 barrel racing reached the ultimate event during that time, the annual Madison Square Garden rodeo."[1] However, in researching this eastern venue for girls, it was discovered that barrel racing was strictly in conjunction with a rodeo queen contest involving only representatives from nearby New York dude ranches. In addition to choosing a queen, five 'sponsor girls' were picked. The sponsor girls ran the barrels at each performance, while the queen had a contract to perform with Roy Rogers and Dale Evans during the sixteen-day, twenty-eight performance rodeo.[2]

In 1955, the dude ranch barrel race was held again during the Madison Square Garden rodeo. In 1955 there were forty-five entrants eligible. The five women with the fastest times, held during a preliminary contest, competed for prizes in each of the twenty-eight Madison Square Garden rodeo performances.[3]

After 1939 the Fort Worth Southwestern Exposition and Livestock Show & Rodeo eliminated the popular ladies' bronc riding. This was much to the disappointment of Tad Lucas, a local cowgirl, and other women that had excelled in the event. Protests were made, and in 1940 Fort Worth held a glamour girl contest during the rodeo. It was more than just a beauty contest; the women were required to compete in rodeo-type activities such as roping and riding against time. Margaret Montgomery Owens won the title. Later she became the first president of the Girls Rodeo Association.[4]

Women's events were discouraged at the Fort Worth rodeo for some time, except for ranch girl or glamour girl-type performances. It wasn't until 1955 that Billy Bob Watt introduced barrel racing at the Fort Worth rodeo. His real reason for adding the event is questioned, but some believe Watt realized the excitement and thrill of watching women race against the clock was good entertainment. It was billed as the Fort Worth Invitational Ranch Girls Barrel Race. The women were invited based on their beauty and horsemanship; therefore, it was considered an 'amateur event.' Not just anyone could enter unless they were invited and sponsored by a ranch or civic organization. Those were the Fort Worth rules.[5]

Gene McJunkin (Livingston) went to the Markham Ranch with thirty-five other invited women in 1955 to compete with the understanding the one that won would represent Fort Worth at the Southwest Exposition and Livestock Show in the Invitational Ranch Girls Barrel Race. Gene went on to win and later recapped the experience.

"Everyone made four runs," she said. "The top twenty would go to the semi-finals, and then the ten with the fastest runs would go to the finals. In the end, I won third."

She also said there were no entry fees, and each woman that competed was paid, but winners were paid more.[6] The rodeo put up $1,700 for the purse as it was a timed event.[7]

When asked if they were required to wear fancy clothing, Gene's response was, "It was more of an expectation. We were always inspected, but in those days, you never saw blue jeans in barrel racing. Everyone dressed up."

Gene McJunkin on *Sis*, owned by L.C. Hopper, was the winner of the barrel race to determine who would represent Fort Worth at the first barrel race during the Fort Worth Fat Stock Show & Rodeo in 1955. *Photo courtesy of Gene McJunkin Livingston.*

Gene competed a second time in 1963 after she won the Arkansas State Barrel Racing, and they were her sponsor.[8]

In 1995 Delbert Bailey, publicity director for the Southwestern Exposition and Livestock Show, said there were no plans to change from an invitational to an open barrel race in the future.[8] Fort Worth Invitational Ranch Girls Barrel Race event was held for the last time in 2003.[9] Since 2003 the barrel race during Fort Worth is sanctioned by the Women's Professional Rodeo Association.

When the sponsor event at Stamford was first held in 1931, before barrel racing became so popular as it is today, it indeed was a glamour gal event. The women were considered to be in the event because of their beauty and fashion. It added much color and femininity to a sport that had none of that. Even when the timing first became important in barrel racing, many people still considered the event more of a novelty, like performers in rodeo engaged in trick riding, Roman riding, and trick roping. These specialty acts, people always dress in glitzy colorful costumes, and therefore it was expected of this 'new event' for women . . . barrel racing.[10]

Chapter Ten
Canadian Barrel Racing

Barrel racing was a new event at the 1957 Calgary Spring Horse Show. Dean Mayberry of Hanna, Alta., had spread the word that anyone interested should come to a meeting in the alley of the horse barn to form a barrel racing organization.[1] Ten or twelve women attended, and the Cowgirls Barrel Racing Association (CBRA) was founded. Willa Beebe was the first president and Isabella Miller, age sixteen, became a director.

The first barrel racing champion was Ingrid Hewitt. She was a barrel racer for years and was instrumental in getting barrel racing becoming a part of professional rodeo. Forging a competitive liaison with the PRCA in the United States. Later, she became a steer roper.[2]

In 1962 the organization was renamed Cowgirls Barrel Racing and Rodeo Association (CBRRA). Pearl Borgal, a leading businesswoman in public relations and organizations, was chosen president. At this time, the group expanded to include and approve events in goat tying, calf roping, and cow riding. Cutting horse and steer undecorating were added in 1964 and 1966, respectively. The cutting horse was dropped in 1974 due to a shortage of competitors. From 1962 to 1969, barrel racing had senior, intermediate, and junior circuits, but due to an influx of new barrel race circuits in other organizations, the intermediate group was eventually dropped.[3]

In 1967 the CBRRA again had a name change to Canadian Girls Rodeo Association (CGRA). The CGRA held its first Canadian barrel racing championship finals in 1968. The top ten barrel racers from across Canada were eligible to compete for prize money and receive an array of added awards. Since 1974 the Canadian Barrel Racing finals have been held in conjunction with the Canadian National Finals Rodeo.[4] Senior barrel racers ran for Canadian championship points on the Canadian professional cowboys' circuit called Cowboys Protective Association which later changed to Canadian Professional Rodeo Association (CPRA).

In 1971 the CGRA had a working agreement with the WPRA in the United States. This allowed a CGRA member to count points earned on the Canadian circuit towards WPRA standings. If she finished in the top 15 money-wise, she would have the opportunity to compete at the National Finals Rodeo in Oklahoma City for the World Championships. This agreement was later terminated.[5]

In 1984 the Canadian Professional Rodeo Association (CPRA) officially took on members in their organization, calling it the Canadian Ladies Barrel Racers, on a money-won point system. Jerri Duce, a CGRA nine-time Canadian barrel racing champion, was instrumental in this change.[6] The CPRA has accepted the previous CGRA barrel racing champions from 1957 through 1983 in their organization. CPRA has inducted into their Hall of Fame, CPRA, and CGRA Canadian barrel racing champions. Those barrel racers inducted are; Jerri Duce, Isabella Miller, Ruth McDougall, Elaine Watt, Gina McDougall, Viola Thomas, Dee Butterfield, and Rayel Robinson.[7]

Besides CGRA's senior Canadian champions, they have other divisions, such as Junior members competing in CGRA rodeo events, intermediate members (sometimes named 'circuit,' 'novice,' or 'Alberta' members), and they raced in non-professional rodeos, jackpots, and other open events. In 1969 due to the influx of new barrel racing circuits, the Intermediate was dropped, and efforts concentrated on the senior and junior members.[8]

In 1999 Monica Wilson won the right for cowgirls in Canada to vote as members of the Canadian Professional Rodeo Association (CPRA). She convinced the CPRA to give women barrel racers equal status in the professional rodeo circuit. Because of her efforts, barrel racers now qualify for the same prize monies accorded to men for winning their individual rodeo events. She was the ladies barrel racing director for the CPRA for thirteen years. An active lobbyist for her sport and an exceptional athlete, Monica was presented the coveted Cowboy of the Year award by CPRA in 1999. She is a professional barrel racer and makes her way from rodeo to rodeo all summer long on a circuit that stretches from Vancouver Island to Morris, Man. She drives a $40,000 pickup truck which pulls a $70,000 trailer. Her entire world is in tow – her horses, her family, her tack, her bed, and her computer. Doesn't that sound familiar? She was also the only Canadian honored by being invited to judge at the Miss Rodeo America contest in 2003. She also trains barrel horses and hosts workshops and clinics for beginners.[9]

The Canadian National Finals (CFR) features the ten leading money-winners in barrel racing and the first and second-place finishers during the last ten rodeos of the Canadian Tour season. Those twelve contestants are contested over six days, featuring six rounds. Before 2006, only Canadian residents were able to compete in the CFR. International contestants (including United States barrel racers) are now eligible to compete in the CFR; if they qualify, contestants have to compete in fifteen Canadian CPRA rodeos to be in the top ten money winners. One hundred twenty qualifiers compete in seven performances, but this includes one performance which is the Rising Stars Junior Canadian Finals Rodeo.[10]

Lindsay Sears became the first Canadian barrel racer to win the barrel racing champion title at the National Finals Rodeo in the United States in 2011. She won $139,002 at the National Finals and a total of $323,570 for the year. She also finished third in the average.[11]

Lisa Lockhart won the Guy Weadick Award at Calgary Stampede in 2016. This honor is very special in Calgary. Weadick was the ramrod that produced the first Calgary Stampede in 1912 and continued working with Calgary for some time. The Guy Weadick Award is presented to one chuckwagon or rodeo competitor 'who embodies what the cowboy stands for, and best typifies the Calgary Stampede's spirit. It is based upon ability, appearance, showmanship, character, sportsmanship, and cooperation with other cowboys, the arena crew, media, and the public. Lisa Lockart and Monica Wilson, a Canadian barrel racer who won it in 1996, are the only two women who have won this prestigious award since it was started in 1969. Lisa won the barrel racing at Calgary in 2017 and again in 2019.[12]

In the 2018 barrel racing finals, there were eight Canadians and four Americans. The Canadian Finals Rodeo barrel racing champion was Callahan Crossley from Hermiston, Ore.[13]

The Calgary Stampede, since 1912, has been held in July each year. The prize monies have soared through the years, and this outdoor rodeo is considered the richest, in Canada, with $2 million offered in 2019. It is an international rodeo including Canadians, WPRA contestants, PRCA cowboys from the United States, and the Professional Bull Riders and Brazil. On the last day of these important events, the four top contestants in each event competed for $100,000. Calgary barrel racers' points count in circuit standings toward the Canadian Pro Rodeo Finals.[14]

One hundred twenty rodeo superstars were invited to compete in six events, including barrel racing.

The 2019 Calgary Stampede ladies barrel racing contestants were:

Brittany Barnett – Bakersfield, Calif.
Taci Bettis – Round Top, Texas
Ivy Conrado – Hudson, Colo.
Callahan Crossley – Hermiston, Ore.
Kaylee Gallino – Wasta, S.D.
Hailey Kinsel – Cotulla, Texas
Lisa Lockhart – Oelrichs, S.D.
Emily Miller – Weatherford, Okla.
Nellie Miller – Cottonwood, Calif.
Amberleigh Moore – Salem, Ore.
Brittany Pozzi Tonozzi – Victoria, Texas
Carman Pozzobon – Savona, B.C., Canada
Jessica Routier – Buffalo, S.D.
Jennifer Sharp – Richards, Texas
Diane Skocdopole – Big Valley, B.C., Canada
Jimmie Smith – McDade, Texas
Shelby Spielman – Dalhart, Texas
Jessie Telford – Caldwell, Ida.
Sarah Rose Waguespack – Brunswick, Ga.
Kylie Whiteside – Longview, Alb., Canada

At Calgary, the WPRA barrel racers' money won does count in the WPRA tally.

Day money was first-$5,500, second-$4,500, third-$3,500, fourth-$2,500 and fifth-$1,500.

After racing each day, at random, someone's horse is tested for drugs.

At the 2019 Calgary Stampede, the Canadian dollar was worth 75% of the American dollar.

Pool A (four runs constitute a go-round, which they call a pool)
First place: Ivy Conrado, Hudson, Colo.
Second place: Nellie Miller, Cottonwood, Calif.
Third and fourth places were tied by: Jessica Routier, Buffalo, S.D.; Brittney Barnett, Bakersfield, Calif.; and Jessie Telford, Caldwell, Ida.

Pool B (four runs)
First place: Hailey Kinsel, Cotulla, Texas
Second place: Jennifer Sharp, Richards, Texas
Third place: Emily Miller, Weatherford, Okla,
Fourth place was tied by: Lisa Lockhart, Oelrichs, S.D., and Amberleigh Moore, Salem, Ore.

The top four in each pool go to the Semi-finals on Sunday's final day. The rest go to wild card day, and the top two for the day go the the semi-finals.

Those who qualified for the finals were:
Jennifer Sharp, Richards, Texas
Hailey Kinsel, Cotulla, Texas
Nellie Miller, Cottonwood, Calif.
Emily Miller, Weatherford, Okla.
Lisa Lockhart, Oelrichs, S.D.
Callahan Crossley, Hermiston, Ore.
Ivy Conrado, Hudson, Colo.
Jessica Routier, Buffalo, S.D.
Amberleigh Moore, Salem, Ore.
Jessie Telford, Caldwell, Ida.

The winner of the $100,000 was Lisa Lockhart
Second place, winning $25,000, was Hailey Kinsel
Third place was Nellie Miller winning $15,000
Fourth place with $10,000 was Emily Miller.

Lisa Lockhart, when getting her winnings said, "Yes, I've been crying. It means so much to me. I think the older you get, the more it means. It is not just the money. It is what it transpires." She also said in another interview, "I didn't expect this; the horse I had been riding didn't seem right, so for the finals, I changed to my other horse and hoped to do our best. I was shocked for this to happen."

Ruth Quinn stated that Lisa had been so much a part of Canadian Pro Barrel Racing they think of her as part of their Canadian/US family. She won by 3/1,000 of a second over Hailey Kinsel.

The Canadian Finals Rodeo for 2019 was held at Red Deer, Alb., from October 29 through November 3.

The winners were:

Place	Name	Winnings
1st	Brooke Wills of Kamloops, BC	$60,657.37
2nd	Stacey Ruizicka of Bluffton, AB	$55,831.67
3rd	Taylor Manning of Yellowhead County, AB	$49,309.26
4th	Justine Elliott of Lancombe, AB	$48,951.17
5th	Mary Walker of Ennis, Texas	$43,870.55
6th	Jennifer Sharp of Richard, Texas	$42,014.91
7th	Angela Ganter of Abilene, Texas	$41,229.41
8th	Shelby Spielman of Dalhart, Texas	$36,011.63
9th	Jackie Ganter of Abilene, Texas	$32,314.93
10th	Bertina Olafson of Hudson Bay, SK	$30,293.80
11th	Jenna O'Reilly of Millarville, AB	$19,962.02
12th	Lynette Brodoway of Brooks, AB	$18,050.64

Average Winners:

First – Stacey Ruizicka; Second - Shelby Spielman; Third - Jennifer Sharp; Fourth - Mary Walker; Fifth - Brooke Wills; Sixth – Jackie Ganter; Seventh – Justine Elliott; Eight – Lynette Brodoway; Ninth - Taylor Manning; Tenth – Bertina Olafson; Eleventh – Angela Ganter; Twelfth – Jenna O'Reilly.

Canadian friend Ruth Quinn shared the following:

> We took in the final day of the Canadian Finals in Red Deer. Jackie Ganter, on her grey horse, absolutely stunned the crowd. Even the cowboys said after, 'That is the most perfect run they have ever seen. Even though this is the second year for the finals in Red Deer – Jackie set a barrel racing record on the last day. She rode her horse straight and cool around those barrels and home. What a team; her horse was just perfect inches away from the barrels and straight on her way to cross the finish line. So smooth, there was no flinging/flapping around.[15]

Chapter Eleven
States Begin to Form GRA Chapters

The Girls Rodeo Association in 1960 started encouraging states to form member chapters. Some states preferred to keep barrel racing as an open or amateur event and some states had already formed independent state barrel racing organizations, like California. Connecting to GRA was enticing to most states, as well as California, which merged with GRA in 1960. After the California Barrel Racing Association merged with GRA, it was reported that another group had been started called the California Open Barrel Racing Association. This non-professional group would compete with men's non-professional rodeos.[1]

Charlene Jespersen was crowned, for the second year, champion barrel racer of the GRA's California chapter. She finished the season with $2,025 and rode her horse *Lotta Dollar*, a Quarter Horse stallion owned by her father, Hoke Evetts. Janice Montgomery was second; third place was Phyllis Bryant with Jean Libby Sharp capturing fourth; fifth was Roxy Freeman; Betty Van Allen was sixth; seventh place went to Debby Miller.[2]

Sammy Fancher Cole (later Brackenbury) of Las Vegas was appointed the GRA representative for Nevada in 1960.[3] The Reno, Nev., rodeo was held annually from 1919 to 1923. Then took a break until 1932. Barrel racing was introduced in 1960 and was won by Sammy Cole. The following year thirty-nine women entered the event. Judy Marshall of Tulare, Calif., and Jean Sharp of Fresno, Calif., tied to win it. In 1962 it was not held, but it came back in 1963 and was won by Judy Messerly.[4]

The Arizona GRA started with help from Phyllis Turnage of Seligman and Gloria Underdown of Wickenburg. It started with seven women attending the first meeting. By 1986 there were sixty members.[5] Barrel racing had finally become a nationwide competition, and many young women were interested in competing in this exciting new sport.

Some of the independent organizations in barrel racing in the 1960s were the Wyoming Girls Barrel Racing Association with Karen Reynolds as the president; the Oregon Barrel Racing Association was formed in Klamath Falls, and the West Texas Barrel Racing Association had headquarters in Lubbock.[6]

Lydia Moore saw her first barrel race at a St. Louis RCA rodeo in the mid-1950s. Wanda Bush came to compete, but there were very few entries. Fannie Mae Cox and Boots Tucker were the only other entries. Wanda went to Valley Mount Ranch near St. Louis, a prominent facility for all things western owned by Benny Kraus, father to Dottye and Norita Kraus. She put out an appeal to horsewomen in the area to participate. Barrel racing was not well known in that area at that time, although it was a GRA-approved barrel race. Lydia and Percyna Moore's dad, Percy, worked for Kraus at the time.[7] St. Louis was home to many prominent horse-related events and shows.

Sammy Fancher Cole won the first Reno rodeo barrel race in 1960. *Courtesy of the WPRA.*

The Missouri GRA chapter was founded in the late 1950s by two wealthy philanthropic horsewomen from St. Louis, Martha Volz Fisher, owner of Volz Packing Company, and Millie Hamm, daughter of a prominent trucking company owner. They had traveled to San Antonio to an RCA rodeo and saw their first cloverleaf barrel race. They were very interested in getting barrel racing established in their part of the country. On their return, they contacted as many horsewomen as they knew. Since Percy Moore, was also Martha Volz Fisher's trainer, Percy's daughter, Lydia, and sister, Percyna, were asked to help organize it and joined immediately. Dottye Kraus Goodspeed and Norita Kraus

Dottye Kraus Goodspeed barrel racing in Fort Smith, Ark., in 1960. *Courtesy of the WPRA*

Henderson held the first jackpot and chapter events in their area. The 1959 Missouri barrel racing champion was Dottye Kraus Goodspeed with $498 for the year.[8]

By the mid-1960s the Missouri GRA chapter had a sizeable membership base. When it came to the end of the year they wanted to present awards to the top women in the orgainization at a public event. The St. Louis Fireman's Rodeo (which was a large RCA-sanctioned indoor rodeo during that time) was produced by Tommy Steiner. Lydia Moore, Missouri GRA chapter president, went to Steiner and asked if they could have the awards presentation while the barrels were being set up during the last performance. He happily consented. One of the top rodeo photographers of the day, Bern Gregory, took photographs. Lydia later became the chapter secretary and awards chairwoman.[9]

The 1960 GRA officers and directors were Florence Price Youree, of Addington, Okla., president; Berva Dawn Taylor, Dublin, Texas, vice president; Manuelita Mitchell, of Lohn, Texas, secretary; barrel racing directors were Wanda Bush, Mason, Texas;

Mildred Farris, Iowa Park, Texas; Janet Dudley, Perryton, Texas.

Florence went to the RCA convention in Denver and got several new rodeos to include barrel racing. According to Florence, it seemed there was greater interest than ever in including barrel racing.[10]

Willard Porter wrote in his column, "Two Wraps and A Hooey" in the *Hoofs and Horns*, January 1960 issue:

> *Denver's National Western Stock Show and Rodeo announced a $2,000 purse in the girls' barrel race, The Girls Rodeo Association came of age. We believe this high–purse trend will continue, and other top rodeos, following the example of Denver, will continue to offer higher and higher purses. The girls who make up the GRA membership are to be complimented. We don't think it just simply happened that Denver gave this big purse. Through the years, the GRA has probably gathered more bruises than bouquets. And for a while, the going was pretty rough on the self-styled professional cowgirls. But they stuck with it; they fought for what they thought was right, and today their perseverance is paying off. Because these girls had and still have a right good idea of what the word "professional" means, they have been accepted by the public. And that's something that's taken a long time. Today the GRA membership is made up of skillful riders on quality horseflesh. They're colorful when they perform, and probably the most important phase of this color is the way they dress. Flashy shirts, bright trousers, big hats, neckerchiefs, fancy boots, gay jackets, tailored suits – all of this is the mark of a pro. And the professional performer is the one whom rodeo management wants to put before the public. It all adds up to this: the GRA cowgirls have stuck with their ideas through some pretty lean years, but now it looks as if 1960 is going to be a pretty fat year for them.*[11]

By the time it was held the purse had $2,400 plus the entry fees – largest purse ever offered in barrel racing. Sherry Combs won the most monies with $653.49, followed by Jane Mayo with $591.01, Mildred Farris third with $492.94, and Billie Ann Evans with $483.93.[12]

The Rodeo Cowboys Association, Inc. Articles of Association,

By-laws and Rules had in their 1960 book the following: "No contestant memberships shall be issued to women, and female contract members will not be eligible to compete except in the case of contest trick riding and trick roping."[13]

This did not affect barrel racers since they were GRA members, and approved by the RCA. This ruling was directed toward women interested in contesting in other male-oriented RCA events.

In 1960 GRA initiated the change to put permanent markers in the arena ground for the duration of the rodeo. At first, GRA directors were responsible for the task; then, it was transferred to the GRA members because directors couldn't be at every rodeo. Today the rodeo judges handles that job.

Jane Mayo, a GRA barrel racing champion, for three consecutive years, 1959 through 1961, had a book published called *Championship Barrel Racing*, by Cordovan Corp., Cypress, Texas. It sold for $4 and stated it contained "vital how-to information needed if you plan to win consistently in this exciting contest!" She also opened her own new western wear store in Okemah, Okla.[14]

During this era, the "Sage Hens and Cow Ponies" column in *Hoofs and Horns* reported news from most barrel racing organizations in the various states and news from GRA. In the February 1962 issue, it was reported that the Houston Livestock Show & Rodeo had a barrel racing purse of $3,230 plus entry fees of $50 per contestant. All contestants must have a veterinarian's health certificate for their horses before entering the rodeo grounds. The same issue reported a South Dakota GRA meeting in Sturgis, and the Arkansas Barrel Racing Association elected officers for 1962. Also in the February issue was an article "Montana's Triple Threat," telling of three Montana barrel racers having success in the event. They were Barbara Dear of Simms, Lila Mae Stewart from Missoula, and Fay Hanes from Hot Springs.[15]

Sue Ann Hubbard, the "Sage Hens" reporter, announced in the May 1962 issue an all-girl rodeo (Girls National Rodeo Association) at Brewster, Wash. The Ohio Girls Barrel Racing Association awarded the championship saddle to Mary Acton of Sterling. Ahead in the California GRA standings was Sammy Thurman of El Monte, Calif. Sammy was also expecting a baby soon.[16]

The *Quarter Horse Journal*, the official magazine of the American Quarter Horse Association, had a column in their December

1963 issue entitled, "Girls Rodeo Association Highlights." The secretary-treasurer of GRA, Billie McBride, reported and not only gave current barrel racing outcomes; she listed the top fifteen GRA barrel racers; first was Loretta Manual, winning $5,437.52; second was Wanda Bush with $5,315.10; third — Sherry Combs, $4,848.10; fourth — Sissy Thurman $4,698.99; fifth — Fay Ann Horton, $4,300.11; sixth — Diana Chapman $4,068.78; seventh — Sammy Thurman $3,020.87; eighth — Boots Tucker, $2,197.15; ninth — Mildred Farris, $2,160.45; tenth — Billie Edwards, $1,824.53; eleventh — Norita Henderson, $1,783.51; twelfth — Dorothy Snow, $1,778.51; thirteenth — Janet Dudley, $1,725.92; fourteenth — Donna Mullins, $1,473.69; and fifteenth — Sis Armstrong, $1,450.95 [17]

Sherry Combs and her husband, Benny, were trying to get to the rodeo at Little Rock, Ark., and the traffic was terrible. Once they reached the rodeo grounds, they knew they were running out of time. Benny told Sherry, "Go to the announcer's stand and ask him to put you last in the barrel race. I'll get *Red* (Sherry's horse) ready and bring him to you."

When Sherry was making her way almost there, she heard her name being announced. Tim Apodaca was a pickup man standing next to his pickup horse. Sherry said, "Tim, let me use your horse."

He handed her the reins in amazement. Sherry realized the stirrups were way too long for her, but she loped the horse into the arena and made the barrel pattern. When she came out of the arena, she saw Benny standing with *Red*. He was stunned, as well, but Sherry made her entrance on time, and despite the long stirrups, she loped the horse around the barrels and stayed in the average. Don't ever underestimate a barrel racer.[18]

In the mid-1960s, according to the GRA rulebook, the standard barrel pattern was sixty feet from score line to the first barrel, ninety feet from first to the second barrel, and 105 feet to the third barrel. From the 1980s through the mid-1990s, rules allowed for a bigger pattern for larger arenas — ninety feet from score line to the first barrel, 105 feet from the first barrel to the second barrel, and 120 feet to the third barrel.

Cowtown, N.J., located in the Woodstown/Pilesgrove area in the southern part of the state, began holding rodeos during the summer of 1955 every Friday and Saturday night. Barrel racing

Frances Smith receiving her GRA Champion Barrel Racing saddle for 1967. To her left is Gene Pruett and the men on the right are unknown. *Courtesy of Dude Smith.*

was not held as a standard event until after their new arena was built in 1965. Before that, they only held a barrel race two or three times a summer, starting in 1960, but never consistently.

Most barrel racing in New Jersey during the 1950s were held at jackpot events and were strictly amateur. Rodeo was part of this community early in the twentieth-century as part of the Salem County Fair, but once World War I started in 1918, it was canceled. Cowtown, N.J., brought rodeo back in 1930. Stoney Harris and later Howard Harris Sr. organized and hosted it.[19]

Willard Porter wrote in his article "Two Wraps & a Hooey" in the December 1967 issue of *Hoofs and Horns* that he thought Jane Mayo of Okemah, Okla., was the first to organize and conduct a barrel racing school. "Then came Sammy Fancher Thurman, who, as far as I know, still conducts barrel racing schools in California. Both Sammy and Jane are top riders and always work with the best of Quarter Horses or Thoroughbreds," said Porter.

The National Barrel Racing Clinic held its eighth annual event

Hoof and Horns, Sept. 1968 cover promoting Cowtown, N.J. Barrel racing started there in 1965 after the new arena was built. *Courtesy of Hoof and Horns*.

on the grounds of Colorado State University at Fort Collins in 1968. The event was entitled "Barrel Racing Fever" and was sponsored by the Colorado State University Rodeo Association. Throughout the clinic, speaker demonstrations were held and featured Frances Smith, Margaret Clemons, and Ardith Bruce, champions in barrel racing. Also held were a fashion show, a barrel horse sale, a barbeque, and a western dance. These clinics were popping up around the country and did much to educate young barrel racers and their parents.

Men's jackpot calf roping and team roping were held one day. No doubt of interest to some of the fathers and brothers. On Sunday, GRA and jackpot barrel racing were on the agenda. For this clinic, more than 250 girls attended, with seventy-five youngsters entered in the amateur barrel racing event, with all other events carrying large entry numbers.[20]

A photo of the first barrel racing clinic held in the East, sponsored by Eastern Barrel Racing Association in Bethany, Conn., was in the *Hoofs and Horns*, August 1968 issue. Attendees were from Rhode Island, New York, New Jersey, and Connecticut and as far away as Ontario, Canada. Martha Josey instructed, and her husband, R. E., assisted in correcting mistakes the racers had picked up.[21]

The next month's issue had a picture of Victoria Soden of Farmingdale, N.J., on the front cover of *Hoofs and Horns*. She was dressed in the proper attire and was to prove there is as much activity in the East as in the West. The photo was taken at

Cowtown, N.J.[22]

Missy Long of Duncan, Okla., joined the GRA in 1968. She was only twelve-years-old and had competed in Quarter Horse shows since she was six and found the transition to barrel racing easy. In early 1969, she didn't compete much because of school, except when she could compete close to home. But by May, she was number fourteen in the GRA standings. That urged her to see if she could improve her standing, and shortly she moved to number four. In August she had a terrific string of Colorado wins, eleven out of thirteen rodeos, including Colorado Springs and Pueblo. At Pueblo, she caught Mildred Farris, who had led all year.

Missy went to the National Finals Rodeo in first place. She was the youngest, age thirteen, to compete at the NFR and broke every record in the GRA at that time. She placed in eight of nine go-rounds — a record — and won the average, winning over $1,500 — a record — which gave her total winnings for the year of $9,783 — another record. Missy only competed in fifty-two rodeos that year to become the World Champion Barrel Racer.[23]

Chapter Twelve
Barrel Racing at the National Finals Rodeo

The first National Finals Rodeo was held in December 1959. Much cussing and discussion had gone on with the powers that be in the Rodeo Cowboys Association about having a specific end to each year. Some cowboys felt if rodeo expected to grow it needed to hold a finals with the top cowboys in each event. Other cowboys said the RCA was formed so that any member could enter any rodeo — regardless of his standing in the association. But after three years of pros and cons those wanting a final rodeo, to end the year, won out. It was scheduled to be held in Dallas, Texas, the day after Christmas and would include the top fifteen contestants in each event, based on season winnings.

The events to be held in Dallas included bareback riding, steer wrestling, saddle bronc riding, calf roping and bull riding. There were ten performances over a five day period with two performances held each day. The finals for steer roping, team roping and barrel racing were not included in the Dallas event, instead were scheduled to take place in Clayton, N.M.

The RCA formed a National Finals Commission that met in Tulsa to discuss and set the format for the three events not held in Dallas. The members included: Bill Harlan, a team roper from Clayton, N.M.; John Van Cronkhite, producer of the NFR; Dale Smith, team roping director and Clark McEntire, steer roping director. Carl Arnold was chosen as arena director and Chuck Sheppard and Joe Crow Jr. as flaggers. Prize money was set at $5,000 for the steer roping and team roping, but the barrel racing was only $1,950. There were only four rounds of barrel racing, and six rounds of team roping and steer roping.[1]

The top fifteen barrel racers for the 1959 year that qualified to compete were: Mildred Farris, Jane Mayo, Jo Ann Crosby, Janet Dudley, Sissy Thurman, Billie McBride, Fay Ann Horton, Sis

Armstrong, Sherry Combs, Wanda Bush, Martha Ann Symons, Billie Ann Evans, Manuelita Mitchell, Betty Ray and Florence Youree.[2]

The Clayton event was held November 13 and 14 and weather was bitter cold. Clayton is in the northeastern part of New Mexico. The area is basically prairieland and almost no trees. During that time of year nothing stops the wind from blowing and it can feel like the wind originates in the Arctic. In fact, the rule that required all barrel racers to wear a hat was waived, but competitors were allowed to wear head-scarves.

Jane Mayo placed in all four rounds, with two firsts, one second and a tie for third and fourth. She also won the average in 77.9 seconds in four runs. Each of her runs were timed 19.7; 19.2; 19.7 and 19.3 seconds. Mayo's National Finals earnings were $663. She placed first at the finals and won the barrel racing world championship with total earnings for the year of $5,814.

Mildred Farris was reserve world champion but won her second place position before the NFR was held. Farris only won $19, with a fourth place tie with Sis Armstrong, in the second-

Billie Ann Evans competing at the first National Finals in 1959. Note she is wearing a bandana, the wind was so strong the hat rule was waived. *Courtesty of Joleen Steiner*

round.

Wanda Bush also placed in all four rounds, with one first, two seconds and a third place win. She also won second in the average with 78.4 seconds on four runs. The first three of her runs were 19.5, and the last was 19.9 seconds. Her winnings were $546 placing her sixth for the year with $1,975.

Janet Dudley finished third at the finals with one first, a second, third, and a fourth for a total of $507. She placed third in the average with 78.6 seconds over four rounds. Dudley also finished third for the year with total winnings $2,950. The other contestants didn't win a dime at the finals.[3]

In 1960 the second National Finals for the team roping and barrel racing were moved to Scottsdale, Ariz. The steer roping went back to Clayton, with the prize money for the three events remaining the same.

Seven of the top fifteen barrel racers in the country chose not to

Sammy Thurman competing at the second National Finals Rodeo, held in Scottsdale, Ariz., in 1960. *Photo by Devere Helfrich, courtesy of the Natonal Cowboy & Western Heritage Museum.*

compete at the finals in Scottsdale. Those who did compete were: Jane Mayo, Sammy Thurman, Nancy Farqhuar, Jody Thomas, Sis Armstrong, Pat Marr, Tana White, Wanda Bush, Mildred Farris, Sherry Combs, Frances Moates, Billie Anne Evans, Florence Youree, Jo Ann Crosby and Phyllis Turnage.

Jane Mayo again won the world title, after splitting first and second in the average with Sammy Thurman with a time of 107.0 seconds in six rounds. Jane had a final total for the year of $7,833, winning $746 at the Finals.

Mildred Farris won reserve champion again with $7,034 total, including NFR winning of $52. Sherry Combs won third for the year, winning $207 at the finals, and $3,850 for the year. Fourth was Sammy Thurman who won $759 at the finals and $3,777 for the year.

The 1961 NFR was held in Santa Maria, Calif., and the prize money was raised to $2,205. Jane Mayo won the barrel racing World Champion for the third consecutive year and Sammy Thurman was second. The women winning third, fourth and fifth for the year were Mildred Farris, Sherry Johnson, and Faye Ann Horton. Farris, Johnson and Horton did not compete at the finals because the women felt the prize money offered would not justify the time and expense to travel to California.

The 1962 NFR for barrel racing was moved to Dallas and the prize money was increased to $3,226. Sherry Combs won the world championship with $7,899 for the year, winning $504 at the finals. Reserve champion was Wanda Bush with $6,942 and she won second in the average with $242 won during the finals. Fay Ann Horton won third, and Mildred Farris won fourth. The average at the finals was won by Sissy Thurman, who won $988 and had the fastest run with 17.6 seconds.[4]

The barrel racing finals was moved from one location to another each year, but never considered to be a part of the National Finals Rodeo which finally settled in Oklahoma City, at the State Fair Arena (later renamed the Jim Norick Arena), in 1965 and eventually the Myriad Convention Center. It was held in Oklahoma City until it moved to Las Vegas in 1985.

Florence Youree was president of the GRA from 1960 through 1964, and was aware of how important barrel racing had become in professional rodeo. She knew in her heart that it should be a part of the National Finals Rodeo, along with all of the other events. She prepared herself thoroughly and went to visit with Stanley Draper, who was the head of the Oklahoma City Chamber of Commerce. Draper and the Oklahoma Chamber of Commerce were in charge

Top fifteen barrel racers for 1967, the first year the barrel racing was held as part the National Finals Rodeo in Oklahoma City. (Top Row L to R) Fay Ann Leach, Roxy McFarland, Sis Armstrong, Kay Whitaker (Vamvoras), Frances Smith. (Middle Row L to R) Florence Youree, Sherry Combs Johnson, Mildred Farris, Sammy Thurman. (Front Row L to R) Judy Marshall, Sissy Thurman, Loretta Manual, Ardith Bruce and Patty Mack (Prather). Allene Gaylor is missing from the group. *Photo Courtesy of Ferrell Butler.*

of the National Finals Rodeo along with Clem McSpadden who had become the announcer for the 1965 and 66 finals.

Youree told them that to see "beautiful girls wearing colorful lamé and rhinestone costumes as they raced around the barrels at the finals would be an additional asset and draw more fans who would want to come to the National Finals to see the girls."

She also offered that the barrel racers would also be available for the grand entry and carry flags during each performance. Draper agreed and another $1,000 was added to the purse for 1967.[5]

Draper added the following year that barrel racing be held at the National Finals as long as it was held in Oklahoma City, with a minimum purse of $2,500.[6]

Lydia Moore moved to Oklahoma that year from Missouri, where she had been very active in the rodeo world. She was hired by Stanley Draper to be liaison for the barrel racers at the National Finals Rodeo in Oklahoma City. Eventually she became involved with the GRA directly and served as their calf roping director, Southern region director, then bull riding director. In 1973 she became the executive secretary for GRA/WPRA and held that office until 1995.[7]

Texas barrel Racing Association RoundUp held in Clifton, Texas, in the early 1960s. (Standing L to R) Barbara Smith, Edith Eggleston, Sadie Lacey, Gene McJunkin Livingston, Paulette Allen, unknown man and two unknown cowgirls, Jo Walling and Bertie Dutton. (Kneeling L to R) Loraine Adams, Carolyn Cartwright, Barbara Cummings, Jackie Thompson, Fay Oglesby, Sharron Reeves and Dawn Tripp. Notice the fancy dress and hats worn by the cowgirls of that era. *Courtesy of Gene McJunklin Livingston and photographer unknown.*

Chapter Thirteen
Roll Out the Barrels

Once barrel racers were included in the National Finals Rodeo and barrel racing had spread across the country, it was evident there was no holding those barrel racing cowgirls back. They were getting more and more publicity, but not just about their horsemanship. In the January 1969 *Hoofs and Horns* an article entitled "One Girl Style Show" the best dressed barrel racer, chosen by her fellow state GRA members was Nancy Rodewald from Craig, Colo. She and her fellow racers had emphasized the individuality and the personal competition by choosing to be style pace-setters in the rodeo world. Nancy made her own clothing and made many fancy yokes and notch work, belt loops and many other intricate sewing styles."[1]

In the beginning, when barrel races were called sponsor races, the serious cowgirls who prided themselves on their horsemanship, not beauty and fashion, put much more emphasis on the racing than how they were dressed. Of course, the GRA had a say in the dress code, so there were no shabbily dressed barrel racers. Four decades later they found a happy medium, where these talented cowgirls could seriously compete and look good at the same time. An article in the November 1970 issue of *Hoofs and Horns* entitled "What They Are Wearing, Barrel Racing Styles," by Robert Freedheim, it said in part:

> *The rapid growth of barrel racing at major rodeos owes some of its success to the good looks and colorful fashions of the contestants. G.R.A. barrel racer Joyce Shelley Burk, who was voted Best Dressed Cowgirl at the 1969 National Finals Rodeo, and who is riding high in the standings this year – having a terrific history in rodeo – has more than a little to contribute to the barrel racer fashion style concept.*

A former Miss Rodeo America, 1963, and an All-Around Champion at the All-Girl Rodeo at Duncan, Oklahoma, Joyce said "To keep a wardrobe always ready G.R.A. gals have to give considerable attention to their outfits." Their colorful garb and high style are very much a part of their appeal to the rodeo public. Add this to the outstanding professional riding these girls demonstrate, and you have plenty of show to sell to committees. Joyce won the 1970 world barrel racing championship and the average at the NFR with $10,629.[2]

Loretta Manual won the world champion barrel racing title in 1963 and 1967. She was off to a great start at the National Finals in 1970. Manual split first and second with Anita Kilgore, in the first go-round. She went on to win four more rounds, plus a fourth and a second in two other rounds. In the fourth go-round she failed to

The 1973, '74 and '75 world champion barrel racers at the 1975 NFR. (L to R) Gail Petska on *Dobie*, Jeana Day on *Excuse* and Jimmie Gibbs Munroe on *Billy*. *Photograph by and courtesy of Kenneth Springer.*

follow the correct barrel racing pattern. The judges did not catch her error and gave her a time. Realizing what she had done, Loretta went to the judges and explained she had not correctly followed the required pattern. The judges gave her a no-time for that round.

Loretta was disqualified for the average, which she would have won, had she not been so honest and turned herself in. She finished fifth in the world standings.[3]

When Judi Fields, Loretta's longtime friend was told of this she said, "I'm not at all surprised. Loretta has always been a 'straight arrow' and followed the 'letter of the law'— no matter what."

Cowgirl honesty came into play fifty years later, when Jackie Crawford, in the first breakaway roping held during the National Finals in 2020, had an illegal head-catch, which the judges did not call, and they gave her a time. Once she told the judges of their mistake, she received a no-time for that round, which put her out of the average race. But in spite of it, Jackie won the first world champion breakaway roping to be held during the National Finals Rodeo. Martha Angelone won the average with 34.8 seconds on ten head. Angelone also became the reserve world champion.

There are people in this world that feel being honest, even if the judges miss their error, is more important than winning.

Joleen Hurst had a good horse for barrel racing, but it wasn't until her sister married and quit barrel racing, and gave Joleen her horse, *Hot Shot*, she seriously hit the rodeo road. She joined GRA in 1970 and picked rodeos to go to that added the most money. She was having fun and couldn't

Joleen Hurst Steiner at the National Finals Rodeo in 1971. *Photo courtesy of the Steiner family.*

find a single negative about her rodeo days. She admitted she never practiced. "I just hung on to *Hot Shot*," she laughed, "and if I didn't knock over a barrel we generally got in the money."

Joleen was having a good year and her dad promised her if she won the Cow Palace rodeo, in San Francisco, he would buy her a trailer with living quarters. She won the 1970 Cow Palace, and she qualified for her first National Finals. For the finals she won three seconds and two first places and finished seventh. Her dad bought the trailer. During the 1971 season her mom traveled with her preparing all the good home cooked meals that are missed on the rodeo road. "We stayed on the rodeo grounds with *Hot Shot* and it was easy and lots of fun," said the straight-talking cowgirl.[5]

The following article was in the April 1972 issue of *Western Horseman*:

> *During the National Finals Rodeo at Oklahoma City in December fifteen barrel racers from nine states were racing the 'cans' to determine the final 1971 standings of barrel racers in the Girls Rodeo Association.*
>
> *Donna Patterson went into the Finals with $11,017, a lead of $483 over Karen Greenough who had $10,534. Jeana Day was third with $10,396; and Joleen Hurst was fourth with $10,394. Any one of these top four girls could have emerged as the world champion for '71 if she turned the barrels fast enough at the Finals. As a result the audiences were treated to some of the finest runs ever?*
>
> *Donna Patterson, with pressure on her and on a world championship stage made barrel racing runs that only a real professional can make. She won four fourths, one second, and topped the average with a total of 168:79 seconds on her ten runs. With the average paying $485 and a go-round paying $223, Donna successfully out-raced all others to win the championship barrel racing for 1971. Her winnings for the year totaled $11,952. Jeana Day won three go-rounds, and placed second three times to move into second place for the year. Karen Greenough had the misfortune of knocking a barrel over in the sixth-go which put her out of the average--- and dropped her down to fourth for the year's final standings.*
>
> *Joleen Hurst, making consistent runs, won three thirds*

and three seconds to finish the year in third place.

Although Martha Tompkins, Dublin, Tex., had no chance to win the year-end championship, she made some sensational runs. She started off with a slow run in the first go-round, but then her gelding really 'caught fire.' Of the remaining nine go-rounds, Martha won six of them (go rounds 4, 5, 6 & 8, 9, &10), was third in two go's, and fourth in one go.

Martha pocketed $2,019, and finished the year in sixth place with $6,456. She also took home the Ann Lewis Memorial Trophy for the Rookie of the Year, and the Sissy Thurman Memorial trophy for the fastest run at the Finals, with a 16.33 seconds run.

Winner of the hard-luck trophy was Celie Whitcomb, Sterling, Colorado, whose horse got sick; and the winner of the Best-Dressed Cowgirl trophy was Lee Natale, of Patterson, New Jersey.[6]

Gail Petska, of Norman, Okla., made quite a showing at the 1972 National Finals Rodeo. She won seven go-rounds and placed second in two. Not only did she win the world championship, but also won the NFR average with 167.41 seconds in ten rounds. Her total monies for the year were $17,104, with winnings at NFR of $2,503.

The following year at the National Finals she won six go-rounds, plus one second place and split third and fourth in one round. She again won the world with $19,448, winning $2,236 at the finals.[7]

Petska did not compete the next year; instead she was becoming a mother. But twenty years later she and her twenty-year-old daughter, Tye, were going down the barrel racing rodeo road together. Tye, qualified for the 1994 NFR and came in eighth for the year, and second in the average at the NFR.[8]

Wendy Potter, mother of Sherry Cervi, and wife of Mel Potter, a great roper of his era, also competed in barrel racing and did quite well, according to her husband, Mel. He owned Rodeo Inc., along with Jack Brainard, John Snow and later Maury Whyte and they they were putting on rodeos at that time. He said, "Wendy never competed in more than twenty-five rodeos a year, and made the National Finals in 1970, 1971 and 1972."[9]

Lynn McKenzie making a run in 1983. *Photograph by Murray Tinkleman and courtesy of Stan Searle and Hoof and Horns.*

Carol Goostree on *Dobre*.
Photo courtesy of Kenneth Springer.

In 1971 Jimmie Gibbs Munroe took her young, green, three year-old horse, *Billy*, to college with her. Jimmie roomed with another barrel racer Vicki Adams, at Sam Houston Sate University in Huntville, Texas. They both decided they were doing well enough in barrel racing to get their GRA cards.

Jimmie applied and sent her money in, then found out Vicki had failed to send her money in because she realized she couldn't go to the winter rodeos. Since they had planned to go to GRA barrel races together Jimmie called the GRA office, and talk to Lydia Moore, the executive secretary, asking if she could get her money back. She found that it was too late to do so. Fortunately for Jimmie she qualified in second place and went to the National Finals Rodeo that year, finishing third in the world. Not bad for someone who had tried to get her money back and not join the GRA earlier in the year.[10]

As barrel racing became more professional more innovative ideas came into the sport. At first the timing was done by a watch, with a second hand. Timers or secretaries usually timed the event.

Tommy Steiner, ramrod of Steiner Rodeo Company, had hired Mildred and John Farris to work for the Steiner Rodeo Company. Mildred was a rodeo secretary and timer, but she was also an excellent barrel racer. Tommy felt that some folks might think Mildred was favored in barrel racing in some way at the Steiner Rodeo Company rodeos. He looked for something that would prove the racers were all timed and treated equally. Tommy had seen an electric eye used at the race track and felt that using an electric eye during the barrel races would eliminate anyway of having favoritism in the event.[11]

Steiner and John Farris went to the horse race track in Shreveport, La., to examine how they timed horse races, which was with an electric eye system. John Farris remembered that Tommy ended up buying one in 1964 or '65. During the barrel racing when Mildred was competing, either Beverly Steiner or Bonnie Bostian timed the event. Another barrel racing perk that the Steiner rodeos allowed was if the racer's horse fell, they were given a second run.

John Farris also said that it was his responsibility to set the electric eye up at each rodeo. He said the eye had to be positioned exactly right on each side of the arena to work properly. He remembered sometimes it was difficult to get the red light to come on if it wasn't aimed directly at the eye apparatus on the other side of the arena.[12] In time the electric eye became an extremely important tool and standard equipment to time barrel racing runs.

Electric timers did not become common until the 1970s. However, Ardith Bruce, a well known barrel racer from Colorado and 1964 world champion barrel racer, remembered that her husband, who had been in the Navy, had a real stopwatch that he used for his duties while in the Navy. The rodeo judges or secretaries would borrow it for the barrel races. She also said, "Our Colorado chapter instigated the electric timers in their areas. She recalled, "In the mid-1960s we had one built for us. It weighed 100 pounds and ran off car batteries."

They continually made improvements on the Colorado 'creation' and in time dropped the need for the heavy car batteries which made it more portable.[13]

The 1970 GRA rulebook lists electric timers as allowed but

Jimmie Gibbs Munroe on *Billy* in 1978.
Photo courtesy of Kenneth Springer.

certainly not mandatory. By 1973 the GRA approved a rule requiring the use of an electric eye along with a backup stopwatch.[14]

The first sponsor that bought electric eyes for GRA was Nestea in 1979, according to Jimmie Munroe. They donated enough money to buy twenty electric timers. The GRA distributed them to stock contractors throughout the country.[15]

In 1981 GRA barrel racers paid, in addition to their entry fee a $2 timer fee, for the person responsible for putting the timer in play at each rodeo and maintaining it. This $2 timer fee continued until 2008.[16]

By 1975 there were 460 rodeos approved by the PRCA with 362 offering barrel racing, but of those rodeos only forty-two added equal money for barrel racers compared to the pay-off of other events.[17]

In 1975 the Rodeo of Rodeos program, sponsored by the Phoenix Jaycees, Jeana Day Felts was featured on the girl's barrel racing page. It also noted the purse was $1,100 and the entry fee was $50. Jeana Day was born October 24, 1954, in Woodward, Okla., and joined the GRA in 1969. She was offered three scholarships to attend college but chose barrel racing instead. Jeana rides a bay gelding, *Poco Excuse*, who was eleven-years-old and 14.1 hands tall. She started him in 1967 and he is her main horse. She was reserve champion in the GRA for four years and became world champion for 1974.[18]

In 1976 a major change occurred at the National Finals Rodeo, with the PRCA changing the format for determining the world championships. The world champion would be determined by the person in each event that won the most monies at the NFR, instead of for the entire year, as it had been since the RAA started keeping track of monies won in 1929.

The WPRA went along with PRCA in this format; however the WPRA had a second set of winners those three years and actually had two champions. One championship was based on NFR winning monies only at the finals, and another for winning the most money for the entire year which was called the WPRA national champion.

The WPRA world champions were determined by the most monies won at the National Finals Rodeo, as ruled by PRCA.

Those three champs were; 1976 – Connie Combs; 1977 – Jackie Jo Perrin; and 1978 – Lynn McKenzie.[19]

The WPRA national champions for those years: 1976 and 1977 – Jimmie Gibbs Munroe; 1978 – Carol Goostree.[20]

The PRCA after 1978 changed the way yearly world champions were determined back to the competitor that won the most money all year long in each event, including the finals. The three year change, 1976, '77 and '78, was greatly criticized and has never been repeated.

Lynn McKenzie who became the WPRA world champion in 1978 holds a unique record. She won the world but did not become Rookie of the Year in 1978. That title went to WPRA national champion, Carol Goostree. Lynn won the National Finals with $6,500 won at the NFR and a total for the year of $15,500. Carol Goostree won $29,651 for the year.

Another innovation in professional rodeo, in the late 1970s, included the way contestants were allowed to enter professional rodeos. Until PROCOM was started rodeo contestants traveling the rodeo road had to telephone the rodeo secretary or a committee person to enter each rodeo. Certain times were required, which was not easy to do before cell phones became available. It required stopping in a town, finding a pay phone and hoping to reach the person taking entries, or hoping the number was not busy so that another call was necessary. PROCOM centralized entering on a toll-free number. Call-backs for positions now come via email. The WPRA also has a website that lists details regarding upcoming events.[21]

An additional attempt for safety purposes was tried at the 1977 NFR for barrel racers. They used barrels that had a covered top, but no bottom. It was done, no doubt, in an attempt to have the barrels be lighter to handle. Realizing they might turn over too easily Clem McSpadden had two boards crossed, like an X, and placed on the bottom, to make it more stable.

Vicki Adams, riding her famous stallion, *Firewater Flit aka* Milo, hit the second barrel and he stepped in it with his hind leg, cutting it badly. But since the competition for the barrel racing event had started with the barrels designed in that manner, with no base, they had to continue to use them through the ten performances. They were never used again.[22]

Chapter Fourteen
Barrel Horses: Find — Train — Win

In the early days of barrel racing the horse a young girl used was a ranch horse also used for different ranch chores. On occasion the horse might have been used at rodeo competitions, but doubtful. Horses used on the ranch had to be versatile — one minute they are cutting out cattle from a herd, and the next minute they may be dragging a calf to be branded. The following day that same horse might be at a rodeo helping a young woman race around the barrels or be ridden by a hazer to keep a steer running straight.

Once the American Quarter Horse Association was formed the breeding of ranch horses started being discussed more and more. Previously a horse buyer was more concerned with how well the horse was broke and how he performed. If he raised him from birth he knew more about the sire and dam and their abilities, and maybe the next generation would have those same traits, but maybe not. But once the era of specialization started the breeding of the horse became more important — roping horses, bulldogging horses, barrel racing horses.

Jimmie Gibbs Munroe said when she started, as her barrel racing improved they began looking for a better horse for her. Her family went to see Rebecca Tyler, of Uvalde, Texas, who owned *Flit Bar* and his progeny. Tyler had some impressive horses from the *Flit Bar* breeding. Tyler showed them a five-year-old gelding that she thought would be good for Jimmie. While Jimmie was riding the horse and her dad was watching, Jimmie's mother, who had a good eye for horses, had seen a three-year-old gelding saddled in another pen that impressed her. When she suggested they look at the three-year-old Jimmie and her dad looked at it briefly but didn't give it much thought. Jimmie's dad never took a trailer when they went to look at a horse because he felt that encouraged the owner to know he was interested in buying and possibly might raise the price. On the way home Jimmie said, "All mother could talk about was that other horse. So when we got home my dad called Rebecca Tyler and asked her what she wanted for the two geldings."

The price was $1,000 for the five-year-old and $400 for the three-year-old. Mr. Gibbs bought them both. The three-year-old gelding, *Billy*, turned out to be the best barrel horse and took Jimmie to her first world title. Mother knows best![1]

In a 2018 April *WPRA News* an article entitled, "Impact of Barrel Racing Blood-lines in the WPRA" by Jolee Jordan said, "That all changed in a tremendous way, first because of the GRA's promotion of the sport in professional rodeo and later, with the growth of futurities and eventually even divisional format barrel racing. The growth of events and prize money opened the market for trainers, virtually non-existent in barrel racing before the 1950s, and for breeders."[2]

Some of the bloodlines that were mentioned in this article were: *PC Frenchmans Hayday* (called *Dinero*), *Three Bars*, Hancock, and Skeet bloodlines, *Lena's Bar* (dam of E*asy Jet*), *Sugar Bars* (sire of *Flit Bar*) and *Rocket Bar* (the grandsire of *Dash for Cash*), *Dee Gee*, *Oklahoma Star Jr.* (siring *V's Sandy* and *Star Plaudit*), *Leo*, *Gills Bay Boy* (aka *Scamper*) and more.[3]

That being said, there is always that 'unknown' horse that has no specific breeding background or tendencies to attract attention, or even be considered to run the barrels. It may be found at birth, or years later. Once 'an unknown' is shown the basics of running barrels the owner occasionally finds the horse has an amazing talent for the sport, or it doesn't make an impression at all.

The combination of the 'right' horse with the 'right' rider can often make anything happen. Is it because they both have the drive and determination to win? The size of the heart of a horse is often credited with the ability to out run and out maneuver their competitors. Actually the physical size is not in question. It is the tremendous willingness and ability at speed and precision at going around those three barrels and the deep relationship between the horse and rider that make them winners. This can seldom be determined until they have had enough time practicing, learning about one another and enough time in the arena in competition.

The barrel racing horse has been said by many barrel racers, to be as much as 90% of whether a barrel racer wins or not. Some people have said, "If you have enough money, you can buy a well-trained barrel horse and win no matter who is riding it."

But statements like this are always questionable. There is no doubt; the horse is a very important part of winning a barrel race. But so is the rider! Below are some of the articles and opinions of various outstanding barrel racers through the years.

In an article in *Hoofs and Horns,* Jane Mayo, who won the barrel racing championship at the National Finals Rodeo in 1959, 1960 and 1961 said about her horse, *V's Sandy.* Jane said it wasn't a difficult chore to get him to run her style but it takes a long time for a horse and rider to come to an understanding. "A horse and rider must think together to win," said Mayo.

When discussing *V's Sandy* she said, "He can run faster a farther distance and turn closer and better than any horse I know of." She also said of him, "He has all of his 1,200 pounds of power ready and willing to use in a split-second. He has brains, know-how, ability and most of all a heart. He tries to do anything I ask of him. As far as barrel racing is concerned, he will run the course full speed and I never have to take hold of him."

She also added, "In traveling he can be put anywhere and he will eat and drink and not get hurt. He will always load, no matter where you are or how tired he is. He works equally well indoors or outdoors. If you ask me if I think he's the best barrel horse in the country, I'll just say — 'what do you think'?"[4]

In four summer issues of *Hoofs and Horns,* 1969, Jimmie Hurley featured information she gleaned from Sammy Thurman as to How to Choose a Barrel Horse; Equipping Your horse; Faults in Horses and Riders; and finally How to Handle Problem Ground.[5] Sammy's articles have been condensed by the author.

Sammy pointed out that in the barrel racing event the difference between times of racers are generally figured in one hundredth of seconds. In other rodeo events there may be five or ten seconds between first and fourth place winners. She also gives the horse 85% of the credit for winning If the horse has had the proper training. The first thing she looks for in a horse is speed. This is needed for short distances and therefore Quarter horses are a good choice, but she also knows she wouldn't rule out other breeds. She knows a horse with a long stride has speed, but they do need to know how to shorten up a long stride - to get around a barrel. This is taught by the exercises you practice with the horse. She stressed it is important to analyze the conformation of the horse you are considering and make sure they have no structural faults. Between mares, geldings and stallions she found mares to be moody, but if you have one with a good disposition and they don't try to resist they generally give you all they have. A mare generally has more staying power than a gelding, although geldings have a more even disposition and when finding one with a lot of heart he can't be beat. Stallions are different. If he wants to be a barrel horse, he will give you all he has consistently. But you can't train one to want to be a barrel horse if he doesn't have the desire. Former race horses have speed but if they have been racing for awhile it is hard to train them to slow down at a barrel. Picking one with speed from breeding is a good choice. Sammy's best luck in training is to find a horse that was trained to be a stock horse. These horses have been taught to respond or taught how to learn. The best way to the pay window is to buy a horse trained for barrels and is a proven winner. They can run into four and five figure costs but they can save you a lot of heartache and disappointment.[6]

> *Equip Your Horse:* Equipment for the horse and rider should fit both of them and be in top condition at all times. Check each piece of equipment before a run — and again after the run. Sammy likes a light saddle, it can help even a few tenths of a second, and it is worth it. Make sure you have a pad that fits your horse's back. Stirrups should hang in the right place — definitely not behind you. Sammy prefers a bend in her knee just enough to lift her to a three-inch clearance in the saddle. She designed her favorite saddle — it is lightweight due to a hollow fiberglass tree, light leathers and no back cinch. A reasonably high swell which is cut away for better leg grip and is not built up in the front of the seat. This enables you to move in the saddle and use your body to cue the horse. Light leathers are helpful, but swing easily, so Sammy uses tie-ups on her stirrup leathers to make sure her feet don't get behind her. She prefers a ¾" rigging with a short seat, scant

skirts for lighter weight. Monte Foreman designed a breast collar she likes. She uses a tie down with a strap to the breast collar. Using a tie-down directly to the breast collar tends to make the horse's nose pull back toward his chest. Sometimes you have to use a variety of options to see what works best for each horse. The choice of bit depends entirely on the individual horse. Sammy works her horses more from cues. If you use a severe bit, don't use it often. You definitely don't want your horse to give you no response when you pull. She does not use spurs to make her horses run. In fact if a rider does not use spurs, don't start. Learn to use spurs correctly. She uses run-down boots on his front legs. They are made of neoprene so they can be snug to hold in place yet have enough elasticity to keep from hurting. She uses skid boots on the back legs. Tendon boots protect a horse that interferes up high on his legs. If the horse has a tendency to overreach you can use bell boots or over-reach boots.[7]

Faults In Horses and In Riders: Sometimes the fault lies with the horse, but often the horse is trying to do what is expected of him but the rider is keeping him from it.

Common Faults Found in Green Barrel Horses: It has seen the barrels and at first it is normal for him to shoulder into the barrels or come in too close. If so, it will fail in getting around the barrel without losing time. In correcting this, move it away from the barrel with your inside foot, use a spur only if necessary, until you are ready for it to drop in. When starting to encourage more speed, they may get chargey, so do it slow and easy, building up his speed when you feel the horse can handle it. Discipline is something that has to be schooled into a green horse. You are the boss; always make it do what you want it to do your way. Be fair, don't let it get away with anything, but don't pick at it or antagonize it. When you do discipline it, do it hard and you won't have to do it often. Don't lean too far forward and get your spurs up in the horse's flank. Learn to use the saddle horn to be with your horse. It is wrong to rein across its neck; this causes a horse to make a roll back or an inside roll with its nose tipped away from the turn. You are probably using the reins and you will be pulling it back when it should be driving out. Sammy tries to look for her next barrel when she is 3/4th of the way around the barrel. She starts driving her horse then and it leaves the barrels hard. She also sets it up for the next barrel by going straight to where she wants it to be placed coming into the next turn. Don't over-ride your horse. It is a common problem with beginners. Don't over-whip, over-spur or over-rein your horse. Give them a chance to do something on their own. Once you get a horse trained leave it alone and let it do it himself — just help it a little. Look at the course before you run it — and make sure the barrels are up. Sammy always took her horse the shortest distance from the starting line to the first barrel, but you must give your horse enough angle to make a smooth turn around the barrels. After turning 3/4s around the last barrel she would have a spot past the scoreline which was the shortest and most direct and send her horse to it. The only time that doesn't work is when the gate (where you come in and go out of the arena) is too close to that spot. Your horse may fight to go out the gate. If it is too close let it go out the gate. Be sure your horse is running when it goes past the timer going and coming from the barrels.[8]

In *Western Horseman*, January 1972, issue was an article "Sammy Thurman Describes the Ideal Barrel Horse" by Jimmie Hurley, with a drawing by Karin McNulty of what Sammy described. In part, Sammy said:

> I'm not asking for a beautiful horse. I don't give a darn what he looks like if he can run and I can get the money in the barrel racing purses. I've never seen a horse with perfect conformation and a beautiful head that could do anything. Since I want my horse to have

what I consider perfect conformation, I must have one fault. I want that fault in his head because I want the rest of his body to be able to perform perfectly.

He should be a fairly good-sized animal . . . . around 15 hands and weigh between 1,100 and 1,200 pounds. I want him to have good, flat bone . . . not too refined, yet not too heavily boned.

White feet tend to be soft and won't hold a nail; therefore, I prefer black feet. I like a fair length of the pastern . . . not too much and not too little of an angle. A horse with too much angle to the pastern is subject to tendon troubles because he puts too much pressure on the tendons. If it is too straight, the horse would be rough to ride and put too much jar or stress on the bone structure.

The angle of the hind leg seems to have more than a little importance. A horse with a real straight hind leg usually has high speed but can't keep his feet under him to turn and maneuver. However, if the angle is too severe, he would have maneuverability but would lack speed. The perfect hind leg for a barrel horse would be somewhere in between these two; not too straight and yet with not too much of an angle. A horse with a long stride is assured of speed; however, you want this same horse to be able to collect that length of stride or shorten it up well enough to be able to turn around a barrel. I believe the angle of the hind leg determines if the horse will have a balance of both speed and maneuverability around the barrel.

Low knees and hocks on a horse seem to give him more speed and maneuverability than the average horse.[9]

* * *

Sharon Camarillo has an approach to training called her Performance Horsemanship Program which is to encompass performance evaluation and the mental game of competition. In a recent article in *Rodeo News* by Sharon and Donna Irvin, a nationally acclaimed intercollegiate horse show coach and more, entitled "Ride To The Top" they use six building blocks for their

Sharon Camarillo competing at the Cheyenne Frontier Days Rodeo. *Photo by Jan Spencer and courtesy of Sharon Camarillo.*

training pyramid.

Rhythm and Forward: The ability to move your horse forward without resistance is the foundation to everything we do. Cadence in a walk should be smooth and four beat; the trot is two beat; and the lope should be consistent and three beat in both leads.

Suppleness: The ability of the horse to learn to give and move off of rein and leg pressure. Flex in the head and neck along with bend that incorporates the horse's shoulder rib cage and hip. Being supple with rhythm and forward builds the foundation.

Contact: Requires the horse's trust and acceptance of the bit in the rider's hand enabling to connect the hindquarters to the forehand. Consistency, patience and timing in applying pressure and release is key in establishing confident horses.

Impulsion: Forward propulsion from the power

generated from the hind end forward which creates more powerful forward energy for maneuvers such as transitions, laterals, rating, stopping, etc.

Straightness: The ability to align the horse's body on both straight and curved lines. It requires attention by the rider and application of the rider's seat, legs and hands and the skills provided by the prior levels to allow the rider to position the horse's entire body aligned and balanced between their legs, seat and hands.

Collection: The reward of applying the skills provided by the training pyramid is to teach a horse to carry its body with an athletic frame for balanced, efficient movement, strengthening your performance results by understanding and evaluating each level of the pyramid.[10]

Sharon also has a book by *Western Horseman, Barrel Racing, Completely Revised, The A.R.T. of Barrel Racing, Applied Riding Techniques for Work, Play and Competition.*

* * *

Amberley Snyder, a young barrel racer, from Utah was injured badly in an automobile accident in 2010. She was thrown from the vehicle and hit a post causing her to have no ability below her waist. She is now confined to a wheelchair, when not riding her horse and competing. She required much rehabilitation as well as time to decide what her future path might be. She chose to get her Masters in Counseling and does a great deal of motivational speaking.

Before the accident she and her dad found a horse for her to train to barrel race when she was in high school. His name was *Power*. He was high strung and had a short attention span. *Power* was turned out for eighteen months after Amberley's accident until she decided she was ready to get back on him.

"This horse became my 'one in a million' horse. He took care of me above himself every run," Amberley said.

Amberley knew winning on a horse she had trained was more rewarding than winning on one someone else trained. She now has *Legacy*, who can spin and stop and felt so athletic to her. She knew she needed a horse that was a free runner, honest, and could figure out how to just listen to my hands and voice.

It took time to figure out how to communicate with her horse since she is not able to use her legs. She won her first buckle with *Legacy*, and has renewed faith in herself that she can still train a winning barrel horse in spite of the fact she is strapped in her saddle, cannot kick, and is still in her wheelchair.[11]

* * *

There are many savvy cowgirls who competed in the past and are now holding clinics to train the up and coming barrel racers of tomorrow. Each and everyone one of them has the desire to help the untrained become better and some trained barrel racers to improve their skills. Martha Josey, world champion barrel racer, has been teaching and training for over fifty years and her schools and clinics are well-known.

Martha and her husband, R.E., (now deceased) have long lived in Karnack, Texas, for years. She and her staff are well-advertised and offer a great deal to students in so many ways. She has also written books which can help barrel racers learn so much about their event. *Running to Win, How to Win at Barrel Racing Both Inside and Out*, was published in 1985 and answers many concerns and advice that is still important today. Another book by Martha is *Run to Win with Me in Barrel Racing*.

* * *

Many trainers have remarked on the way Celie Whitcomb Ray trained her horses during her era. Her ways of training barrel horses was quite different from most trainers. She was one of the most successful futurity trainers of her day. She also learned a great deal from Allene Gaylor-Mourne about training barrel horses. Celie was consistent and she understood horses, it was just second nature to her. Her good friend and trainer Dena Kirkpatrick said, "She was always in the right mindset. She had ice water in her veins — nothing bothered her."

Celie did not believe in starting the horse's turn around the barrel too soon. "You don't want your horse running to the barrel looking at it with their left eye," she said. When she did her rollbacks she did it away from the fence, not into the fence. It was to keep the hip under the horse. She liked the horse's hips square and took the horse a little straighter to the pocket than most. Libby Hurley,

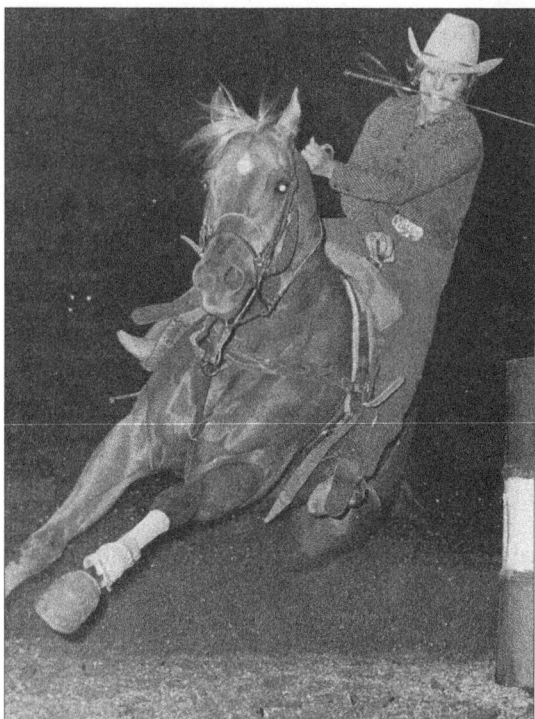

Celie Whitcomb running a 15.5 at Inglewood, Calif. *From the July-August 1971 issue of Hoof and Horns. Photo by Mattocks.*

who worked with Celie, said, "To go around a barrel on a horse Celie had trained was like riding a motorcycle and you had your inside leg on the ground, and the motorcycle was pivoting around your inside leg in a perfect circle; coolest feeling."

Celie expected her horse to know the arena was a place of business. She never overrode her horse. She never used her feet in a run, nor did she use her hands to check a horse. Celie's horse knew the sleight of hand with the pinky going in to the neck and body was their cue to turn. Picking up that inside rein picked up the horse's shoulder, rib cage and hip and they would make a perfect turn. Celie sat square in the middle, never leaning and just barely tipping her shoulder down in a turn.

She said, "If they are giving you all they've got and your still flogging them, they'll eventually quit. Don't over-spur a horse to get it to go, it shortens their stride."[12]

* * *

Florence and Dale Youree have been breaking and training barrel horses since they married in 1950. Both, Florence, former GRA president and all-around champ, and Dale, 1978 Old Fort Days Futurity winner and AQHA barrel racing champ twice, have won many awards in the barrel racing world. Their ranch is made up of three generations and all are involved in training barrel racing horses. In 1981, Florence and Dale were invited to run barrels in Washington, D.C., at the Folklife Festival in an exhibition on the National Mall. Their daughter Renee and husband, James Ward; granddaughters Cassie Ambrose, Kylie Weast, and Janae Ward Massey are all involved.

Cassie prefers to stay on the ranch and train horses, but does compete occasionally. Their operation is in Addington, Okla., and is based on training solid fundamentals slowly and at a rate the horse can handle. The horses will be trained to hunt and rate barrels, work around and dig out of the barrels and know how to make a quick run home. This family was given the WPRA Lifetime Family Heritage in Rodeo award in 2011.[13]

Chapter Fifteen
Dirt

One of the constants in rodeo barrel racing is that the 'playing field' is dirt. The earth is made up of many different types of dirt — sandy, loam, marl, clay, silt and rocky. It can be moist, muddy or extremely dry. In the beginning of barrel racing there was not much thought about the surface dirt of an arena. The women merely did their best on whatever dirt was under the barrels.

In the early days of barrel racing most were not concerned with the ground conditions, the weather, and other problems that could interfere with a good run. The professional barrel racers of today are extremely aware and concerned with every aspect of their run, including the ground and much more.

In an interview with Joleen Hurst Steiner, who was one of the top fifteen barrel racers in 1970 and '71, and a National Finals Rodeo competitor, was asked about the ground conditions in the rodeo arenas during her competing days. With a quick and ready answer she laughed and said, "No one complained about the ground conditions in my day. If it was too sandy, too hard, or whatever we just dealt with it."[1]

The arena dirt was not of much concern to most cowgirls and cowboys in the earlier days. Usually the heavy equipment needed to improve the dirt in an arena was either too expensive to rent or own, or too scarce.

As barrel racing became more popular and rodeos kept becoming more professional, the need to have the arena ground worked for safety purposes and for the best conditions for every event, especially barrel racing, became a more important concern.

People having to deal with dirt brought into an indoor arena, that generally was concrete not soil, had to consider what kind of dirt they needed. Often it might be important to have additional kinds of dirt brought into an outdoor arena and spread around. A

Charmayne James and *Scamper* making a run.
Photo by and courtesy of Kenneth Springer.

tractor drag eventually became a must. No rules were in evidence on how many barrel racing runs could take place, before the ground had to be re-worked, until the mid-1970s. Since then numerous pieces of equipment, in addition to the tractor drag, specifically for working the ground for rodeo events has been developed.[2]

Rollie Gibbs was the president of the Helldorado Rodeo, in Las Vegas, in the mid-1980s. He remembers having only a day and a half to prepare for the first performance held in the Convention Center. University of Las Vegas had their commencement just two days before. Getting the dirt in place was the first thing they did to get ready.

He said they laid a base of clay (harder dirt) down first, and then on top of that was a mixture of dirt and sawdust. He said it worked real well and required very little watering. He also had three men with rakes at each barrel and after each run the men would rake around each barrel. He remembers the producer, Mike Cervi, wasn't too happy with this extra effort of raking around the barrels, since producers like to keep the rodeo going. But, Rollie felt it important that each barrel racer have the same conditions as those before them.³

Tom Feller, director of event marketing for Justin Boots, had the idea to approach WPRA in the early 1990s about partnering on a program that would focus on the health and well being of the horses. They call it the Justin Best Footing Awards by Justin Boots partnering with WPRA. It keeps horses performing at top level, but also recognizes the hard work and numerous hours rodeo committees put into making their ground safe as possible for the barrel horse and all rodeo livestock.

Every year they recognize the top three rodeo committees in all twelve circuits, as well as the rodeo that has improved the most, in each circuit. Awards provided by Justin include cash bonuses (ranging from $350 to $1,000), plaques and at certain award levels, a pair of Justin exotic boots. Additionally, a name of each winning rodeo from all twelve circuits is put into a drawing for an additional $1,500, from Justin Boots. The awards are presented at

Charmayne James and *Scamper* making a run in Memphis, Tenn., in 1986.
Photo by Bern Gregory and courtesy of the National Cowboy & Western Heritage Museum.

the WPRA Star Celebration Luncheon at the NFR.[4]

The Abbeyville, Kan., PRCA Frontier Days rodeo committee received first place for the Prairie Circuit in the Justin Best Footing Award in 2015. The WPRA Star Celebration Luncheon is held each year during NFR weekend. As the Frontier Days committee accepted their plaque, Louise Knoefel, representing the committee, told the audience of the committee's extreme efforts to be sure the dirt in the arena is the best it can be for the animals partnering with their cowgirl or cowboy for each event.

She gave Bob Jones, of Abbeyville, credit for taking care of the ground for years, plus others in his family after he passed away. She also said that the John Deere representative in their town gave them a brand new tractor every year to use in working the dirt.

Abbeyville has hard ground so in the spring, usually April, Bob would begin reworking the arena ground, so that when their rodeo time came in late May the dirt would be as good as it could be. She also said they were fortunate to live in a community with companies that support their rodeo in such important ways, that if they had to hire people to do these things it would have been impossible.[5] They also have a Pee Wee division that starts at the age of eight.[6]

An article in *Hoofs and Horns*, October issue, 1969 entitled, "How To Handle Problem Grounds" as told to Jimmie Hurley by Sammy Thurman, covered lots of information for the barrel racer to give her mount the most knowledge about each and every rodeo's arena ground.

Sammy explained, "I want my horse to have a chance to feel the ground out before he is expected to make a run on it." Her suggestion was to ride in the rodeo grand entry. She also said due to weather the ground may be different from day to day. A slick spot near the barrels can cause a horse to slip and slide and possibly turn over a barrel. Some horses will go out wide from the barrel, to avoid a slick spot, while others will slow way down almost to a stop. A solid horse will take care of himself on slick ground when making a turn, shortening their stride but not slowing down too much. Some horses have this natural ability, but some do not. Keep your horse collected, close to the barrel, and keep urging him if he slows down too much. A horse will learn in time how to handle slick ground. Deep heavy ground, such as damp sand, or boggy mud, will slow him so keep urging him. Sometimes the ground is more manageable than it looks. Wet grassy arenas are much like slick ground. Dry grass is different from any type of ground. A horse can't get his feet into it, but an experienced horse will figure it out. At many rodeos you are expected to come in to the arena running. Sammy likes her horse to see the first barrel when she enters so she'll run her horse down the alley on the opposite side of her first barrel. The horse sees the barrel early and puts him in a position to run to the barrel in a straight line. The lighting in an indoor arena can confuse a horse, especially if you are running in from outdoors. Get the horse into the alley before he starts to run. Also check the barrels and know if they are normal metal barrels or very light. Sammy tipped one and reached back to set it up and almost threw it into the stands. If your horse makes a major mistake in the arena, try to get him back in the arena soon after the performance. Practice with your horse until he does it right.[7]

As the sport has become more professional, with numerous ways to improve the horses, tack and rider and properly preparing the ground conditions are constantly being addressed. In the earlier days it was seldom discussed unless it was a comment here and a criticism there, and then forgotten.

Once rules regarding ground conditions in professional rodeo began being enforced in the mid-1970s, today's arenas tractor drags and all kinds of equipment are used diligently to prepare the ground to be the best it can be, not only for barrel racing, but other events as well.[8]

Mel Clark, Inc., is the guru of arena dirt being perfect for all rodeo events and so much more. Mel Clark is an old cowboy who still ropes. He grew up with Hereford cattle and his dad sold thoroughbred horses to wealthy people in California to use as polo horses.

Mel's business is dirt. He has been in charge of preparing the dirt in Thomas & Mack Center at the University of Nevada, Las Vegas, where the National Finals Rodeo has been held since the Finals moved to Las Vegas in 1985, with the exception of being held at Globe Life Field, in Arlington, Texas, in 2020 due to the Covid pandemic.

He orders seventy-percent clay and thirty-percent percent sand

Lynn McKenzie and *Magnolia Missile* competing at Cheyenne Frontier Days in 1981. She won the world title in 1978. *Photo by and courtesy of Kenneth Springer.*

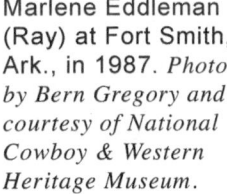

Marlene Eddleman (Ray) at Fort Smith, Ark., in 1987. *Photo by Bern Gregory and courtesy of National Cowboy & Western Heritage Museum.*

and mixes them in a mill together with the amount of water recommended. It sits in a big pile and they go in and mix it again and again blending it with water until they finally put it in the arena at Thomas and Mack.

He said by then the dirt is perfect. Once he places it in the arena it is important that the right people, tractors and equipment are used, because if they aren't strong enough, they don't go deep enough in the dirt to keep it the way it should be. He uses the same dirt each year and just adds sand to it. He said the barrel racers are the most particular competitors about the dirt, and rightly so.⁹

Wanda Harper Bush helped get equal money for the barrel racers at the major rodeos in Texas. Wanda holding the Coca Cola Woman of the Year trophy in 1989. *Photo by and courtesy of Kenneth Springer.*

Chapter Sixteen
Girls Rodeo Association Becomes Women's Professional Rodeo Association

In 1981 the Girls Rodeo Association changed its name to the Women's Professional Rodeo Association.

The board of directors decided it was to their advantage to give the organization a more professional name. The women were determined that they be taken seriously and were willing to do whatever it took to get what they wanted. The name change was expected to be a more fitting name, and of course they wanted others to realize they were no longer in the arena just to show off their beauty in decorative clothing. First and foremost, they were excellent horsewomen and barrel racing professionals.

The name Charmayne James became synonymous with barrel racing in the 1980s. She was just barely a teenager in 1984, but was a force to be reckoned with in the barrel racing. She won the barrel racing average at the Nationsl Finals and her first world championship. James also won the rookie of the year title, and if that didn't impress fans, she got their attention the following year.

As she entered the arena at the NFR in round seven in 1985, her great horse, *Scamper*, caught his bridle on the side of the gate. It caused the screws to come out of the bridle and by the time she rounded the third barrel, *Scamper* had spit the bit out of his mouth and the bridle hung uselessly around his neck. They won the round, in spite of the mechanical failure, and guess what? It was Friday the Thirteenth!

Jimmie Gibbs Munroe became the president of GRA in 1977 and held the office until 1993, and was chosen again in 2011 and 2012 to hold the top office, and again in 2021, in what had become the Women's Professional Rodeo Association. Jimmie qualified for the National Finals Rodeo eleven times. She won the world

Ardith Bruce receiving her trailer for winning the world championship in 1964.
Photograph by and courtesy of Ferrell Butler.

title her second year to qualify, 1975, and won the WPRA national championship in 1976 and 1977. In 1984 she won five consecutive go-rounds (and hasn't been done again since then) and placed in three more rounds. Her winnings at the NFR that year were $15,792. Munroe finished third in the world and fourth in the average. Her total earnings were $39,836 for the year.

Also, in 1984 the National Finals Rodeo used rubber barrels with the purpose of helping the barrel racing contestants to be safer. It was a common occurrence for a competitor to accidentally hit a metal barrel with their legs at the knee or below. It can cause quite a bruise or worse. Some racers even wear protection on their legs. Also, the horses on occasion would be injured on the metal barrels. The barrels were made of hard rubber on top and bottom. They collapsed easier because they were soft in the middle and tipped over more easily. Once a barrel falls over it causes competitors to get an additional five-second penalty. The rubber barrels were never used again after that year at the Finals.[1]

The WPRA honored Liz Kesler in 1984 for her contribution to the organization, which involved requiring every PRCA rodeo in Montana to hold a barrel racing event. Liz and husband, Reg Kesler, three-time Canadian all-around cowboy, who continued his career by becoming a rodeo producer and stock contractor. They lived in Missoula, Mont. and Rosemary, Alb., Canada, and held many of the professional rodeos in the state.

Florence Youree, president of the newly formed Barrel Futurities of America, better known as BFA, announced that the BFA and the Oklahoma City Chamber of Commerce would hold their first championship futurity in December 1986, at the Fairground Arena. The purse was at least $300,000 with $50,000 added money.[2]

Charmayne James and her horse, *Scamper*, won ten world championship titles in a row (1984-1993). This was the most world championships won by any barrel racer, and consecutively — an amazing feat. She also was the first woman to qualify to wear the Number one back number at the NFR in 1987. This means she won more money during the regular season, than any of the event qualifiers, male or female!

Charmayne got *Scamper* when she was only fourteen, and he had a reputation of being hard to handle. But the two found a partnership that allowed them both to do things no barrel racer had done before. It has been said Charmayne was way ahead of her time. She was also into all kinds of food supplements and additional things to help *Scamper* be the best horse he could be.[3]

* * *

An old-timers rodeo was held in Phoenix, Ariz., January 3 and 4, 1987, sponsored by Mera Bank and other supporting sponsors, and held in conjunction with the Arizona National Livestock Show. Tom Nesbitt was rodeo chairman and Andy Womack coordinated the rodeo clowns who included Leon Coffee, Jess Franks, and Randy Munns. Some of the former world champions competed such as Benny Reynolds and Ronnie Rossen in the bull riding. Dennis Reiners and Benny rode saddle broncs. Monte Montana performed. The barrel racing was split with ages forty to forty-nine with Janeen Johnson, Sharon Ferguson, Pat Spratt, Gerry Neugebauer, Susan Olson and Dottie Jordan. The next group, ages fifty and over were: Phyllis Jones, Ev Brenneman, Ruth Nettleton, Leta Rasco, Earline Herring, Ethel Jones and Ardith Bruce.

* * *

A lawsuit was filed by Lance Graves against GRA in 1980 to allow men to enter the barrel racing at GRA rodeos. The GRA won and it was costly, but worth the battle when those that testified proved there would not be barrel racing in PRCA rodeo if men were allowed to compete in the barrel racing.

There were many places men could barrel race, especially in futurities and derbies — but not in the GRA/WPRA. However, he filed another lawsuit against the Cowboys Regional Rodeo Association in McAlester, Okla., in 1988, to fight the decision to keep him from competing in the barrel racing event.[4]

There are many places a man who enjoys barrel racing can compete today, just not at WPRA sanctioned rodeos which are generally held in PRCA rodeos.

PRCA rodeos totaled 620 in 1987 and only eighteen did not include barrel racing.[5]

Wendy Potter competing in Tucson, Ariz.
Courtesy of the Potter Ranch.

Chapter Seventeen
Equal Monies — Or We Don't Compete!

In 1980 the GRA board of directors decided the time had come to start working toward a larger payout for barrel racing participants. Realizing this was a major undertaking the board adopted a long-term goal. "It was a five-year plan," said Jimmie Gibbs Munroe.

Gibbs Munroe, elected president of the GRA in 1978 and she continued to lead until 1993. She said the board informed all the rodeo committees of the plan to bring the barrel racing purses up by 1985 after it was put in motion.[1]

Under the plan, rodeo committees had to bring their added money to half of the amount offered to the lowest of the Professional Rodeo Cowboys Association events within a year. The committee had until 1985 to add prize money equal to the least amount of money given in any men's event.[2]

The argument in favor of the extra prize money was sound. Barrel racers were paying just as much, if not more, in expenses to compete as their male counterparts but winning, at some times, as little as ten percent of the prize money.

Jimmie recalled, "We stood firm in our requests. Those rodeos we lost came back later, and we accomplished a lot of good things."

The PRCA board members were not opposed to the request by barrel racers. Byron Walker, steer wrestling world champion, was instrumental in encouraging the change.[3]

When the GRA changed their name to Women's Professional Rodeo Association in 1981, it continued to stand for the same ideals. Although they had been involved in professional rodeo for over two decades they still were not getting equal money compared to the prize money in the men's events. Less than ten percent of all professional rodeos holding a GRA barrel race in 1975 were offering prize money equal to the men's events in the PRCA.[4]

The GRA/WPRA board in 1981, took a stand requiring all rodeos to offer at least half the amount being offered for the lowest paying men's event, which at the time was team roping. Within five years they were requiring all rodeos to pay equal money to be approved for barrel racing. Of the 490 approved rodeos by the PRCA in 1981 there were 239 offering equal money, 175 rodeos offered to pay half, and seventy-six rodeos did not include barrel racing.[5]

Jimmie asked Wanda Bush, who had been on the WPRA board previously and a former world champion barrel racer, to return to the board. Wanda had a good relationship with the larger Texas rodeos, sanctioned by the PRCA. The board knew these larger rodeos would have the most trouble raising the monies to be equal, as they had all ready raised the monies in other PRCA events to such high amounts.

The big rodeos' management held a great deal of respect for Wanda. Her presentation to the rodeo committees for more money, would be much more acceptable, than from someone they did not

Kristie Peterson competing at the National Finals in 1999 aboard *Bozo*.
Photo by and courtesy of Kenneth Springer.

know. Despite the concerns, Wanda hit the problem head on. She visited with Mary Nan West, the head of the San Antonio Stock Show & Rodeo, and Lewis Pierce, head of the Houston Livestock Show and Rodeo. Wanda and husband, Stanley, had been involved successfully, in the cutting horse world for some time, in addition to Wanda's outstanding career in the GRA/WPRA.

Wanda is credited with getting Houston to include the first barrel racing years earlier. Although it was a large gap to overcome, rodeos were able to meet the five year deadline. In fact, every Texas and Turquoise Circuit rodeos made the 1985 deadline.[6]

All the GRA/WPRA directors put in a lot of time committed to this five-year plan. Each director worked with all the rodeos within their circuit. It was a great collaboration between the WPRA board and the rodeo committees. Some of the areas of the country had not had barrel racing that long. After getting approval to hold a barrel race, the directors had to come back to their committees and ask for equal money in a short period of time. It was a tough job, but the women were committed.

Not only did they work closely with each rodeo committee in their area, they also worked hard and creatively and found additional sponsors for those rodeos. The WPRA got Dodge, Coors and Purina to step-up as sponsors, as well as their local distributors, which helped rodeo committees get the additional money required.[7]

Cindy Rosser, western regional director for the GRA, remembered some rodeos that were tough. In face the entire state of Utah was exceptionally difficult. The Utah Barrel Racing Association (UBRA) was strong and many of the Utah PRCA rodeos were holding UBRA barrel races instead of a GRA barrel race. Cindy and Kay Davis, a director from the northwest, worked together to convince Utah rodeos to add a GRA barrel race, then shortly after they received approval for that the directors had to ask for equal money.[8]

In 1985 December issue of *The Ketch Pen*, in the "Jean Curtis Gathering the News" section the following was reported:

> *For the first time in the history of the Oklahoma City State Fair, the women will not have a barrel racing event during the rodeo. This is indeed a shame, and all because of a mere*

> $2,700.00. - - - - - - All the ladies wanted was the same amount of prize monies in their event, that the men received in all of their events, which is $5,400.00. They offered the ladies half that much, and they refused it. - - - - - So hey look, all you committeemen, and civic minded leaders, get over that feeling of 'keeping 'em home, pregnant and barefooted' and recognize these women for what they are. They are professional cowgirls, doing a good job, lend a lot of excitement and color to a rodeo, and are definitely a crowd pleaser.

The article went on to say that the WPRA had also boycotted rodeos in Denver, Colo., Reno, Nev., Salinas, Calif., and a couple of Washington state rodeos because they refused to give the barrel racing equal monies. However, Reno notified them that next year monies would be equal.[9]

By WPRA's 1985 deadline, ninety-eight percent of the 601 PRCA approved rodeos met that requirement.

The following statistics show WPRA strides to get equal purse money:

Date	# PRCA Rodeos	# Give Equal $	#Have No Barrel Race
1975	460	42	98
1981	490	239	76
1984	511	410	13
1987	620	ALL	18[10]

Once the PRCA rodeos had accepted equal pay for barrel racers, it was time to take on the National Finals Rodeo. WPRA president Jimmie Munroe asked in January, 1984, for the National Finals Rodeo Commission (now called the Committee) to discuss the barrel racing money being equal to the other events. The timing of Jimmie's request was not good.

The decision to move the National Finals Rodeo to Las Vegas was taking place and many pros and cons had to be considered in making the decision about the move. Munroe was told that the PRCA board determined how the NFR purse was to be distributed. When the decision was announced the barrel racing was lacking.

The WPRA secured help from Purina, who came on as a sponsor and brought the barrel racing money to half of the money offered in the team roping. Purina also became the official feed supplier of the National Finals Rodeo.

The following year equal money for barrel racing was again denied. The WPRA again got sponsors, Wrangler and Purina, to add $15,000 each. Wrangler and the WPRA formed the Wrangler Bonus Program which helped, but still equal money to PRCA events at National Finals hadn't happened. Munroe and her WPRA Board continued to push for more money for barrel racing.[11]

The barrel racers and team ropers finally received money equal to all other events at the National Finals Rodeo in 1988. The total National Finals added money for each event was approximately $512,300. The previous year the team roping and barrel racing events received approximately $303,080 in prize monies, while other events were in the $484,900 range.

Finally, after a tremendous effort by the competitors and their directors, team roping and barrel racing were finally on an even playing field with the other events. It had been a long difficult and strenuous time, but the rewards were worth it.[12]

In 1989 the WPRA began a drug testing policy at some of the major rodeos. The board decided to keep every issue in barrel racing equal, plus it was done to make sure the equine partner was treated humanely in every regard. Previously professional rodeo had started to test cattle as well as horses. The results were good and in time WPRA stopped drug testing. Testing has still been done randomly and some rodeos continue to require testing.[13]

Jimmie Gibbs Munroe was the president when WPRA decided to begin drug testing. In 1991 at the National Finals Rodeo testing was done to the winner of each round and randomly a second barrel horse. The drug testing team consisted of Kathleen Gentry D.V.M., and Robin Waltrip and both wrote letters to WPRA saying the women were gracious and helpful and the team was treated with courtesy and cooperation.

Munroe got the nicest letter from the president of the American Humane, Animal Protection Division director, Dennis J. White congratulating her, on behalf of the WPRA in their action toward preventing abuse to animals. At that time she went to various livestock and rodeo organizations, on request, to talk about drug testing, the results, and how it humanely protects the horses and the sport. But Munroe said recently she had not done that in some time. A few rodeos do still drug test.[14]

In March of 2012 the WPRA board established a drug-testing committee with the goal of finding a feasible way to enforce Rule 18.1 (in the WPRA rule book) that stated no horse shall be ridden in competition that has been administered a prohibitive substance unless such substances have been administered as a therapeutic measure for the protection of the health of the horse.

The WPRA had a rule concerning the use of certain drugs on horses being competed on since the early nineties, but had not had testing or hearing procedures since then. Guidelines needed to be drawn up where the WPRA could enforce the rule in a fair manner. By having their own rules for standardized testing and hearing procedures that were to be applied at all WPRA approved events where there is testing, they felt they could prevent rodeo committees or other third parties from imposing drug testing rules on their own initiatives.

The WPRA felt the program benefited the contestants by assuring fair competition and removing doubts concerning the use of performing enhancing drugs among top contestants. It benefited the WPRA by making a statement that they were concerned with the well-being of the equine athletes and capable of policing their events themselves with fair rules that their members could abide by and compete under.[15]

The *WPRA News*, August and September 2018, had a two-part article entitled: "The Fight for Equal Money in the Barrel Racing." It was extremely informative and explained historically how difficult and yet, how important it was that the women in professional barrel racing receive equal money compared to what the male competitors in other events received. It was not decided to expect equal money because barrel racers were women, but because their rodeo expenses were the same as in any of the men's events that hauled horses. The barrel racing event is considered the second most popular event for fans, right behind bull riding.

Chapter Eighteen

Barrel Racing Sponsors

Early in barrel racing history and even the beginning of the Girls Rodeo Association no one thought much about sponsors, except to help put on an all-girl rodeo. To find sponsors, usually local retailers, to support the prize money given and other rodeo costs, was always a necessity. But rodeo competitors didn't really think about sponsors for themselves. They were busy trying to decide which direction they could go to compete at the next rodeo, and maybe how they were going to get there.

Ardith Bruce said, once she became a barrel racer that won her share of the races she was given a saddle, a two-horse inline trailer, some Tony Lama boots, and some horse vitamins, obviously provided by sponsors.[1]

Sherry Combs Johnson said that when she was competing, and married to Benny Combs, he was a Wrangler representative and the whole family received Wrangler clothes. This was such a help for the family at the time. Sherry did design a barrel racing saddle, and the Fort Worth saddle maker sent her a percentage check each time he sold a saddle from her design. Her daughter, Becky's photo was on a box of 707 Vitamins and they received free vitamins from 707. But there weren't many sponsors who supported contestants on a regular basis. Wrangler has been one of the most prolific sponsor in professional rodeo.[2]

Jimmie Gibbs Munroe said her first sponsor was Purina. They picked Jimmie to represent them as a barrel racer, and Tommy Lyons of the cutting horse world was also chosen, as was Bruce Davidson an equine event coordinator. They called these three individuals "Influentials." Jimmie was the first woman to be picked for this prestigious position with the company.[3] She also wrote, "Until 1976, there was not one major national corporate sponsor involved with the WPRA. Winston was the first."[4]

These women had become champions and were the cream of the crop. They earned the right to be sponsored and the sponsors were proud to sponsor them. It was a win-win situation. But it is strictly an individual decision and some women have sponsors, but some do not.

On June 1, 1990, the PRCA began a patch program. One of the pioneers of the this effort was Dave Appleton, originally from Australia, a world champion all-around cowboy. His first sponsor was American Airlines. Dave came from Australia to compete in rodeo and earned the sponsorship based on his bareback and saddle bronc riding success, but he, no doubt, received plenty of time with his sponsor flying back to Australia from time to time.[5]

The patch program allows contestants to have companies sponsor them individually. The agreements are between the contestant and the company, however to protect exclusive and first-right sponsors of the PRCA, any contestant competing in a PRCA arena, must register their sponsors and be approved by the PRCA in accordance with the patch program rules. This also includes all WPRA members. Registration has to be done on a yearly basis, or it will expire on January 31 of the next year.

Carolynn Vietor, two-time president of the WPRA, said she did not have sponsors, and individual competitor sponsors were not happening in her era often enough to remember.[6]

Wrangler started picking rodeo contestants to be their endorsees in 1947 when the company, then named Blue Bell, took an eighteen-wheeler to Madison Square Garden, in New York City, and gave away jeans and jackets to the cowboys participating in the rodeo. At first Wrangler 'representatives' were strictly for cowboys to be in their advertisements, but the relationship between Wrangler and professional rodeo has grown and does include barrel racers. Wrangler now has the prestige of being the title sponsor of the Wrangler National Finals Rodeo.

Sherry Cervi said her mother, Wendy Potter, never had sponsors during her rodeo days. Sherry also said when she began she didn't have sponsors, but in time, she added them and they became a vital part of her success. She said sometimes she approached a sponsor and other times they approached her. Sherry said some of her sponsors provided finalcial support, while other donated product.⁷

Justin has been a major sponsor of professional rodeo for many years and have been making boots since 1879. But in 2019, they released a new campaign and added a new casual line they claimed would return energy to the foot, giving a trampoline effect with every step. WPRA barrel racers Sherry Cervi, Mary Walker and Ivy Conrado were included in their advertising, along with other endorsees.⁸

There is no information regarding the number of barrel racers that have sponsors, but it certainly can be a help, because there are so many miles put on their pickups and trailers to get from one rodeo location to the next. There is also many other expenses involved including horses, tack, feed, and vet bills, not to mention, the motels and meals along the way for the barrel racer.

But with sponsors come additional responsibilities. The women have to keep their positions in rodeo and reporting back to the sponsor is a necessity. Promoting their sponsors in various ways can take time away from practice and other responsibilities. It is definitely an individual choice.

Chapter Nineteen
The Last Decade of the Twentieth Century

The WPRA decided that effective December 1, 1990, for the 1991 season, WPRA members must be at least fourteen-years-old. Five years later, December, 1996, the WPRA ruled: effective for the 1997 season members must be at least eighteen-years-old. No doubt this was a ruling based on laws regarding liability. An eighteen-year-old can make their own decisions regarding entering sporting events. Prior to age eighteen, parents are involved in decisions being made for their children.

The 'new kid on the block' so to speak was Kristie Peterson, from Colorado. She joined the WPRA in 1991 and won world barrel racing titles in 1994, '96, '97 and '98. She was reserve champion three times, and won the average at the Wrangler National Finals five times, 1994 consecutively through 1998. Her mounts, *Bob* and later *Bozo*, were the partners in her success and it was evident that she had trained them well.[1]

* * *

In 1994, the barrel racing world lost a great competitor and trainer, Celie Whitcomb-Ray, to cancer. She was only forty-five-years-old. Many admired her abilities as a trainer, as well as a competitor. In talking with her daughter, Mary Cecelia Tharp, she said that after her mother passed away, she was in competition with one of her mother's favorite horses, and he did not perform well. Her dad who witnessed the scene said, "If your mother had been riding him, instead of you, the horse's head would have been hanging mighty low right now."

Tharp knew this to be true and said the horses her mother trained were always trying to please her and when they failed you could tell the horse was totally disappointed in himself. This was not because of her scolding them, they just knew she strived for perfection, and they had not done their job to her satisfaction.[2]

* * *

At the National Finals in 1995, Sherry Cervi reached the top, as did Charmayne James eight years before. She became the second barrel racer to wear the number one back number at the finals. She was leading all qualifying contestants going into the NFR with more than $129,000 won during the regular season. At that year's finals she placed in four rounds and was fourth in the average, winning $27,588 during the ten-day competition with her two gelding partners, *Troubles* and *Hawk*. And if that wasn't enough, she won the world championship with a total of $157,172 for the year.[3]

* * *

In 1996, another first in the rodeo world for the barrel racing event, *Scamper*, Charmayne James' phenomenal horse, was inducted in to the ProRodeo Hall of Fame in Colorado Springs,

Sherry Cervi competing on *Troubles* at the National Finals Rodeo in 1994. She won her first world title the following year. *Photo by and courtesy of Kenneth Springer.*

Colo. This was the first and only honor for barrel racing at this museum for the next twenty-one years. But, *Scamper* was so deserving of this honor.[4]

The first induction at the ProRodeo Hall of Fame was in 1979, shortly after the opening of the museum. A number of cowboys and livestock were inducted in the inaugural class. In the livestock category that year they inducted saddle bronc horses: *Descent, Hell's Angel, Five Minutes to Midnight, Midnight, Steamboat* and *Tipperary*. Only one bareback horse, *Come Apart*, was chosen. Timed event horses inducted were: *Baby Doll, Baldy, Bullet, Peanuts* and *Poker Chip*. Only two bulls were included: *Old Spec* and *Tornado*.

After the initial class, the only two others in the livestock category to be inducted before *Scamper* were bulls, both in 1990, *Crooked Nose* and *Red Rock. Scamper* deserved to be inducted, but this was the first barrel racing horse that was considered. He not only took Charmayne to ten consecutive world championships, he also won the Houston rodeo ten times for Charmayne.

* * *

In 1998 for the first time the barrel racing event paid out the

Scamper being inducted into the ProRodeo Hall of Fame. *Photo by Steve Gray and courtesy of the ProRodeo Hall of Fame & Museum of the American Cowboy.*

same amount as all the men's events at the Wrangler National Finals Rodeo in Las Vegas.[5] In the NFR program for that year Steve Hatchell, commissioner, of the Professional Rodeo Cowboys Association said in his letter to fans and contestants, "We are proud that the 1998 NFR has a total of $4.2 million and that all contestants are competing for equal prize money."[6]

The breakdown in 1998, by event, was $512,304, except the team roping which was $1,024,608. Team roping had double the amount due to headers and heelers being paid the same as in the other events. Each round paid $39,408 in all events, and double for team roping. The breakdown for each go-round in barrel racing was: first place - $14,936; second place - $11,192; third place $7,448; fourth place - $3,744; fifth place - $1,261; sixth place - $828.

The NFR average was a total of $118,224 and double for team roping. The barrel racing average breakdown was: first place - $32,512; second place - $26,837; third place - $21,280; fourth place - $15,724; fifth place - $10,049; sixth place - $5,557; seventh place - $3,783; eight place - $2,483.

The other timed events were the same amounts of money across the board. The three roughstock events, however, had different amounts in the go-rounds, and the average, but the totals were all the same amounts.

The barrel racers and officers and directors of WPRA had worked on getting equal status and money for so many years. They refused to give up and never quit working for equal pay for the women in rodeo. The payoff was worth all the telephone calls, letters and discussions with potential sponsors, and the 'powers that be' with the PRCA, plus just brain-storming constantly with other members on how to accomplish this all-important issue for barrel racers. The 1998 season just happened to be the fiftieth-anniversary of the GRA/WPRA. What a gift!

Also in 1998, the WPRA started a saddle rotation program to celebrate the fiftieth-anniversary of the GRA/WPRA. The program was to award a trophy saddle to each of the top-fifteen barrel racing contestants. The saddles have been donated to the program by the nation's top saddle makers and their endorsees. There are also saddles donated for the reserve world champion, WNFR fastest time contestant and the WPRA rookie barrel racer of the

Celebrating the 50th anniversary of Women's Professional Rodeo Association in 1998. (L to R) Charmayne James, Jimmie Gibbs Munroe, Joyce (Burk) Kernick, Sherry (Combs) Johnson, Jane Mayo, Billie McBride, Wanda Bush and LaTonne Sewalt. *Photo by and courtesy of Kenneth Springer.*

year. The saddles are on display at Las Vegas during the Wrangler National Finals in the WPRA booth at Cowboy Christmas, held in the Convention Center, except the day of the WPRA luncheon when they are displayed on stage.[7]

The following year, 1999, Sherry Cervi won her second world championship title, but in addition to that she won more money in barrel racing than any other contestant competing at the finals — male or female! Sherry's earnings for the year were $245,369 which was $27,000 more than Fred Whitfield, 1999 all-around, calf roping champion and the high-money winner for the PRCA.[8]

Barrel racing professionally had finally become financially lucrative with the strides made and increased money to equal what all the other events were paying. Now, what is in store for this exciting event of barrel racing in the twenty-first century?

Chapter Twenty
Barrel Racing in the Twenty-First Century

In 2000, Kappy Allen, who had only been to the Wrangler National Finals Rodeo one time previously, won the world champion barrel racing title by placing in nine rounds and winning $95,112 during the ten-day event. Her total winnings for the year was $145,204. She also won the average with a total of 140.01 seconds in ten-runs. During those amazing ten days in December at Thomas & Mack Center in Las Vegas, Allen almost tripled her winnings for the year.[1]

* * *

The Pendleton Round-Up put barrel racing into their performances for the first time in 1962. It replaced chariot races that were held previously.[2] However, the Pendleton Round-Up's arena is grass and used for high school football, when the rodeo is not in town. After the 1962 attempt to hold barrel racing on grass, they found that it was just too dangerous for the horses and the riders and it was cancelled.[3]

In time the barrel racing became so popular that women from the northwest were clamoring to have a barrel racing included again at the Pendleton Round-Up. They let the people on the Round-Up committee know they were definitely interested in barrel racing coming to Pendleton.

A committee was formed to look into having barrel racing and see if they could work out a pattern. Their conclusion to have the race as safe as possible, was they would put the barrels on the dirt race track that surrounds their grassy arena.

Steve Corey was in charge of the committee to talk with various key people in barrel racing to seek their approval. Carolynn Vietor, WPRA president from 1997 to 2002, came to Pendleton, as did Columbia River Circuit director, Rosanne Strobele.

An unidentified barrel racer makes a run at the Pendelton Round-Up, which features a barrel racing pattern twice the size or more of most rodeos. *Photo by Mikal Wright and courtesy of the Pendelton Round-Up.*

PRCA pro judge Jade Robinson encouraged the committee to work out a pattern that would be safe. Steve Corey and his assistant, Jodi Hack, flew to Tucson and met with the PRCA commissioner, Steven Hatchell, to discuss what they had in mind for barrel racing. They also met with Sherry Cervi, well known barrel racer, and talked about their Round-Up plan. They also discussed it with the racers from the northwest whenever possible. Everyone they talked with agreed the addition was a good thing for the Pendleton Round-Up, for barrel racers and for professional rodeo.[4]

Jack Shaw, Pendleton native, handled the groundwork. He knew the barrels would have to be placed on the dirt race track that surrounds the grassy infield. They wanted twenty-one feet between the barrels and the fence. Once they got it laid out to everyone's satisfaction, the distance between barrels one and two, more than doubled the size of the standard WPRA barrel racing pattern. It is 288 feet between barrel one and two and 288 feet between the second and third barrel, and sixty feet from the score line. The committees also were not sure the electronic timers would reach as far as necessary for their oversized pattern. An electric timer was sent to them and when they tested it, they found it would work quite well. The event returned to the historic northwestern rodeo in 2000.[5]

Many of the barrel racers that go to Pendleton Round-Up and compete say that it is a different and challenging race, but they enjoy competing there. Jack Shaw did admit once in a while it does get a little 'western' when the racer's horse wants to get to the barrel as quickly as it has on other patterns. Jack said that a barrel race time of twenty-nine seconds and occasionally twenty-eight seconds is common presently, but some run higher. In 2018 the prize money was $32,000.[6]

Although the Pendleton Round-Up barrel racing pattern is certainly a challenge to all professional racers, they still enjoy the run. Cheyenne Allan, at the age of sixty-one, of Mabton, Wash., won the barrel racing at Pendleton Round-Up in 2018 for the first time. She had run the big pattern fourteen times in the last seventeen years. Winning the Round-Up barrel race was definitely on her bucket list. She earned $10,888, finishing second in both go-rounds with times of 28.76 seconds in the first round, and 28.62 seconds the second round.

"It's quite an adrenaline rush to run here," she said. Her partner, *Molly* was a thirteen-year old sorrel mare that was born on the Allen place. *Molly's Honor* knows her barrel racing job and does it well, but she does have an attitude and is a bit frisky. But when she is running the barrels, speed is the name of the game to *Molly*. The racers call the Round-Up's barrel pattern "The Green Mile."[7]

* * *

In 2001 at the NFR, Janet Stover won the world title by placing in nine rounds with four first place go-rounds, three second place wins, a third, and tied for fourth and fifth. Her total winnings for the ten days was $126,934. Her total for the year was $186,812.[8]

* * *

In 2003, Janae Ward, granddaughter of barrel racing and trainer Florence Youree, GRA president from 1960 to 1964, came

Sherry Cervi on *Dinero* at the 2005 Wrangler National Finals Rodeo. *Photo by Dan Hubbell, courtesy of the Potter family.*

into the National Finals in fourteenth place. She won the world championship by placing in eight rounds and winning $111,908 during the ten-day NFR. Her total money for the year was $155,792.[9]

* * *

Amazingly in the first four years of the twenty-first century, three of the world champions in barrel racing qualified to the National Finals Rodeo and won nearly twice as much as they had won all year in their ten-days in Vegas. Kappy Allen had $50,092 by NFR time and won $145,204 for the year; Janet Stover had $59,878 by NFR time and won $186,812 for the year; and Janae Ward had $43,884 won for the year before the first performance at the NFR and ended up with $155,792.[10]

An article in the 2005 *WPRA Media Guide* entitled "Professional Barrel Racing" reported that "today WPRA has more than 2,000 members and sanctions some 800 barrel races a year, paying out prize money exceeding $3 million dollars."[11]

* * *

Mary Burger, of Pauls Valley, Okla., won her first world title in 2006 at the age of fifty-eight, the oldest member of WPRA to win a world title at that time. Then, she did it again in 2016 at sixty-eight. Her barrel horse in 2006 was the AQHA Barrel Horse of the Year, *Rare Fred*. Her winnings for the year were $189,195 and $277,554 in 2016.[12]

* * *

In 2006 Charmayne James decided to have her barrel horse, *Scamper*, cloned. She did her research regarding cloning for seven years before she made her decision. Cloning is defined as a group of genetically identical cells descended from a single common ancestor. This is done scientifically in a laboratory. The result of the cloning was a stallion Charmayne named *Clayton*. He was not used in barrel racing competition but to carry on *Scamper's* genetics.

* * *

In 2007 the Professional Rodeo Cowboys Association made a decision that only lasted one year. They formed a new organization called Professional Women's Barrel Race (PWBR). When notifying barrel racers, the PRCA explained that PWBR was under the PRCA umbrella and all competitors at PRCA rodeos and the National Finals would be totally equal. Only the members of PWBR would be eligible to compete at the Wrangler National Finals.[13] Of course, all the top barrel racers in the WPRA joined the newly established PWBR, because there was so much money being offered at the WNFR.

Brittany Pozzi-Pharr won the world title that year and the average with 140.18 seconds in ten runs. She won $95,192 at the Wrangler National Finals, and $259,713 for the year. Others that qualified were: second - Lindsay Sears; third - Jill Moody; fourth - Terra Bynum; fifth - Lisa Lockhart; sixth - Maegan Reichert; seventh - Deb Renger; eighth - Vickie Solmonsen; ninth - Brenda Mays; tenth - Codi Baucom; eleventh - Molly Powell; twelfth - Brandie Halls; thirteenth - Sherrylynn Johnson; fourteenth - Tana Poppino; and fifteenth - Brittany Hofstetter.[14]

The WPRA lost a majority of their best barrel racers to this new organization and it made quite a dent in the GRA/WPRA fifty-nine year history. WPRA filed a lawsuit against PRCA over the forming of PWBR.

On the first ruling, the WPRA lost their case. However, they pursued the issue further and in the end WPRA received a cash settlement from the PRCA. The WPRA also made an agreement with the PRCA that the PRCA would not start another barrel racing organization for the next ten years.

More than ten years has gone by since that agreement was made and the two organizations continue to work together without incident. In fact they seem to be more compatible today than ever before.[15]

* * *

June Holeman had qualified for the National Finals in 2005 at the age of sixty-one and finished twelfth. In 2010 riding her twenty-one-year-old horse, *Sparky*, and Holeman was sixty-six, she won second in the barrel racing at the Black Hills Stock Show & Rodeo in Rapid City, S.D.

June lived west of Arcadia, Neb., all her life and started her competition in area horse shows and in a saddle club. Later she ran barrels in junior rodeos and the Nebraska Cowgirls Association and eventually competed in the Prairie Circuit of WPRA.

June and *Sparky* won the Prairie Circuit in 2005. She got *Sparky* when he was twelve. She admitted *Sparky* needed more rest when they got to their barrel racing destination. And the hauling was harder on him. She felt she owes much of her success to *Sparky*. He was also Molly Powell's back up horse at the WNFR in 2004 and 2006. June and *Sparky* are both very inspirational to us all.[16] June passed away December 3, 2018.

* * *

Lindsay Sears, of Nanton, Alb., became the first Canadian barrel racer to win the WPRA Barrel Racing World Championship at the Wrangler National Finals Rodeo. In 2011 she placed in eight rounds at the ten-day WNFR, winning five rounds. She placed third in the average, and won $139,002 at the WNFR and won a total of $323,570 for the year. The WPRA and the Canadian Professional Rodeo Association have an agreement that allows CPRA barrel racers to compete at the Wrangler National Finals Rodeo if their regular season monies is more than that of a barrel racer from the U.S.

Before 2006, only Canadian residents were eligible to compete in their Canadian National Finals Rodeo. However since 2006, American contestants can compete at the Canadian Finals if they win enough money in Canada. To qualify all contestants have to compete in at least fifteen Canadian CPRA rodeos during the year to be in the top-ten money winners.[17]

* * *

Sherry Cervi, of Marana, Ariz., out did herself in 2013 when she placed in all ten rounds at the WNFR. She had three go-round wins and won a total of $155,899 during that ten-day competition. She set a WPRA record for the most money won at the WNFR and the 'icing on the cake' was her fourth world championship, with $303,317 for the year. She was just the fifth barrel racer in finals history to have placed in ten consecutive rounds.[18]

* * *

In 2014 the American Quarter Horse Association started to require helmets for the protection and safety of riders under eighteen-years-old. Fallon Taylor, who had sustained a serious head injury in a 2009 horse accident, knew how invaluable this requirement was for the safety of anyone participating in any sport where injury could easily happen.

Fallon had her own style and always stood out because of it. Her outfits chosen for competition were 'over the top' and always unusual and unique. She decided when she qualified for the National Finals she should wear a helmet. When she got through the first round and realized that the helmet was as comfortable as it was, she hurried around Las Vegas buying up helmets. Then she decorated them with bling and colors to match her riding outfits for the rest of the WNFR rounds. She later designed a helmet and sold it for riders, designating a portion of the proceeds to go to charity.[19]

* * *

Mary Burger had the honor of wearing the number one back number at the WNFR in 2016 for only the third time in history for a barrel racer; preceded by Charmayne James and Sherry Cervi. Not only had she won more money than any other WPRA or PRCA contestant during the year, but at age sixty-eight she became the oldest world champion, man or woman.

Her total money for the year was $277,554. Her mount was *Mo* (full name – *Sadiesfamouslastwords*). Mary knew he was not one-hundred-percent, but her veterinarian was present and checked the seven year-old buckskin gelding often, during the ten day competition. *Mo* was also was named runner-up to the AQHA-WPRA Horse of the Year *Tibbie* ridden by Ivy Conrado. *Mo* was named the Scoti Flit Bar Rising Star Award that was awarded during the WPRA Star Celebration luncheon.[20]

During the 2016 Wrangler National Finals Rodeo, Mary was seen wearing her gold buckle she received ten years earlier when she earned her first world championship. She seldom wore it and she said the reason was, "I never figured I'd get another one, and I didn't want to scratch it."[21]

* * *

Amberleigh Moore set a new WPRA record for the most money won at the WNFR in 2016 with $187,692. Hailey Kinsel topped that in 2017 with a record $189,385. There were only two other WNFR contestants that won more money than she did in 2017, Marcos Costa, a tie down roper, and Sage Kimzey, world champion bull rider.[22]

In addition to the money record Hailey made in 2017, she also set a new record for the fastest time in National Finals barrel racing history. In round three Hailey and *Sister*, her amazing Palomino, ran the barrels in 13.11 seconds.

"I don't set goals to win stuff," said Hailey, but she won plenty that year. She won the The American rodeo, hosted by RFD-TV, in February, she was a college champion, and won $50,000 at the Days of '47 in Salt Lake City, Utah, just to name a few of her wins during the year.[23]

* * *

In 2017 Taci Bettis was back in business after her ten-year-old gelding was injured and had to have surgery in the fall of 2016. Taci had been trained by Tammy Fischer, her rodeo coach, since high school. She finished second at Reno, and broke a thirty-four-year-old arena record at the Ogden Pioneer Days, by making a 17.05 run.

At the end of the year she went to the WNFR and came in third, to become the WPRA Barrel Racing Rookie of the Year. Then she got an invitation to the RFD-TV's, The American rodeo in 2018, held in the AT&T Stadium in Arlington. This rodeo is unique in that as a competitor, you can be invited, or you can qualify by competing in preliminary events to qualify for the semi-finals and from there, The American.

Taci had tried to qualify the year before but did not make it. On her invitational 2018 first run at The American she came in fourth, and in the shoot-out round she won and received a check for $100,000.[24]

By the end of the year she had again qualified for the WNFR. She won round-eight and came in second in round-nine. She fiinished seventh in the world with $191,538. Her experiences the last two years with the Wrangler National Finals and The American were awesome.

* * *

Lisa Lockhart had won just about every major rodeo in the country and lots of smaller ones as well. But she hadn't won a

Lisa Lockhart competing at the Wrangler National Finals in 2013.
Photo by and courtesy of Kenneth Springer.

National Finals championship or the Ram National Circuit Finals. She had qualified for fourteen years for the Circuit Finals but just hadn't won it.

The WPRA rules state you are allowed to count 100 rodeos a year toward your season's earnings. In 2018 Lisa had only picked forty-three rodeos. She has three children that also have responsibilities and competitions in rodeo. Therefore, after the major winter rodeos, Lisa generally goes home to assist her family in their commitments and desires.

The winnings for 2018 qualified Lisa as a National Finals contender as well as a National Circuit Finals qualifier. Prior to the actual Circuit Finals, held in March 2019, Lisa's main barrel horse, *Louie*, suffered an injury at the Houston rodeo earlier in 2019. It was necessary that Lisa take her greener horse, *Cutter*, whose registered name is *Prime Diamond* out of *Hugos Diamond* by *Prime Talent*.

She had ridden him at four 2018 rodeos and he had done well, but Lisa had no idea if he could hold up to the Circuit Finals demands. Happily he did, she did, and they won it all. Lisa said, "You go in with all these expectations, you win it with the least expectations of all time, and it turns out to be more than amazing."[25]

Chapter Twenty-One
Tragedies — In the Barrel Racing World

History repeats its self again and again when cowgirls and cowboys are trying to get to as many rodeos as possible. Traveling in the dead of night, so as to not waste time, through a countryside that is generally too dark to see or unfamiliar to the driver, has taken it's toll of rodeo folks in various ways. It has always been a way of life for rodeo folks, to travel from one rodeo to the next at night, and continues to this day. But there have been other ways terrible things have happened to barrel racers throughout the years. Here are just a few:

* * *

The hard luck trophy awarded by the Odessa, Texas, Junior Chamber of Commerce in 1959 was aptly presented to Kathy Burton. Kathy, on her way home from Pecos, Texas, lost her good barrel horse when the trailer broke loose from the car.[1]

* * *

In 1968 two of the leading barrel racers, Ann Lewis and Sissy Thurman, were in a horrible pickup-camper accident near Hope, Ark. They were driving from a Little Rock, Ark., rodeo to a Waco, Texas, rodeo to run the next night. Ann Lewis, from Sulphur, Okla., and Sissy Thurman, of Bryan, Texas, were traveling with the Lewis family. They had stopped earlier to eat and were driving leisurely on Highway 67 about 1 a.m. planning to stop later to rest and continue on the next morning to Waco.

A semi-truck and trailer heading east had hit two cows, jackknifed and turned over. Unknowingly, the Lewis family and Sissy came upon the wreck unexpectedly and hit the truck and a fiery crash occurred. Ann, age ten, and Sissy, a well-respected competitor and director of the GRA, plus Mrs. Lewis were killed at the scene. Jan, Ann's twin sister, died five days later. The two barrel horses in the trailer, behind their vehicle, had to be put down. Survivors included Ann's dad, Bob Lewis, and brother, Randy, and Sissy's husband, Doug, and daughters, Karen and Vanessa.[2]

* * *

One of the more positive outcomes as noted "From the Editors Desk," in the *GRA News*, June, 1969:

> *Lee Matale had a freak accident on her way to a quarter horse show, while traveling on one of the busiest highways in New Jersey. Her trailer broke loose from the pickup and went flying down the middle of the highway on its side. Her good barrel horse, Reed, was in the trailer and it took more than an hour to get him out. It sure didn't hurt him much as he is already back to winning barrel races again.*[3]

* * *

Sunday morning, May 26, 2002, near Webbers Falls, Okla., Maggie Green of San Antonio, Teza and Gail Shanahan, of Stockdale, Texas, were returning home from the Old Fort Days Futurity and Super Derby, at Fort Smith, Ark., hauling their horses in a trailer, on Interstate 40. It was Maggie's forty-seventh birthday.

They had gone to Fort Smith to watch horses, Gail had trained, and were being ridden by Kay Blandford, who had won $7,000. Unknown to Gail and Maggie two connected barges guided by a tugboat had just struck the bridge spanning the Arkansas River and toppled a 500-foot section of the bridge into the river.

There wasn't enough time for police to arrive to warn drivers, or barricades to keep them from continuing to drive on the bridge that had been destroyed. Seventeen vehicles plummeted into the rain-swollen river, including the Blandford trailer. Gail and Maggie, plus eleven others were killed, as were Gail's three horses.

Gail Shanahan, age forty-nine, was considered one of the better barrel horse trainers and had been a Texas Youth Rodeo champion. She also mentored many barrel racers. It was reported that Kay Blandford traveling in another vehicle some distance behind them heard of the accident and tried to reach them by cell phone to alert them, but failed.[4]

Blandford qualified to compete in National Finals seven times from 1993 and later qualified for the 2002 National Finals.[5]

* * *

In 1956, Tina Sikes Hodge, age fifteen, was ranked in the top fifteen barrel racers in the spring. She went to a rodeo at West, Texas, and had her horse saddled and ready for the barrel race to begin. A boy she knew came along and asked her to go get a soft drink with him, which she did. When she returned, she heard the announcer call for the barrel racers and got in the saddle ready to compete.

When she rode into the arena she thought her mount, *King*, was acting strange but dismissed it and concentrated on her run. When she got to the first barrel *King* didn't turn and he didn't stop , running directly into the fence. When *King* hit the fence, Tina landed in front of the saddle horn, and the reins were around the horn under her legs.

King was completely wild and ran around the arena several times. Tina's dad, Joe Sikes, whistled, which normally would stop the horse in his tracks, but it didn't faze him. Finally James Bynum, a champion steer wrestler, grabbed the horse and got him settled enough to get Tina rescued. They discovered that *King* had been drugged.[6]

* * *

Diane Moore of Butte Falls, Ore., is blind. When the eleven-year-old's horse aimed at a nipping dog and kicked her instead, Diane never saw again. Instead of becoming an invalid, her accident was merely an interruption in her goal to become a professional horse trainer.

Before her bandages were off she was out in the pasture with her horse that blinded her. Horses were her living. Her proficiency in training horses ranges from barrel racing, English pleasure, jumping, and roping.

Before moving to Butte Falls, she worked for Bill Shadwick at Medford. Ore., who said in a 1973 article in *Hoofs and Horns*,

"Diane is good . . . damn good. Something happens to a horse around her. They learn something about humans. She trusts them, most of us don't. They know she's blind. You bet they do!"

Diane was noted as one of the best horse trainers in Southern Oregon. She has some sort of an inner radar mechanism. In familiar surroundings, she slithers under, over and around obstacles like a cutting horse and has an almost telepathic sensitivity toward her horse pupils.[7]

* * *

It is so easy to be hauling horses to a rodeo, and often in the dead of night, and if something goes wrong, especially in the trailer, the driver might not know it for some time. That happened to Nellie Miller, of Cottonwood, Calif., in 2008, shortly after she bought her permit in the WPRA.

Nellie said, "*Blue Duck* and I were having a stellar year until" . . . Nellie was driving from one rodeo to the next when her great horse, *Blue Duck*, whose registered name is *Reba's Smokey Joe*, a half brother to her present horse, *Sister*, somehow, unknown to Nellie, got one of his hindlegs out through the window of the trailer. It was the middle of the night and Nellie didn't discover it for some time. She didn't know if he was tired, had a major melt down, or what caused him to get his leg caught outside the window. Fortunately he was in the front stall and the trailer had an escape door, so they did get his leg out of this strange predicament. He was injured for almost a year and a half, but he did recover in time and took Nellie to her 2017 world championship.[8]

* * *

Tina Ellis was a typical country girl. She was born in Tyler, Texas, on July 31, 1959, to Cecil and Wanie Ellis. The family moved to Belton, Texas, when she was five, to be near her maternal grandparents. She loved horses and rode as often as she was able. She had a Shetland, named *Frosty*, when she was small.

Her grandfather often took her to horse shows and entered her in pleasure classes on normal sized horses. In fact her grandfather, a horse trader, liked to have Tina ride his horses in front of potential buyers so they could see how well-trained they were. She also went to play days where she competed in goat tying, steer undecorating and ribbon roping.

When she became a teenager she started barrel racing. Tina made all the small rodeos and high school rodeos around Central Texas. She loved it all! Her dad made sure she got to all these rodeos before she could drive.

Cecil was a rodeo clown and bullfighter, and often worked the rodeos, too. Tina attended Belton High School and was named to "Who's Who Among American High School Students." She was president of the Belton 4-H horse club and chosen as the Belton rodeo queen by her fellow students.

Tina Ellis competing in the goat tying in 1972 at Florence, Texas. *Photo courtesy of the Ellis family.*

On April 16, 1978, she and a friend went to a play day rodeo at nearby Gatesville, where Tina entered the barrel race. She mounted her horse, *TJ (Tina Junior)* and charged into the arena, her blonde hair flying. Around the three barrels she went without a flaw. When she raced across the finish line and headed to the gate, she did not see that the gate was closed. *TJ* slammed into it, and Tina flew headfirst into the heavy gate.

As she lay crumpled in the arena, cowboys and medical personnel rushed to her side. "Is there a doctor in the house," the announcer asked over the loudspeaker.

There was a doctor there and he accompanied her to the hospital in the ambulance, as she slipped into a coma. There was very little he could do. She was transferred to Hillcrest

Hospital in Waco. Her parents were called and they rushed to her side.

She was in one hospital or another until July. At that time the doctors told her parents it would be best if they made arrangements to place her in a nursing home because it was very doubtful she would ever recover or come out of the coma.

Her dad, Cecil, said, "Doctor, I believe you have underestimated us."

They brought her home with all the hope that the doctors were wrong. They converted their garage into a room for Tina, equipped with a hospital bed, bathtub, plus a bed for Cecil, a cook stove and kitchen table and chairs.

Cecil put together a heavy metal lift, with steel and parachute fabric to be able to lift her gently from the bed to the bathtub. Wanie, her mother, and/or Cecil were with her constantly, talking to her about every possible thing they could think of. Eventually, they realized they needed help, but a nursing home was never an option. They hired a woman named, Blossom, who came to assist them, and lived in a trailer behind their house. Wanie worked at the bank, and Cecil owned Ellis Glass Company. Shortly, Wanie retired, and Cecil put his company up for sale. They insisted on being with Tina full time.

The Ellis family tried to go through the proper channels, including senators and representatives plus other officials to hire appropriate help, but nothing happened. Cecil heard about three sisters from Mexico that had fled to Houston and needed work. He brought them to the Ellis home, where they lived as part of the Ellis family. The oldest sister was only fifteen years-old when they arrived at the Ellis home.

Tina lived in a coma, for thirty-one years, before she passed away peacefully on July 13, 2009. Although she never responded or spoke again after the accident, it was evident to her family and caretakers that she was aware of some things. She kept her eyes open, when not sleeping, would react favorably to her daily bath, laugh on occasion, and showed disapproval of a few things.

Cecil took a van seat and made it into a wheelchair for her so they could take her outside. For a time she went to a therapist in Fredericksburg, but nothing about her changed. They placed her in a lounge chair during the day. She had Ensure Plus every meal through a feeding tube in her stomach. The family, which included the women who cared for her, ate every meal in Tina's room at the kitchen table.

Her mother, Wanie, said Tina was relatively healthy the last thirty years, she just was not responsive. The love of her mother and dad, her brother, and the girls who were her care-givers was absolutely amazing. The care she was given could not have been better. Cecil and Wanie never once considered letting anyone but themselves, and their Mexican girls, take care of Tina. They have no regrets.[9]

Now, the loving vigil has ended. Left are the precious, unforgettable memories of the fair-haired, smiling girl. Their cowgirl who went to her last rodeo way too early in life — but left that final rodeo while doing what she loved, running barrels to the cheers of fans. Tina had finished her last ride.

The three Mexican girls became part of the Ellis family and lived with them until they married. They were truly loved and cared for by the Ellis family and they cared deeply for Tina and her parents. Cecil passed away in 2019. Wanie still considers the girls that lived with them and their families, as part of the Ellis family and they call her 'Grandma."

In the program at Tina's funeral was the following poem:

He Only Takes the Best
God saw she was getting tired
And a cure was not to be.
So He put his arms around her
And whispered, "Come with me."
With tear-filled eyes we watched her
Suffer and fade away.
Although we loved her deeply,
We could not make her stay.
A golden heart stopped beating
Hard-working hands put to rest
God broke our hearts to prove to us
He only takes the best.[10]

Chapter Twenty-Two
ProRodeo Hall of Fame Inducts Barrel Racers & Horses

By 2017, barrel racing had become well established in the professional rodeo world. They had been a part of the National Finals since its beginning in 1959, and had moved to the main National Finals Rodeo location for the major events in rodeo in 1967. By 1985 all PRCA rodeos were paying barrel racers equal monies that were paid in the men's event.Finally, in 1998 the barrel racers at the National Finals Rodeo got the very same amount of prize money as each of the other events. All these results had proven that the barrel racing event was as popular, if not more popular, than some of the other rodeo events.

The ProRodeo Hall of Fame and Museum of the American Cowboy, is the museum that houses everything PRCA deems worthy, located in Colorado Springs, Colo., along with the PRCA offices. Champions for each year in all events, plus those that are chosen for induction each year have items on display. It is the history of professional rodeo from; stock contractors, the broncs and bulls, plus the important horses from various timed events, the contestants, the announcers, bullfighters, barrelmen, laugh-getters and other important people in rodeo.

The 'powers that be' had decided it was time that the ProRodeo Hall of Fame invite the Women's Professional Rodeo Association to choose barrel racers and their mounts to be inducted for the class of 2017. After all they were partners in rodeos and should be represented in the Hall of Fame.

First inductees were: Wanda Bush, Charmayne James, and *Star Plaudit aka Red*, Sherry Combs Johnson's horse. Wanda Bush was the most decorated cowgirl with thirty-two world titles, including two barrel racing titles and nine all-around titles. Wanda was truly an all-around cowgirl. She qualified in barrel racing at the National Finals seven times, although her two world titles were won before the NFR started in 1959. Her best horses were *Dee Gee*, her main barrel racing horse, and *Flying Eagle*, a versatile horse.

Charmayne James won eleven barrel racing world titles, the first when she was only fourteen-years-old in 1984. She also won seven NFR average titles. James was the first barrel racer to win over a million dollars in one year, and the first woman to wear the number one back number at the 1987 NFR. Her horse *Scamper* took her to ten of her world titles and was inducted in to the ProRodeo Hall of Fame in 1995.

In 2017 Wanda Bush was one of the first barrel racers and WPRA members to be inducted into the ProRodeo Hall of Fame. *Photo courtesy of the Women's Professional Rodeo Association.*

The third WPRA barrel racing inductee was *Star Plaudit*, called Red, a bay gelding, ridden by Sherry (Combs) Johnson. Although he was an outstanding barrel racing horse, he was originally trained and ridden in steer wrestling competitions. Benny Combs and other steer wrestlers rode him at the same time Sherry was running barrels on him. *Red* helped his mounts win three world championships in one year. Sherry won the barrel racing title, Tom Nesmith won the steer wrestling and all-around titles in 1962.[1]

The WPRA Inductees in to the 2018 ProRodeo Hall of Fame Class were Billie McBride, Kristie Peterson and *French Flash Hawk aka Bozo*. Billie McBride won four world championships in a row, 1955 through 1958 on her mare, *Zombie*. In ninety-nine runs she only knocked over one barrel. Her record of four consecutive world titles remained for thirty years. She was also instrumental in getting barrel racing to be a part of the National Finals Rodeo.[2]

Kristie Peterson and her great horse *French Flash Hawk, aka Bozo*, were inducted together. Kristie, too, won four world barrel racing titles, 1994, 1996 through '98 on *Bozo*. They also won three reserve world titles, five consecutive NFR average titles and four National Circuit Finals. *Bozo* was the American Quarter Horse Association

Florence Youree was inducted into the Pro-Rodeo Hall of Fame in 2019 in the Notable category. *Photo compliments of the ProRodeo Hall of Fame*

Charmayne James was inducted into the ProRodeo Hall of Fame in 2017. *Photo Compliments of the Pro-Rodeo Hall of Fame*

Sherry Price Johnson holding the trophy for her horse, *Red* (aka *Star Plandit*), inducted into the ProRodeo Hall of Fame in 2017. (L to R) Lisa Lageschaar, Miss Rodeo America, Johnson, Karl Stressman, PRCA commissioner, and Kent Sturman, executive director of the ProRodeo Hall of Fame. Johnson was inducted into the ProRodeo Hall of Fame in 2023 for her accomplishments in barrel racing.

"Horse of the Year" five times, 1995 through 1999. He also won the WPRA "Horse with the Most Heart," four times, 1995-1998.[3]

The inductees for the 2019 ProRodeo Hall of Fame included Jimmie Gibbs Munroe who was the NIRA barrel racing champion twice. She was also the world champion in 1975 and WPRA champion in 1976 and 1977, plus in 1978 she came in runner-up for the WPRA title. She has held the office of president on three occasions and during that time was instrumental in getting the barrel racers equal money at the National Finals Rodeo, the use of electric eyes for accurate timing and better conditions in the arena.

Sammy Thurman Brackenbury was an all-around contestant, competing not only in the barrel racing, but also roping events. She qualified for the National Finals eleven times and won the world in 1965. She was the California circuit director for the WPRA and in the GRA served as all events director, vice president then president of the GRA in 1976.

Florence Youree was the third recipient and received the "Notable Award." She competed at the first National Finals Rodeo, was president of the GRA, then became secretary and was instrumental in getting the barrel racing to be held at the National Finals in Oklahoma City. She was an excellent administrative person and organized the first barrel horse futurity, has held clinics for youngsters on barrel racing and has spent her life with her husband, Dale training barrel horses. Their daughter, and two granddaughters have qualified for the NFR.[4]

Barrel racing will continue to grow. It is so popular that thousands of contestants are practicing rounding the barrels hours on end, day after day. Jackpot barrel races, amateur and open rodeos, as well as professional rodeos have barrel races. Barrel racing futurities and derbys are also popular. It is not just a woman's event at some venues, allowing men to also compete. The WPRA however, is still only available to women and draws the 'top of the crop' of barrel racers.

As for the women, they still have very stringent rules as to what they can wear. This is not just for looks, but for safety as well. But you can bet these barrel racers look their best when they are competing. The rules for WPRA did not allow denim jeans until the 1990s, and at first blue jeans were only allowed during slack or when the rodeo was designated part of Wrangler's tour, which is one of the most important sponsors in rodeo.

The professional rodeos have always required certain clothing not just for women but, also men. Although in today's rodeos there is less glitz and more color coordinated denim and shirts. Barrel racers are using the bling on their horses with fancy beaded and fringed breast collars and headstalls. Their legs are usually in color-coordinated wraps.[5]

Chapter Twenty-Three
Barrel Racing for Fun, Exercise & Peace of Mind

Barrel racing isn't always done with winning the championship in mind. There are numerous women that just enjoy being on the back of a horse and seeing how well they can run around the cans and leave them standing. No pressure, just a relationship between a woman and a horse. Often it is found that the right horse enjoys the experience as much as the person on their back.

Everyone knows the name, Reba McEntire, an amazing singer that has been gracing the country and western music stages for years. Her first professional performance was when she sang the *National Anthem* at the 1974 National Finals Rodeo, recommended by Red Steagall and encouraged by Clem McSpadden. She was nineteen-years-old.

Later that evening her mother, Jackie, asked Red Steagall to help guide Reba in the music world. The rest is history, so the old saying goes.

Reba's daddy, Clark, was a world champion steer roper, (1957, '58 & '61), her grandpa, John McEntire, was also a world champion steer roper (1934). Her brother, Pake, roped steers and is a musician, also. Susie, two years younger than Reba, also became a wonderful gospel singer.

In a conversation with Reba's mother, Jackie McEntire, she said that Reba barrel raced when she was young because she loved the atmosphere of the cowboys and a rodeo, but she couldn't remember that Reba won anything. Reba never had her own barrel racing horse, always using a horse from the ranch. Jackie remembered Reba really didn't have anyone that barrel raced to teach her how to improve.

"Her heart was into her music," said her mother, "and I know I encouraged it. I would tell her to go get on the piano and her music and quit working with those old horses. My family was

Reba McEntire runns barrels at the Fort Smith, Ark., PRCA rodeo in 1975. Her mother, Jacqueline said, "Her heart was in music, but she thouroughly enjoyed barrel racing." *Photo by Kenneth Springer, courtesy of Sharon Camarillo.*

always into music and I know I pushed her."

Jackie did admit their oldest daughter, Alice, also barrel raced and did win some. Alice rode a horse that was mean, explained her mother.

"He ran — when he wanted to — and he won — when he wanted to. Sometimes he'd just run around the arena and leave the arena, not even going around the barrels." Jackie continued, "Clark had his steer roping, rodeo, his cattle and the ranch, and I had my music. Our kids got some of both as they grew up."

You might say 'it was in their genes – jeans.[1]

* * *

Mary Jo Pope Franks, who calls herself a 'backyard barrel racer,' was born October 15, 1956. She grew up on a farm with seven siblings. She enjoyed watching barrel racing as a kid whenever she got to go to a rodeo, but that wasn't often. She didn't start to barrel race until she moved to Santa Fe, N.M., in 1986. She was thirty-years-old, had two children and a job, so she couldn't venture too far from home.

Her first barrel horse, in 1986, was one the family used for ranch work called *Ben*, an eight year-old gelding. It was *Ben's* job, cutting cattle out of the herd, overseeing the herd, and more. Mary Jo bought a Sharon Camarillo barrel racing book, set up the barrels in the pasture in the pattern suggested, and tried *Ben* at barrel racing.

"Hmmm, Ben seemed to like it," she thought.

Ben was bred right, out of *Three Bars* and *Triple Chicks*, and his registered name was *Big Regards*. He was a registered Quarter Horse, a clay-back dun with a dark stripe down his back, and also a registered Buckskin.

When she began competing with him it was at horse shows, gymkhanas, and all-breed horse shows. She entered the barrel race and pole-bending events. She won her first buckle in barrel racing at the Zia Barrel Racing Association in 1989. The American Quarter Horse Association had shows she entered, and won a number of honors from then through 1992, but received only ribbons and buckles — no money.

"In 1992, the National Barrel Horse Association revolutionized the barrel racing industry by pioneering the divisional format, which allows riders of all skill levels a chance to win money and prizes in barrel racing competition," explained Mary Jo, who was a charter member and helped bring the NBHA to New Mexico.

"The entire family can go and compete." she said. "To me the divisional barrel racing helped build confidence and bring accomplishment to a lot of weekend jackpot barrel racers."

"There is no greater feeling than being on a horse running into that arena and connecting with your horse while turning three barrels and running back across the time line with all three barrels standing! You don't care what your time is you are just so happy that you did it," she said with a big smile.[2]

There are thousands of women like Mary Jo that have found the relationship with a horse, the out-of-doors, and the opportunity to meet and get to know other women who enjoy barrel racing. She would find a big void in her life if she had to stop barrel racing. Presently she and husband, Jess Franks, a former rodeo barrelman, live on a ranch near Dora, N.M.

* * *

Lynn Kirby Stokes was born November 1, 1940, in San Angelo, Texas. She was raised on a fourth generation ranch near Sonora and has been around horses all her life. She was involved in 4-H where she raised and showed sheep and did very well. Then she decided to switch animals and work with horses.

She started competing in barrel racing in 1953 when she was thirteen-years-old. She bought a registered Quarter Horse from a breeder who bred horses for cutting, but this horse, named *Cyclone*, didn't take to cutting. They then tried him a few times on barrels before Lynn bought him.

She continued *Cyclone's* training, who she nicknamed *Jimbo*, because it was easier than *Cyclone*. When school was out for the summer she went to six or so summer rodeos and placed in half of them. She continued to compete, but also spent time training two palominos colts. When they turned three she gradually started to use them. One named *Pecos Pete,* and Lynn worked the barrels well for twelve years. When she was a freshman in high school her family moved to Evant, Texas.

She continued to compete when she could find someone to travel with. She went to a GRA rodeo in San Saba, Texas, and was thrilled to see top barrel racers there — Wanda Bush and Jane Mayo. Much to her surprise Lynn and her horse, *Pecos Pete*, placed at the rodeo.

Lynn met John Stokes at Evant High School who already had his RCA card, to ride bulls, by the time he was fifteen. Lynn went with John, with him riding bulls and her barrel racing. John and Lynn were married in 1965 and their life revolved around rodeo and continues to this day. Lynn quit competing when they had their daughter, Tamara, in 1973.

When asked if she missed competing she said, "Oh yes terribly. But we were training barrel and roping horses and there was so much to do."

Plus their daughter started riding when she was three and when she was old enough to compete, they made sure she had the right horse, the right tack, and Lynn enjoyed competing through their daughter, Tammy.

Lynn loved the sport and did it for eighteen years. When asked what it was that made her continue to compete she said, "I always had a feeling I belonged with animals and mainly horses. It was just where I needed to be."[3]

* * *

National Little Britches Rodeo Association (NLBRA) has been having youngsters compete in rodeo events since it was formed in the 1950s. They have three age groups, ages five to eight, which are called Little Wranglers; ages nine to thirteen are the Junior Division, and the Senior Division is ages fourteen through eighteen. The Little Britches organization holds over 500 rodeos a year, all across the country. The finals are held at the Lazy E Arena, in Guthrie, Okla., in July. Presently they have 569 Little Wrangler members and the majority of those at that age are barrel racers.[4]

* * *

In the September 2019 *Rodeo News* issue, "Back When They Bucked," article featured Dixie and Lee Wheaton. Dixie barrel raced and Lee rode bulls and entered other events, also. Although Dixie's main profession was a teacher in Tulsa from 1965 to 1992. She also coached basketball and won coach of the year. The couple continued to rodeo and Dixie also trained her horses.

No major wins came their way, but multi-tasking people seldom have the time to concentrate on one priority. A friend, Florence Youree, entered Dixie in a Senior ProRodeo barrel race. Lee accompanied her and they found many of their old rodeo friends from earlier years also entered.

Lee said, "The senior pros were fun for us. Rodeoing wasn't stressful. When you left home you knew you could pay your bills. You didn't have to win anything."

They both qualified for the Senior Pro Finals in 1980 through 1985. In fact, Dixie won the year-end barrel racing title in 1982 for the senior pros. Just goes to show, sometimes when the pressure of feeling like you have to win is gone, it happens.[5]

* * *

Mickey Brown, age sixteen, was the National Little Britches Rodeo Association 2017 barrel racing champion from Moroni, Utah. She has been competing at NLBRA since she was seven. She has a full plate with school and competing in seven events during

NLB rodeos — barrel racing, pole bending, goat tying, breakaway roping, team roping, trail course and ribbon roping. She admits she likes breakaway and barrels the best.

Barrel racing gives her a rush of excitement. Her horse, *Dasher*, she trained herself, is her barrel and breakaway horse. She practices at home at least three times a week, and rides her horses every evening after school. *Chocolate* is her roping horse and she credits her success to various people that have helped her along the way, but the person that helped her get started is Kendra Sagers.

"She's like a second mom to me," Said Mickey. She also looks up to Amberley Snyder and has known her for a long time. Mickey's advice to other up-and-coming barrel racers and young competitors, "Never let a bad or slow run affect your day. Try your best every time and never get discouraged. It takes a lot more effort than just turning three barrels in an arena. My main goal is to be the best I can be and to never give up no matter what happens."[6]

That sounds like good advice for anyone wanting to compete in barrel racing or any other event in rodeo and beyond.

But please don't think that serious, professional barrel racers don't take time out to have some fun. It can't be all work and no play. Also, many people consider barrel racing just as much fun as it is work.

Chapter Twenty-Four
2018 Wrangler National Finals Rodeo

The Wrangler National Finals Rodeo had been held in Las Vegas since 1985, with the exception of 2020, when it was held in Arlington, Texas, due to Covid.

The 2018 Wrangler National Finals was the sixtieth year since the National Finals was first held in 1959. The WNFR barrel racing in 2018 brought fifteen exceptional barrel racers to Las Vegas.

Hailey Kinsel was in first place before the finals started with $192,834 won for the season. Nellie Miller, champion of the 2017 WNFR, was second with 2018 earnings of $146,834. Brittany Pozzi Tonozzi, with twelve WNFR qualifications beginning in 2003 was third. Fourth place was Lisa Lockhart, also with twelve WNFRs to her credit, who had won $2 million barrel racing, and $1 million of it had been won in finals competition.

Fifth place was Stevi Hillman of Weatherford, Texas, with $110,232 for 2018. Taci Bettis, came in sixth, and had two WNFR qualifications and just joined WPRA in 2017. Seventh place was a first-timer, Kylie Weast, with $101,715 so far in 2018. Eighth place was another first timer, Jessica Routier, with $98,704, from Buffalo, S.D. Ivy Conrado, from Hudson, Colo., was ninth riding *JLo* the 2018 Reserve AQHA/WPRA Barrel Racing Horse of the Year. Tenth place was Tammy Fischer, who won the most money over the Fourth of July, which is known as Cowboy Christmas. Eleventh place was Kelly Bruner, a licensed veterinarian, from Millsap, Texas with $90,515 won. Tracy Nowlin, a first-timer, from Nowata, Okla., was ranked twelfth and joined WPRA in 2006. Amberleigh Moore, of Salem, Ore., made the trip to Vegas ranked thirteenth. She joined the WPRA in 2015 and qualified in 2016 and '17 for the WNFR. Fourteenth place was Jessica Telford, of Caldwell, Idaho, who won $88,342. Her grandfather was the late

PRCA Hall of Fame rodeo clown Gene Clark. Fifteenth place was Carman Pozzobon, from Aldergrove, British Columbia, who won $86,947, and got to the WNFR on her horse *Ripp,* who she trained. She won the Canadian Professional Rodeo Association ladies barrel racing championship in 2017.[1]

The ten days in early December are exciting when Las Vegas is teaming with Resistol and Stetson hats, and cowboy boots in every color. Thomas & Mack Center on the campus of UNLV was the destination for the women who worked their very best and took excellent care of their mounts, with nothing lacking.

No doubt, there were many short nights and long days making sure everything from their horses to their clothes were in the best condition and ready for anything. These barrel racers had made many fans, throughout their careers, including family and friends, but strangers, too, who watched and followed their year in rodeo. The outcome of the year could go to any one of these dedicated women who had traveled the country all year long to get to Vegas. There was so much money available at the Wrangler National Finals Rodeo and with $105,887 the difference between number one, Hailey, and number fifteen, Carman, anything could happen.

The 2018 Wrangler National Finals Rodeo payout was $8,800,000 total per event (per man in team roping). The $1,100,000 go-round breakdown per event (per man in team roping) was $84,615. In 1959 the total amount of the purse for all events was $61,950.

2018 Wrangler National Finals Rodeo Prize Money
(breakdown per event, per man in team roping)

Each Go-Round	Average Pay-Off
1st Place $26,231	1st Place $67,269
2nd Place $20,731	2nd Place $54,577
3rd Place $15,654	3rd Place $43,154
4th Place $11,000	4th Place $31,731
5th Place $ 6,769	5th Place $22,846
6th Place $ 4,231	6th Place $16,500
Ten Go-Rounds	7th Place $11,423
	8th Place $ 6,346

Each contestant received a $10,000 bonus which counts toward their Wrangler earnings, totally 1.2 million. The total purse was $10 million for 2018.[2]

Hailey Kinsel became the 2018 World Champion Barrel Racer,

with four go-round wins. She tied for third in round three, and tied for second in round five, finishing seventh in the average. Her horse, *DM Sissy Hayday*, also called *Sister*, was the 2018 WPRA/AQHA Barrel Racing Horse of the Year. Hailey knew she had the title after the ninth round, so in round ten, she used her backup horse, *Thunder Stones*, aka *TJ*. Her horse, *Sister*, is owned by her parents, Dan and Leslie Kinsel, who own a commercial beef cattle ranch near Cotulla, Texas.

The Kinsels bought *Sister* as a two-year-old, and *Sister* was trained by Leslie and Hailey. At the 2018 WNFR, Hailey won $157,865 and added to her earnings won before the WNFR she ended up with $350,700 for a total in 2018. The only other competitor at the 2018 National Finals to surpass her total monies was Sage Kimzey in the bull riding with $415,263 for the year.[3]

Jessica Routier was the reserve champion for 2018 winning $251,704 and moving up to second-place from starting the WNFR in eighth position. Jessica also won second in the average with

Hailey Kinsel and *Sister* working hard to keep ahead of the rest at the 2018 Wrangler National Finals Rodeo. *Photo by and courtesy of Kenneth Springer.*

a time of 142.6 seconds winning $54,577. It was her first year to qualify for the National Finals. She rode *Fiery Miss West, aka Missy*, owned by Gary Westergren of Westergren Quarter Horses in Lincoln, Neb.

Gary asked Jessica to ride his horses with the ultimate goal of getting one to the WNFR. Jessica said *Missy* was special. She was a natural fit for Jessica's riding style.

Jessica said, "She's one that I never had to really think about how I need to ride her correctly when I go into the arena. It's a natural. The way I want to ride is the way she wants to be ridden."

Jessica also qualified for the College National Finals Rodeo four years, winning the national barrel racing title in 2003. She attended National American University in Rapid City, S.D., on a rodeo scholarship. She graduated in 2006 with a master's degree in business. She is married to Riley Routier and they have five children. Her daughter, Payton, is a trick rider and rides at regional rodeos.[4]

* * *

Florence Youree, was president of GRA from 1960 to 1964, and was honored with the 2018 WPRA National Finals Rodeo's Achievement Award. Florence and husband, Dale, of Addington, Okla., breed, raise, and train barrel racing horses. Generations of horses have been bred and trained on their ranch and continue to win honors and awards going around barrels. They aren't the only ones from the Youree ranch still going around the barrels.

After Florence barrel raced, their daughter, Renee Youree Ward, qualified for the 1985 Finals in barrel racing and finished ninth. Renee's daughter, Janae Ward, also went to the Wrangler National Finals beginning in 2001 then went again in 2002 and became world champion barrel racer in 2003. She was twenty-one and a senior at Oklahoma State University.

Kylie Weast, another daughter of Renee's, qualified for the 2018 Wrangler National Finals. Kylie finished the ten-day competition in tenth place. For Kylie's first experience qualifying for the WNFR, she placed in five rounds. She had some barrel problems in three rounds, but in the tenth-round she was amazing with a run of 13.37 seconds. She won $61,770 at the finals, and ended her year with a total of $173,484.

Florence and Dale also have another granddaughter, Cassie Ward Ambrose, that also competes in futurities on occasion, but her main desire is staying home and training barrel horses. She may change her mind when that 'perfect horse for Cassie' is ready.[5]

Chapter Twenty-Five

2019 Wrangler National Finals Rodeo Seventy-One Years Since Beginning

What an amazing history barrel racing has in a short seventy-one years! The credit must go to the women who chose to pursue the event, develop it, and see that it improved from the beginning to what is has become today.

Who could have guessed that a Cowboy Reunion in Stamford, Texas, in 1931, inviting young ladies, called sponsors from surrounding communities, to their town to dance with the competing cowboys... be introduced on horseback and going around barrels placed in a row, would end up in seven decades as a multi-million dollar rodeo event?

The era when it all started was one of many changes for the country including the Depression. No work, no money, and yet the country and people needed to have fun. Women were beginning to lose ground in the rodeo world as lady bronc riders, trick and fancy ropers, trick riders, and relay riders, were being excluded from many rodeo programs. And yet, with their years growing up on ranches, where the women worked along side the men in their families, women knew they were just as capable of performing and competing.

Who knew that sponsor races, eventually becoming known as barrel races, would become such a popular and important rodeo event and open the door for women to earn the same kind of money in a rodeo arena that cowboys were winning.

2019 Wrangler National Finals Rodeo Prize Money
(breakdown per event, per man in team roping)

Each Go-Round	Average Pay-Off
1st Place $26,231	1st Place $67,269
2nd Place $20,731	2nd Place $54,577
3rd Place $15,654	3rd Place $43,154

4th Place	$11,000		4th Place	$31,731
5th Place	$ 6,769		5th Place	$22,846
6th Place	$ 4,231		6th Place	$16,500
Ten Go-Rounds			7th Place	$11,423
			8th Place	$ 6,346

These are the barrel racers at the end of the 2019 season with the top monies earned. They went in to the Wrangler National Finals Rodeo in Las Vegas in December vying for the 2019 Barrel Racing World Champion title.

Rank	Name	Hometown	Money Won	Rodeos Attended
1.	Nellie Miller	Cottonwood, CA	$154,610.50	28
2.	Hailey Kinsel	Cotulla, TX	$148.866.64	49
3.	Lisa Lockhart	Oelrichs, SD	$146,351.65	47
4.	Shali Lord	Lamar, CO	$111,775.59	55
5.	Brittany Tonozzi	Lampasas, TX	$105,503.40	67
6.	Stevi Hillman	Weatherford, TX	$105,334.82	76
7.	Emily Miller	Weatherford, OK	$ 98,144.73	79
8.	Jessica Routier	Buffalo, SD	$ 96,581.90	54
9.	Dona Rule	Minco, OK	$ 96,407.49	64
10.	Ericka Nelson	Century, FL	$ 93,433.24	65
11.	Ivy Conrado	Nowata, OK	$ 93,269.24	49
12.	Amberleigh Moore	Salem, OR	$ 93,059.51	51
13.	Jennifer Sharp	Richards, TX	$ 91,754.45	94
14.	Cheyenne Wimberley	Stephenville, TX	$ 90,360.85	89
15.	Lacinda Moore	Willard, MO	$ 88,935.85	73

The Wrangler National Finals Rodeo began on December 5 and ran thru December 14. The women were excited, frustrated, thrilled, and experienced ten days full of all kinds of emotions. They had much to do in those ten days. Their horses also experience emotions, however, we are not able to know whether they thought this was 'just' another rodeo or realize it was the most important one. After all they have competed against many of these horses throughout the year and some had been in this arena in previous years. Some contestants take several horses with them, in the event something might happen to their primary mount, others rely on just one four-legged partner.

Also listed are the women that came in sixteen through thirtieth. Doing that well, is also exciting, as popular as the sport of barrel racing is these days, and although they do not get to compete at the Finals, they should be extremely proud of what they accomplished in 2019:

Rank	Name	Hometown	Money Won	Rodeos Attended
16	Leia Pluemer	Los Lunas, NM	$ 79,058.36	91
17	Brittney Barnett	Joliet, MT	$ 76,433.45	100
18	Carly Taylor	Andersonville, TN	$ 72,299.75	85
19	Jimmie Smith	McDade, TX	$ 65,087.68	89
20	Jessica Telford	Caldwell, ID	$ 64,064.16	62
21	Jackie Ganter	Abilene, TX	$ 61,416.89	91
22	Teri Bangart	Olympia, WA	$ 58,228.47	70
23	Megan Champion	Ukiah, CA	$ 57,422.99	86
24	Ivy Hurst	Springer, OK	$ 57,156.81	90
25	Kathy Grimes	Medical Lake WA	$ 52,948.35	41
26	Jill Wilson	Snyder, TX	$ 52,782.86	65
27	Sabra O'Quinn	Ocala, FL	$ 52.000.96	51
28	Destin Devenport	Escondido, CA	$ 51,564.86	64
29	Shelley Morgan	Eustace, TX	$ 50,282.86	70
30	Callahan Crossley	Hermiston, OR	$ 47,690.25	52

Emily Miller won the first go-round, with Lisa Lockhart placing second; Stevi Hillman, third; Nellie Miller, fourth; Jessica Routier and Jennifer Sharp split fifth and sixth place.

Emily Miller placed in the first four rounds, but then didn't place again until the ninth round, when she finished fifth. Nellie Miller who came into the finals in first place had a fourth-place finish in round one, but then didn't place again until the sixth round finishing sixth. She had two more rounds in which she placed, splitting third and fourth in round seven, and fourth in the

Hailey Kinsel
Photo by and courtesy of Kenneth Springer

ninth round.

Hailey Kinsel who was the champion in 2018 and came into the finals ranked second, had a second-place win in the second round, but didn't place again until the fourth round with a sixth-place finish. She then won the seventh and eighth go-rounds, and came in second in the ninth round. Ivy Conrado-Saebens placed in seven rounds.

When the last barrel racer circled the barrels in the final round, the times began to be tallied. The outcome of the world champion barrel racer and the average winners were:

2019 Average Placings

Rank	Name	Time	Money Won
1.	Ivy Conrado-Saebens	138.44	$67,269
2.	Emily Miller	143.25	$54,577
3.	Lisa Lockhart	144.47	$43,154
4.	Nellie Miller	144.63	$31,731
5.	Shali Lord	144.73	$22,846
6.	Brittany Pozzi Tonozzi	144.77	$16,500
7.	Lacinda Rose	145.17	$11,423
8.	Hailey Kinsel	147.42	$ 6,346
9.	Jessica Routier	148.45	
10.	Dona Kay Rule	148.84	
11.	Jennifer Sharp	165.38	
12.	Amberleigh Moore	167.51	
13.	Cheyenne Wimberley	175.22	
14.	Ericka Nelson	175.45	
15.	Stevi Hillman	154.30 on nine	

Final 2019 World Standings

Rank	Name	Hometown	Money Won	Rodeos Attended
1.	Hailey Kinsel	Cotulla, TX	$290,020.49	50
2.	Ivy Conrado-Saebens	Hudson, CO	$264,673.09	50
3.	Emily Miller	Weatherford, OK	$255,798.58	80
4.	Lisa Lockhart	Oelrichs, SD	$250,697.81	48
5.	Nellie Miller	Cottonwood, CA	$235,898.96	29
6.	Amberleigh Moore	Salem, OR	$207,982.30	52
7.	Dona Kay Rule	Minco, OK	$192,392.11	65
8.	Jessica Routier	Buffalo, SD	$191,197.29	55
9.	Shali Lord	Lamar, CO	$173,390.97	56

10. Stevi Hillman	Weatherford, TX	$157,219.44	77
11. Brittany Pozzi Tonozzi	Lampasas, TX	$152,099.55	68
12. Lacinda Rose	Willard, MO	$138 916.62	74
13. Cheyenne Wimberley	Stephenville, TX	$127,860.85	90
14. Jennifer Sharp	Richards, TX	$114,023.68	95
15. Ericka Nelson	Century, FL	$112,317.85	66

The WPRA in partnership with Wrangler awarded bonus checks to the barrel racers at the 2019 WPRA Star Celebration in Las Vegas on December 5. This new Wrangler Network Tour with long standing corporate partner Wrangler brought additional opportunities for WPRA members to compete for bonus money at rodeos they were currently competing at. The Wrangler Network Tour featured eighteen barrel racing events including the finals. A total of $34,000 was awarded in the barrel racing division paying eight places.

1st	$10,000	Nellie Miller
2nd	7,500	Hailey Kinsel
3rd	5,000	Brittany Pozzi Tonozzi
4th	4,000	Cheyenne Wimberley
5th	3,000	Lacinda Rose
6th	2,000	Jessica Telford
7th	1,500	Stevi Hillman
8th	1,000	Shali Lord

The WPRA has had an existing agreement with the PRCA that expired the end of 2019. The two entities worked diligently to craft a new agreement based on currents circumstances and tomorrow's challenges that will work to the benefit of all of our respective members. With regard to barrel racing, this agreement is similar to the agreement that previously existed.

The New Agreement's summary of business terms:
- WPRA will continue to sanction the barrel race at the NFR, RNCFR and circuit finals.
- PRCA will encourage all regular season rodeos to have a WPRA barrel race.
- WPRA will continue to determine and count points towards the world champion barrel racer, but only points earned at PRCA sanctioned rodeos will count for NFR back numbers.

- PROCOM fees for WPRA members will remain the same ($21.00) as PRCA members, subject to equal adjustment if Procom fees for PRCA members rise or decrease in the future.
- Additional cost for technology, entry system of rodeo support services (judging, secretary support, patch system) for barrel race WPRA will pay PRCA 5% of net barrel race card revenue and of the 6%-barrel racing retained prize money.
- PRCA agrees they will work to expand and develop breakaway roping at PRCA sanctioned rodeos throughout the country; the present number of WPRA sanctioned breakaway roping competitions at PRCA rodeos is 35; PRCA will attempt to dramatically increase this number and handle and coordinate taking entries, stock costs, judging secretary support, marketing and other costs associated with expansion.
- Because the PRCA will contribute substantially to the front end development of breakaway roping at PRCA rodeos (in a manner and schedule the WPRA could not fiscally achieve), WPRA will transfer to PRCA 85% of net breakaway card revenue and 6% breakaway of retained prize money to subsidize development.
- Breakaway sanctioning and rules remain with the WPRA.
- WPRA and PRCA will implement a formal process to ensure accountability of judges and stock contractors to ensure our rule book is applied consistently and correctly.
- WPRA retains ownership of all current and future media rights, but grants PRCA an exclusive royalty free license for WPRA sanctioned competitions held in conjunction with PRCA sanctioned rodeos.
- WPRA retains its right to obtain sponsors and distribute its own licensed merchandise (subject to avoiding conflict with PRCA sponsors at PRCA sanctioned rodeos).
- The term for this agreement is six years.

November 30, 2019
From: Doreen Wintermute, WPRA President/CEO[1]

Chapter Twenty-Six
2020 — A Year Like No Other

The 2020 season started October 1, 2019, and was going well, until the eighth performance of RodeoHouston on March 11, when the Houston Health Department gave the rodeo producers, Cervi Championship Rodeo, eight hours to get every animal, cowboy, cowgirl and 'all things rodeo' out of Reliant Stadium.

The Covid pandemic that had started on the other side of the world had come in to the United States with a vengeance. Many other rodeos around the country cancelled after that, especially the big ones that paid the most money. Nationally media was telling everyone in the United States and beyond to wear a mask, stay at home, social distance yourself from others, and use sanitizing liquids and wash your hands often.

The dreaded coronavirus pandemic had begun in China and spread rapidly. From there Europe was affected. Country by country began feeling the force of this new virus, affecting numerous people, even killing some. In no time, the schools were closed, as were churches, restaurants, bars, and more. Sporting events were stopped and the only retailers open were those selling necessities like grocery stores, drug stores, gas stations, etc. Masks were required to enter most of these facilities.

Meanwhile the rodeo world was in a state of upheaval. Cowboys and cowgirls that rodeo on a full-time basis were in limbo. Some had made a good start on the 2020 season, those who were struggling hoped to make the second half of the year up for what they hadn't been able to do earlier. But so many rodeos were cancelled it was extremely difficult for full-time contestants to keep going.

Otherwise, ranches, farms and rural communities were handling life pretty much the same as they did normally. But there were many things that had changed from what we all knew as "normal life." Kids were home from school, there was absolutely no place to go for fun — especially during the summer months.

When things change, with different circumstances, people learn to change from what was their previous way of doing things to what is acceptable, including business. Many companies sent their employees home to work from there. Others had to furlough and lay-off employees. The government tried its best to assist those not working — but there were many challenges.

By July, the PRCA announced there would definitely be a National Finals Rodeo. Slowly a few rodeos started to be held. The Cowboy Channel, owned by Patrick Gottsch, also the owner of RFD-TV, had secured the PRCA contract to air PRCA rodeos on television. This allowed spectators and fans to keep up with what was happening in the rodeo world.

At some rodeos the workers were wearing masks, in other areas they were not. By September Las Vegas Events, an integral part of the National Finals in Las Vegas, announced they could not hold the National Finals in Las Vegas, as they had done for the past thirty-five years. Thomas & Mack Center, where the National Finals is held is on the University of Nevada, Las Vegas, campus was not allowed to host events. Quickly the PRCA turned to other places to find an alternate location.

Texas, and a new facility in Arlington, Globe Life Field, built for the Texas Rangers baseball team was finally chosen for the 2020 Wrangler National Finals. Seating over 40,000 the opportunity to socially distance those attending was possible.

Once the location was decided The Omni Hotel, downtown Fort Worth, was selected for the PRCA convention headquarters. Many fringe events held in conjunction with the Wrangler National Finals, were also held in the area.

The Junior National Finals were held at Cowtown Coliseum in Fort Worth, and many other venues were held in and around the Stockyards, a popular tourist attraction year-round. The Cowboy Christmas Trade Show was held in the Fort Worth Convention Center.

Billy Bob's Texas, billed as "the World's Largest Honky-Tonk," was the setting for the Gala, sponsored by the ProRodeo Hall of Fame, and recognizing the "Rodeo Man of the Year." The 2020

Gala recipient, Bob Tallman, is a long-time announcer and worked for the betterment of rodeo in many ways. Other luncheons for The Ladies of Rodeo Luncheon and the World of Rodeo Luncheon were also held at Billy Bob's Texas.

The top-fifteen barrel racers at the end of the year, September 30, 2020, were:

Rank	Name	Hometown	Money Won	Rodeos Attended
1.	Brittany Pozzi Tonozzi	Lampasas, TX	$86,724.83	41
2.	Hailey Kinsel	Cotulla, TX	$78,460.86	39
3.	Dona Kay Rule	Minco, OK	$67,453.54	43
4.	Jimmie Smith	McDade, TX	$65,022.06	54
5.	Tiany Schuster	Krum, TX	$55,060.38	66
6.	Jill Wilson	Snyder, TX	$53,370.97	35
7.	Shelley Morgan	Eustace, TX	$53,074.95	49
8.	Stevi Hillman	Weatherford, TX	$52,388.69	49
9.	Jessica Routier	Buffalo, SD	$51,370.93	42
10.	Cheyenne Wimberley	Stephenville, TX	$47,039.30	65
11.	Ryann Pedone	Sunset, TX	$42,580.60	70
12.	Emily Miller-Beisel	Weatherford, OK	$42.388.19	47
13.	Lisa Lockhart	Oelrichs, SD	$40,904.14	46
14.	Wenda Johnson	Pawhuska, OK	$39,953.14	24
15.	Brittney Barnett	Stephenville, TX	$39,565.33	84
16.	Jessie Telford	Caldwell, ID	$38,477.00	

Unfortunately, when being tested for Covid-19 just prior to the National Finals Dona Kay Rule tested positive and was unable to compete. Jessie Telford took her place.

Hailey Kinsel won the 2020 World Champion Barrel Racing title with a total time of 170.95 seconds and the average. Although the Wrangler National Finals Rodeo was one of the most unusual since the first in 1959, Kinsel handled every aspect of it with amazing maturity and domination.

The previous thirty-five years the finals had been held in the Thomas & Mack Center, on the UNLV campus, which was a much smaller arena. Every contestant went in to the 2020 finals not sure what to expect — a new location, a new arena.[1]

Kinsel took the lead after winning the first go-round. All together she won five go-rounds. She was runner-up in three more. She did not place in rounds two and six.

In round six she wanted to give her palomino, *Sister*, a rest, so *Sister* would be in top condition for the last four rounds. In that round she rode Cassidy Kruse's eight-year-old gelding, *LeRoy*. Kinsel knew the dirt in the arena in the sixth round was not the kind of dirt *Sister* could gain confidence on.[2]

Kinsel also joined the exclusive list of barrel racers that had won three consecutive world championships with wins in 2018, '19 and '20. Those contestants already on the list were Billie McBride (1955-58); Jane Mayo (1959-61); Charmayne James (1984-93) and Kristie Peterson (1996-98).

She also won the Ram Top Gun Award for winning the most money of any contestant at the Wrangler National Finals, with $349,076. This was just $1,624 less than her season earnings in 2018. Accomplishing these milestones took a tremendous effort and consistency, not to mention that she did not travel to nearly as many rodeos as she had in past years.

The fastest time at the finals was 16.56 seconds run in the eighth go-round by Hailey. Her total time for ten rounds was 170.95 seconds.

She said, "*Sister* is very manual. You can adjust things on her very well. I just give her all the credit." Her plan is to keep *Sister* sound and at her best as long as possible.[3]

But, Hailey was also involved in much more than just the barrel racing at the Wrangler National Finals. She interviewed breakaway roping contestants that won each round in the first women's breakaway roping ever held at the Wrangler National Finals Rodeo.

The breakaway roping was held with four go-rounds on the December 8 and December 9; and two go-rounds on the December 10. The field was narrowed to eight for the next round and then the top-four roped at Globe-Life Field.

There was $187,000 in prize money for the new event, which was won by Jackie Crawford, from Stephenville, Texas, who was six months pregnant.

Five women coming to the Wrangler National Finals in the barrel racing for the first time were: Jill Wilson, Wenda Johnson, Ryann Pedone, Jimmie Smith and Brittany Barnett.

Paige Jones, from Wayne, Okla., won $20,986, to capture the

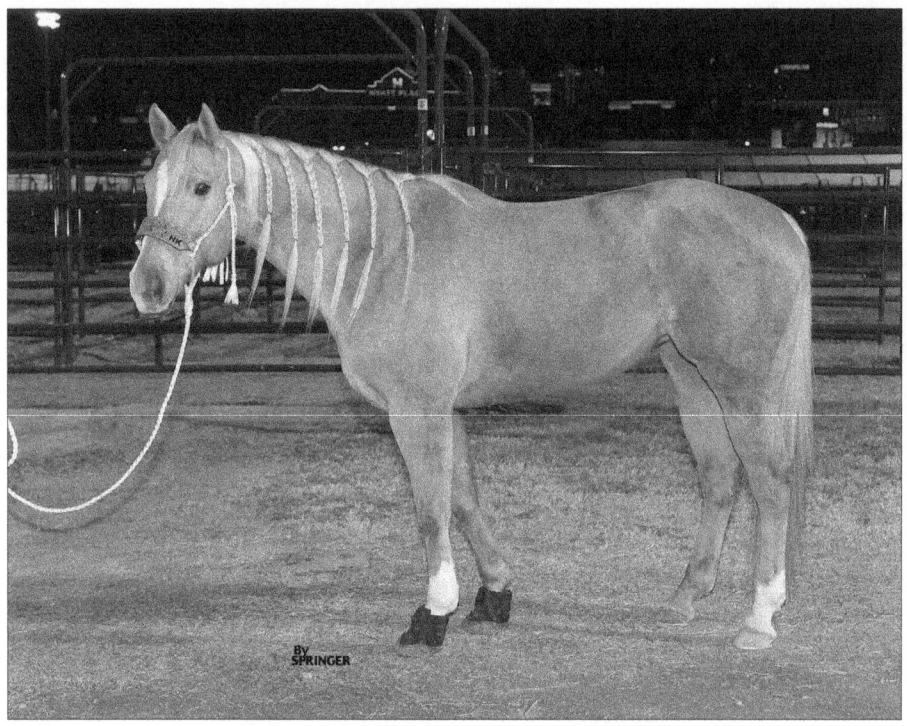

Hailey Kinsel's *Sister* (aka *Sissy HayDay*)
Photo by and courtesy of Kenneth Springer.

Rookie Barrel Racer of the Year title.[4] The "Rising Star Award," presented by Lana Merrick, was won by Brittany Barnett, with her horse *Chicks Keen O Pocopoo*, which she simply calls *Paint*. The award is given, in memory of *Scoti Flit Bar*, and was created by past WNFR qualifier, Lana Merrick, as a way of recognizing the year-long achievements of a horse that is making its first appearance at the National Finals Rodeo. This award is voted on by the top-fifteen barrel racers during the Finals.[5]

Winnings for 2020 for the fifteen contestants and Dona Kay Rule were:

Rank	Name	Hometown	Finals Money	Season Total
1.	Hailey Kinsel	Cotulla, TX	$270,615.39	$349,076.00
2.	Brittany Tonozzi	Lampasas, TX	$114,500.01	$201,224.84
3.	Jill Wilson	Snyder, TX	$112,384.62	$165,755.59
4.	Emily Miller Beisel	Weatherford, OK	$117,038.46	$159,426.65
5.	Jimmie Smith	McDade, TX	$ 88,269.33	$153,291.29
6.	Stevi Hillman	Weatherford, TX	$ 84,884.62	$137,273.31

Rank	Name	Hometown	Finals Money	Season Total
7.	Jessica Routier	Buffalo, SD	$ 82,346.16	$133,717.09
8.	Lisa Lockhart	Oelrichs, SD	$ 78,961.54	$119,865.68
9.	Shelley Morgan	Eustace, TX	$ 63,307.70	$116,382.65
10.	Tiany Schuster	Krum, TX	$ 54,423.08	$109,483.46
11.	Cheyenne Wimberley	Stephenville, TX	$ 47,753.85	$ 94,693.15
12.	Wenda Johnson	Pawhuska, OK	$ 50,615.38	$ 90,568.52
13.	Dona Kay Rule	Minco, OK	Did Not compete	$ 77,453.54
14.	Ryann Pedone	Sunset, TX	$33,269.23	$ 75,849.83
15.	Brittany Barnett	Stephenville, TX	$ 30,730.33	$ 70,296.10
16.	Jessie Telford	Caldwell, ID	-0-	$ 59,477.20

(Although Dona Kay Rule was replaced at the Finals by Telford, she still received the $10,000 for being a WPRA NFR top 15 qualifier.)

2020 Average Placings

Rank	Name	Time	Money Won
1.	Hailey Kinsel	170.95	$67,269.23
2.	Jill Wilson	174.10	$54,576.92
3.	Jessica Routier	174.10	$43,153.85
4.	Brittany Pozzi Tonozzi	175.23	$31,730.77
5.	Emily Miller Beisel	177.72	$22,846.15
6.	Ryann Pedone	177.78	$16,500.00
7.	Jimmie Smith	180.00	$11,430.08
8.	Wenda Johnson	184.92	$ 6,346.15
9.	Cheyenne Wimberley	185.47	
10.	Tiany Schuster	185.72	
11.	Shelley Morgan	189.66	
12.	Brittany Barnett	191.18	
13.	Stevi Hillman	191.84	
14.	Jessie Telford	195.29	
15.	Lisa Lockhart	221.85	

Many things were cancelled, postponed or ended for good, due to the pandemic. But, rodeo and barrel racing continues and will continue as long as there are women who have such strong connections with their equine partners and are challenged by running around a barrel pattern in the quickest time possible.

Chapter Twenty-Seven
2021 — Rodeo World Improving Slowly From Pandemic

The rodeo world was determined to get back to a full slate of rodeos, but it was taking time. The cowgirls were most anxious and taking every opportunity to keep their horses ready to compete.

Martha Josey was inducted in 2020 to the ProRodeo Hall of Fame, but the induction ceremony was not held until 2021 due to the pandemic. She qualified for the National Finals eleven times, on six different horses in four decades. She won the WPRA barrel racing title in 1980 on *Sonny Bit O'Both*, and he was the AQHA World Champion barrel horse. She was part of the United States team that competed at the 1988 Winter Olympic Games in Calgary, and won a bronze medal. The U.S. team won the title, too. She has held barrel racing clinics at her ranch near Karnack, Texas, since 1967 and has been teaching so many youngsters to achieve their goals.

The Wrangler National Finals made its way back to Las Vegas the first week in December and did not lose any of the enthusiasm and excitement that goes with the ten days in the city that never sleeps. So many additional venues that have been added to this important rodeo time of year in Vegas can keep anyone with a love of the western way of life busy way past their bedtime.

The first go-round in the barrel racing was a winning tie between Cheyenne Wimberley and Amanda Welsh with times of 13.77 seconds. The second go-round was won by Dona Kay Rule on her horse, *Valor*, who was picked as the 'Horse With The Most Heart' by the WPRA. Their winning time was 13.56 seconds. Stevi Hillman won the third-round riding five-year-old, *Lemon Drop*, owned by Matt and Vendi Dunn. Hillman said of her, "She's a free running mare and she gets stronger every run."

The fourth round was won by Wenda Johnson, whose mount was named *Steal Money*, with a time of 13.46 second. Round five belonged to Emily Miller-Beisel aboard *Chongo* with 13.43 seconds.

She had given him the night off during the third-round and it paid off.

Another 13.43 second run by Ivy Saebens and steed, *JLo,* won round six. Saeben said, "We can't thank Las Vegas Events for their effort this year to make the ground so good."

Hailey Kinsel and *Sister* won round-seven with a time of 13.45 seconds. Jordan Briggs and her 2021 Horse of the Year, *Rollo,* captured round-eight with another 13.45 seconds run. Round-nine was another tie with Jordan Briggs and Stevi Hillman posting 14.48 seconds each. Hillman also crossed the $1 million mark in career earnings with this win. Dona Kay Rule won her second round in the tenth and final round with a time of 13.59 seconds.

The WPRA barrel racers participated in a program known as 'Tags of Honor' that is run by Gail Mattern. Each barrel racer received tags for a fallen female soldier. Kinsel was riding for Sergeant Nicole Gee who was killed in action in the Kabul bombings in August, a week after she said, "I love my job," and had been photographed with her baby.

Kinsel said, "I got so choked up as it was such a surreal thing. For us to be able to represent people who have fought for our freedom and died for us is just amazing and a true honor."

The top-fifteen barrel racers at the end of the year, September 30, 2021, were:

Rank	Name	Hometown	Money Won	Rodeos Attended
1.	Jordan Briggs	Chilton, TX	$297,460	55
2.	Hailey Kinsel	Cotulla, TX	$281,156	60
3.	Emily Miller-Beisel	Weatherford, OK	$202,565	82
4.	Shelley Morgan	Eustace, TX	$202,202	55
5.	Dona Kay Rule	Minco, OK	$195,575	62
6.	Stevi Hillman	Weatherford, TX	$183,070	73
7.	Amanda Welsh	Gillette, WY	$155,065	59
8.	Ivy Saebens	Hudson, CO	$139,590	65
9.	Wenda Johnson	Pawhuska, OK	$138,345	25
10.	Molly Otto	Grand Forks, ND	$134,698	77
11.	Brittany Tonozzi	Lampasas, TX	$128,200	92
12.	Lisa Lockhart	Oelrichs, SD	$116,845	68
13.	Cheyenne Wimberley	Stephenville, TX	$111,299	77
14.	Jessica Routier	Buffalo, SD	$100,169	49
15.	Nellie Miller	Cottonwood, CA	$85,519	47

2021 Average Placings

Rank	Name	Time	Money Won
1.	Jordan Briggs	136.83 seconds	$69,234
2.	Molly Otto	145.11	$56,171
3.	Hailey Kinsel	146.41	$44,414
4/5.	Emily Miller-Beisel	146.83	$28,086
4/5.	Stevi Hillman	146.83	$28,086
6.	Dona Kay Rule	147.09	$16,982
7.	Shelley Morgan	147.19	$11,757
8.	Amanda Welsh	148.01	$6,532
9.	Brittany Tonozzi	148.27	
10.	Jessica Routier	148.76	
11.	Nellie Miller	148.80	
12.	Ivy Saebens	152.69	
13.	Lisa Lockhart	159.00	
14.	Cheyenne Wimberley	162.93	
15.	Wenda Johnson	167.41	

Jordan Briggs, second generation world champion barrel racer, placed in every round but one. She had two first place wins and set a new record for the fastest time in ten rounds with 136.83 seconds. Her crew included her husband, Justin, daughter, Bexeley, and her four-time world champion barrel racing mother, Kristie Peterson, cheering her on. Jordan's mother, Kristie said, "Jordan has always wanted to be the world champion. Her and her husband are very talented; they speak horse."

In the barrel racing event in 2021 there was $1,132,131 to be won. The ten rounds each paid a total of $87,087: First - $26,996.97; Second - $21,336.32; Third - $16,111.10; Fourth - $11,321.31; Fifth - $6,966.96; Sixth - $4,354.35

The total money paid in the average was $261,261, with eight places paid.

Chapter Twenty-Eight
2022 — The World Of Rodeo Is Back!! Better Than Ever!!

Finally rodeo is back with plenty of rodeos for each and every event. Barrel racing has soared in popularity. The big rodeos were all back in business. Jordan Briggs and *Rollo* won Houston, Andrea Busby and *Blazing With My Dude*, called *Tito* won Cheyenne Frontier Days, Kassie Mowry with *Famous Ladies Man* won Calgary Stampede. Kacey Gartner won Pendleton, that barrel configuration that is twice the size of most, they call 'The Green Mile.' Brittany Pozzi Tonozzi won Salinas for the fifth time in her twenty year career.

Jordan only entered thirty-one rodeos this season, *Rollo* 'got a nod' at twenty-seven of them, and she was in the money at twenty-five of them. Pulling the run-count down will keep *Rollo* rodeo ready for a much longer time. Justin Briggs, Jordan's husband, who trains, said of *Rollo*, "He's consistent with his blazing fast 'efficiency." Rollo was picked as the AQHA Nutrena Barrel Racing Horse of the Year for the second year. He is an eight-year-old sorrel gelding, the pride of Briggs Performance Horses.

Lisa Lockhart passed the $3 million mark, and is the second WPRA member to cross that mark in career earnings, which she did at the Badland Circuit Finals. She went to the Wrangler National Finals for her sixteen consecutive year.

Bayleigh Choate, the barrel racing Rookie of the Year for 2022, qualified for the National Finals, in eleventh place, and won the most money over the Fourth of July time in barrel racing. She won $25,505.

Cindy Rosser, and Ardith Bruce, were two barrel racers that were inducted to the ProRodeo Hall of Fame in July. Ardith, the 1964 world champion barrel racer passed away June 27, just two weeks prior to her induction. Charlene Jespersen passed away on

July 20, 2022. She joined GRA in 1950 and held card number 51.

The Wrangler National Finals payoff for 2022 totaled $10.9 million. Guaranteed prize money was $1.2 million. Competition prize money totaled $9,700,098 and each of the ten go-rounds the money was $93,270 for each event.

2022 Wrangler National Finals Rodeo Prize Money
(breakdown per event, per man in team roping)

Each GoRound		Average Pay-off	
1st Place	$28,913.70	1st Place	$74,149.92
2nd Place	$22,851.15	2nd	$60,159.36
3rd Place	$17,254.95	3rd	$47,567.87
4th Place	$12,125.10	4th	$34,976.38
5th Place	$7,461.60	5th	$25,182.99
6th Place	$4,663.50	6th	$18,187.71
		7th	$12,591.50
		8th	$6,995.27

The top fifteen barrel racers and their money at the end of the season (September 30):

Place	Name	Hometown	Money Won	Rodeos Attended
1st	Jordan Briggs,	Tolar, TX	$177,779	31
2nd	Dona Kay Rule	Minco, OK	$127,442	37
3rd	Wenda Johnson	Pawhuska, OK	$121,594	31
4th	Stevi Hillman	Weatherford, TX	$120,602	50
5th	Hailey Kinsel	Cotulla, TX	$119,390	61
6th	Shelley Morgan	Eustace, TX	$110,467	56
7th	Sissy Winn	Chapman Ranch, TX	$101,348	64
8th	Margo Crowther	N Ft Myers, FL	$96,341	82
9th	Emily Beisel	Weatherford, OK	$93,965	88
10th	Kassie Mowry,	Dublin, TX	$92,553	26
11th	Bayleigh Choate	Ft Worth, TX	$90,893	89
12th	Brittany Tonozzi	Lampasas, TX	$88,432	71
13th	Jessica Routier	Buffalo, SD	$86,863	63
14th	Lisa Lockhart	Oehrichs, SD	$84,871	93
15th	Leslie Smalygo	Skitook, OK	$84,453	50

The RAM Top Gun Award at the National Finals Rodeo goes to the contestant who wins the most money in any single event. This award has been up for grabs since 2010, but in its first year, money earned in multiple events counted. It was changed to wins in a single event in 2011. Only three barrel racers have won the Top Gun Award and they were: Mary Walker in 2012, Sherry Cervi in

2013 and Hailey Kinsel in 2020.

The final results of the Wrangler National Finals Rodeo barrel racing were:

Rank	Name	Finals Money Won	End of Season	Average
1.	Hailey Kinsel	$182,782	$302,172	8-146.06
2.	Jordan Briggs	$96,741	$274,520	4-142.41
3.	Shelley Morgan	$154,563	$265,030	1-137.28
4.	Lisa Lockhart	$168,326	$153,197	3-141.66
5.	Wenda Johnson	$110,266	$110,266	5-142.76
6.	Emily Beisel	$127,753	$221,718	
7.	Margo Crowther	$88,410	$184,751	
8.	Bayleigh Choate	$92,078	$182,971	2-138.98
9.	Dona Kay Rule	$80,126	$171,019	
10.	Leslie Smalygo	$73,890	$158,343	
11.	Brittany Pozzi Tonozzi	$65,729	$154,161	6-143.10
12.	Kassie Mowry	$57,568	$150,121	
13.	Sissy Winn	$47,808	$149,156	7-144.03
14.	Stevi Hillman	$17,462	$138,064	
15.	Jessica Routier	$36,334	$123,197	

Hailey Kinsel won her fourth world championship on *Sister*, her phenomenal partner. She had the fastest run of the Finals in the ninth-round with 13.34 seconds. And in the tenth-round she ran a 13.35. Kinsel's total earning for the week were $182,782.69, making her year-end earnings $302,172.27.

The average was won by Shelley Morgan and her *HR FamesKissNTell* partner with a commanding lead of 137.28 seconds on ten runs. Her first place aggregate payout was $74,149.92 totally for year-end $265,030.

Chapter Twenty-Nine
2023 — It Keeps Getting More Exciting, Year After Year

The Girls Rodeo Association, which changed it's name to Women's Professional Rodeo Association in 1981, celebrated seventy-five years of competition on February 28, 2023. The accomplishments of this organization, which is the oldest women's sports organization in the United States, have been amazing. Thirty-eight women met in San Angelo in 1948 and created the association solely for women, and run by women. Seventy-five years later the barrel racing competition is one of seven events receiving Wrangler National Finals Rodeo payoff of over $11.5 million.

This would not have happened had these women not continued to develop all-girl rodeos as well as convincing the Rodeo Cowboys Association to include barrel racing in their rodeos. They met opposition continually but were never discouraged. Their continued determination finally got equal monies with the other events and proved they could hold their own professionally as well as entertain rodeo audiences.

The year started off with Brittany Pozzi Tonozzi having $25,000 by the end of January, she won the Sandhills Stock Show & Rodeo in Odessa and had the fastest time of the ten-day event with 13.53. But Jackie Ganter riding *Tycoon* and winning Fort Worth topped the standings by the end of February with $36,768. In April, Jordan Briggs won Houston for the second year riding *Rollo* and soared to the lead with $87,895, with Ganter second and Tonozzi third. Jordan held the lead through July, but only went to thirty rodeos for the year.

A special exhibit was on display at the ProRodeo Hall of Fame from May through September of the top barrel racers from the 1960s through 2022. The relationship that WPRA has with the ProRodeo Hall of Fame since 2017 is also a well-deserved plus, since both the PRCA and WPRA call Colorado Springs home.

Emily Beisel banked the most barrel racing money, $25,277, over the Fourth of July week, winning Ponoka, Canada, and Cody, Wyo., with Paige Jones coming in second with $24,776. Taycie Matthews, number eighteen in the standings at the time, won the National Intercollegiate Rodeo Barrel Racing championship.

Two very important members were inducted to the 2023 Pro-Rodeo Hall of Fame, Sherry Combs Johnson and Fay Ann Horton. Both were barrel racers, with Johnson winning the 1962 world championship, and went to the National Finals Rodeo from 1959 through 1968, and again in 1970 and 1991, competing in four decades. She joined her famous horse, *Red*, and her sister, Florence Youree, in the Hall. Horton did not win a championship but was a founding member of GRA, one of the thirty-eight that met seventy-five years ago in San Angelo, Texas. She was a competitor and board member that was instrumental in the development and growth of the GRA/WPRA. Unfortunately Sherry Combs Johnson passed away August 2, just two weeks after the induction.

With so many large rodeos held during the summer months, by August the WPRA magazine cover was Brittany Pozzi Tonozzi and the headline "On Top of The World." She moved to the lead in the standings with $167,404. She won numerous rodeos including Reno, Calgary Stampede, Dinosaur Days at Vernal, Utah, Utah Days of '76, and Dodge City. Her main horse was *Benny* whose actual name is *Jets Top Gun*, owned by Busby Quarter Horses and sired by the late *Blazin' Jetolena*. Tonozzi hit the $3 million mark while competing at Salt Lake City on July 24.

Stevi Hillman won the Pendleton Round-Up and the average, riding *Sandi* whose total name was *Sand in My Socks* of C.J. Lemke's 70 Ranch Performance Horses. She also won Pendleton in 2016 and went to her first NFR that year. Her total win in 2023 at the Round-Up was $11,656.

When the year closed on September 30, Brittany Pozzi Tonozzi had a record of $270,563, which surpassed Tiany Schuster's 2017 record of $250,378. Jordan Briggs was second this year with $160,824.

The 2023 Nutrena Horse of the Year given by the American Quarter Horse Association was *Fame Fire Rocks*, or *Pop Rocks* ridden by Taycie Matthews, ranked fourth in the standings, and owned by Mission Ranch LLC. Taycie won the NIRA barrel racing championship and Salinas. Second to Nutrena Horse of the Year was *Benny* ridden by Brittany Pozzi Tonozzi, and third was *Fiery Miss West*, owned by Gary Westergren and ridden by Jessica Routier.

The Rookie of the Year was Kalli McCall, of Lufkin, Texas, riding *Mohawk*, full name *Dr. Nicks Cash*, who she had during her entire barrel racing career. But, after winning second at Denver in 2023 and the Resistol Rookie Round Up in April, *Mohawk* became lame at Reno. Kalli started the search for a second horse, and had her eye on *Dyna*, which she found in Canada. A purchase was made and she continued her year to be named Rookie of the Year, although she only earned $37,407. Second was Rainey Skelton, daughter of world champion team roper, Rich Skelton, of Llano, Texas, with $29,990.

End of season, prior to the 2023 Wrangler National Finals Rodeo the standings were:

Rank	Name	Hometown	Money Won	Rodeos Attended
1.	Brittany Pozzi-Tonozzi	Lampasas, TX	$270,563	79
2.	Jordan Briggs	Tolar, TX	$160,824	30
3.	Emily Beisel	Weatherford, OK	$158,752	85
4.	Taycie Matthews	Wynne, AR	$144,161	79
5.	Lisa Lockhart	Oelrichs, SD	$134,592	54
6.	Kassie Mowry	Dublin, TX	$133,802	28
7.	Wenda Johnson	Pawhuska, OK	$120,506	57
8.	Jessica Routier	Buffalo, SD	$118,973	54
9.	Summer Kosel	Glenham, SD	$115,682	58
10.	Ilyssa Riley	Hico, TX	$111,473	80
11.	Sissy Winn	Chapman Ranch, TX	$109,022	73
12.	Stevi Hillman	Granbury, TX	$109,015	81
13.	Hailey Kinsel	Cotulla, TX	$105,776	61
14.	Sue Smith	Blackfoot, ID	$105,644	59
15.	Paige Jones	Wayne, OK	$102,968	57

2023 Wrangler National Finals Rodeo Prize Money
(breakdown per event, per man in team roping)

Each Go-Round	Average Pay-Off
1st $30,706.41	1st $78,747.07
2nd $24,267.97	2nd $63,889.14
3rd $18,324.79	3rd $50,516.99
4th $12,876.88	4th $37,144.85

Each Go-Round	Average Pay-Off
5th $7,924.23	5th $26,744.29
6th $4,952.65	6th $19,315.32
	7th $13,372.14
	8th $7,428.97

The Wrangler National Finals Rodeo in Las Vegas had a shaky beginning when a gunman at University of Nevada at Las Vegas, (UNLV) where Thomas & Mack Arena is located, began shooting and killing several on campus December 6. The first performance was scheduled for December 7, but was put off, due to the UNLV area still being considered a murder scene. Actually the cancelled performance, was held the morning of December 13, Wednesday. The audience at that performance was limited due to two performances in one day. The seventh performance was held that evening as usual.

Considering the lead Brittany Pozzi Tonozzi had in barrel racing over the racer in second place, almost $110,000, it might seem to be a 'shoo in' that she would win the Finals, but with such huge amounts at the National Finals being paid, it very well could have been one of the other in the top fifteen.

The final results of the Wrangler National Finals Rodeo barrel racing were:

Rank	Name	Finals Money Won	End of Season	Average
1.	Brittany Pozzi-Tonozzi	$225,935.40	$496,498.82	2-141.18
2.	Lisa Lockhart	$209,096.39	$343,688.04	1-137.18
3.	Kassie Mowry	$188,790.54	$322,592.71	3-141.2
4.	Jordan Briggs	$111,694.33	$272,518.53	5-142.23
5.	Emily Beisel	$87,921.63	$246,674.04	
6.	Sissy Winn	$120,939.28	$229,961.77	
7.	Summer Kosel	$113,015.04	$228,696.65	
8.	Paige Jones	$114,170.65	$217,138.87	4-142.21
9.	Jessica Routier	$75,870.19	$217,138.87	6-142.76
10.	Stevi Hillman	$64,974.38	$173,989.82	
11.	Taycie Matthews	$10,000.00	$154,161.40	
12.	Ilyssa Riley	$28,324.79	$139,798.16	7-144.54
13.	Hailey Kinsel	$48,630.64	$154,406.41	8-148.67
14.	Sue Smith	$28,324.79	$133,968.73	
15.	Wenda Johnson	$10,000.00	$130,505.57	

Fastest time at the Finals was in Round 8 by Kassie Mowry with 13.30 seconds.

Brittany Pozzi Tonozzi won her third barrel racing world championship and runner-up to Lisa Lockhart who won the average.

Sherry Cervi was the first barrel racer to reach $3 million won in competition, having won $3,388,790 through the 2023 regular season; followed in 2022 by Lisa Lockhart with $3,308,970. After the 2023 National Finals Lockhart had $3,518,066 and Brittany Pozzi-Tonozzi $3,077,597.

From the very first sponsor girls that went to Stamford, Texas, to dance with the Reunion cowboys, and rode horseback in a straight line, and called sponsor girls to the colorful and professional barrel racers of the 2023 Wrangler National Finals Rodeo and finished most all their races in thirteen-plus seconds, it's been an amazing history. Where does it go from here and who will be next year's top fifteen? Only tomorrow will tell.

Some Outstanding Barrel Racing Horses to Remember

(This is not to exclude other rodeo barrel racing horses that did amazing things as well.)

An Oakie With Cash aka Louie came to Lisa Lockhart to train when he was four-years-old. His sire was *Bierbers Oakie* and his dam was *Lady Kaweah Cash*. By the time the 2010 National Finals came around, and Lisa was one of the top fifteen, she chose to ride *Louie*. "*Louie's* reputation far exceeds mine," Lisa said. "He is like a photo copy. He runs every run the same and did for eighty-three runs at the NFR – 2010 through 2017." She also described him as "fun loving, mischievious, trainable, wants to please and loves his job." Lisa calls him the 'comeback kid' because he has had to overcome some serious obstacles — stifle surgery, a blood disorder, and other minor injuries. "Few horses have had the consistency of *Louie*, except *Scamper*, Charmayne James' great horse," she said. He was voted by the WPRA "The Horse With The Most Heart" in 2011.[1]

Bozo aka French Flash Hawk. It was a horse named *Blue Whizz Bob aka Bob*, a son of *Tiny Watch*, that Kristie Peterson bought that made her realize how good this race-bred bloodline was for barrel racing. She bought the gelding from a co-worker after *Bob* flipped in a starting gate during his race track training. She took him home to see if she wanted to buy him. He sustained a cut while at her place and she had to buy him, but the minor injury healed well. She ran *Bob* at local jackpots and in amateur rodeos. He was a natural and they were doing well in barrel racing in the Colorado Professional Rodeo Association, when Kristie heard of another *Tiny Watch* horse on the market. *Bozo* was not an expensive horse to buy, which interested Kristie Peterson. When she looked at his papers and saw his breeding, and realized it was so similar to *Bob's*, she bought him. *Bozo's* sire was a *Doc Bar* grandson, *Son Frost*, and his dam, *Casey's Charm*, out of *Tiny Circus*, making her a paternal granddaughter of *Tiny Watch*. *Bob* was sold when the Peterson/*Bozo* team began to do so well. *Bozo* was a broncy stud colt Kristie bought for only $400, in 1989, because it was suspected he might be partially blind. His owner said he was difficult on the ground and extremely skittish. Kristie's husband, Chuck, broke him to ride and Kristie followed by introducing him to the barrel racing pattern. *Bozo* just loved it and took to it easily. The pair went to their first NFR in 1993 and won two rounds and ended up reserve champion. The following year,1994, they won their first title and followed with three more championships,1996, '97 & '98. They also won the NFR average five consecutive years,1994 through 1998. Meanwhile *Bob* was purchased by another barrel racer, and then she turned him out. Kristie knew a family of young girls looking for a proven, youth-suitable mount in Colorado Springs, and they used him in high school rodeo until he was retired. When Kristie learned *Bob* was retired Kristie reunited with the gelding and he and *Bozo* remained companions until *Bob's* death at age twenty-six. Kristie said of *Bozo* and *Bob*, "*Tiny Watch* and *Tiny's Gay* gave them a lot of guts. My favorite cross would be *Easy Jet* with *Tiny Watch* on the mare's side — and if you find a *Frenchmans Guy* and cross it on an *Easy Jet*/*Tiny Watch* mare — I'd want it!"[2]

Bugs Alive In 75 was foaled in 1973. He was a sorrel stallion eligible to run in the All American Futurity in 1975, and that was why he was named *Bugs Alive in 75*. He won the All American, which was the richest purse in Quarter Horse racing, at that time. He was also the 1975 "High Money Earning Quarter Horse." Equistat has continually listed him as the number one leading maternal grandsire of barrel horses and has hundreds of money winning horses contributing to his rating. In the rodeo barrel racing arena two were out of the great mare, *Slash J Harletta*, the dam of *Fire Water Flit*. *Smakabug*, a 1980 foal took Celie Whitcomb Ray and then Jimmie Gibbs Munroe to the WPRA pay window on numerous occasions. The other was *I Got Bugs*, a Palomino gelding that Celie Ray rode to the National Finals in 1987 and 1989.[3]

Cebe Reed was a 1958 foal out of *Bay Canary* bred to a Thoroughbred named, *Frank's Pal*, owned by C.B. Reynolds. *Bay Canary* was a mare that Martha Josey's mother sold to Mr. Reynolds, when Martha's father died suddenly. Reynolds contacted Martha and told her he had started the horse on barrels and thought he had lots of potential. She went to see the stocky bay and agreed to try him. Although she recognized that the gelding had some problems with the first barrel and an odd turning style, she also recognized that he had speed and power that was unlike anything she'd ever ridden. Martha said he would run and turn the first barrel and be ready to leave the arena. "I thought, he thought it was a one barrel race," said Martha, who figured out *Cebe Reed's* problems herself. "I knew if he could be consistent in what he did he'd be hard to beat. One day it just clicked with him. Martha bought him from Mr. Reynolds. By 1964 *Cebe's* unusual running style was set, and he never varied. Martha said, "He was a high-headed horse. He was not a head-giving or neck-bending horse. He'd run to the barrel hard and fast, when he got there his back end would gather, and he would bend in his rib cage sliding around the barrel on his hindquarters, pulling himself with his front end, never losing forward motion. Kenneth Springer, *Barrel Horse News* field editor, said of *Cebe Reed*: "What set *Cebe Reed* apart from the rest was not just that he was a winner. There have been lots of winners. But it was the style in which he did his job — a sliding pivot. I can close my eyes to this day and still see the big, stout bay gelding run as fast as he could, with his neck slightly arched and flexed at the pole, all the way to the first barrel and slide and turn it with Martha's leg often touching the barrel all the way around until he drove away for the next turn. It seemed the harder she ran him to the barrel and the further out in the arena it was, the harder he turned when he got there."[4]

Custer aka French First Watch by *Frenchmans Guy* and out of *Dashing Ta Fame*. There are horses that do such a tremendous job for their rider, even though they might not reach the top. This is a horse that earned the honor of "WPRA Horse of the Year," but never went to the Finals. Jill Welsh of Parker, Ariz., had crippling rheumatoid arthritis at age twenty, and the medicine she had to take made her sick. If that wasn't enough, when she was twenty-six she had a migraine headache for a week. She went to the emergency room where she was being treated when she went into cardiac arrest. Her kidneys were failing and her body was shutting down. When they got her stable they air-flighted her to Phoenix. As they landed, her body went into cardiac arrest a second time. She was diagnosed with kidney cancer and spent the next eighteen months taking chemotherapy and radiation treatments. When all of her treatments were over she felt like she had a new lease on life. A few months later she went to her friend, Rachael Myllymaki, who had been winning on a horse, named *Custer*, she was considering selling. Although Jill was still in a wheelchair and weak, she bought *Custer*. Three weeks later she rode the Palomino gelding, with her brother by her side making sure she stayed on. Several months later she made her first barrel race, but got a "no time." She had two more rodeos that weekend and she finally won the last rodeo, winning all three rounds and the average. She and *Custer* were really getting together when Jill received another medical problem — ovarian cancer. Eight months of treatment this time and finally cancer-free. Jill now has a different outlook on life. She is doing what she enjoys and living a good life with *Custer*. "He has done so much for me, it is so much more than just what he does inside the arena. I'm not saying that he doesn't do great things inside the arena because he does. What he has done for me outside the arena though is priceless," she said. He has also gotten the respect of all the top barrel racers, who voted him the "WPRA/AQHA Horse of the Year," in 2015. He won that title, an amazing feat given that he did not finish inside the top fifteen standings for the year, which is generally one of the horses that receives this award. *Custer* has allowed Jill to live her dream. She can tell he knows exactly how she is feeling and responds appropriately.[5]

Dm Sissy Hayday aka Sister was purchased by Hailey Kinsel's parents, Leslie and Dan Kinsel as a two-year-old. But if it hadn't been for her half-sister *Baja*, that they bought on Craig's List as a two-year-old it might never have happened. "*Baja* ran fast and was really coming on," said Hailey, "We loved her so much we called the breeder, learning he had just one half-sister left — *Sister*." She was by *PC Frenchmans Hayday* out of *Royal Sissy Irish*. Although they admit she was a funny looking two-year-old, she was solid-minded and a good turner. She began to fire at three and four, was strong-willed and Hailey kept her slow and focused at first. *Sister* won her first PRCA rodeo at the Elizabeth Stampede in Colorado in 2015. Her record breaking run at the 2017 National Finals of 13.11 seconds, and her performance at that Finals and the 2018 Finals when Hailey became the world champion has cemented *Sister's* worth. She also won the 2017 "Scoti Flit Bar Award" at the National Finals Rodeo. *Sister* was the 2018 "WPRA/AQHA Barrel Racing Horse of the Year." In 2019 *Sister* was in a three-way tie for WPRA "Horse With the Most Heart," and in 2021 she was second for the "Nutrena Horse of the Year," presented by the AQHA.[6]

Dinero aka PC Frenchmans Hayday was born in 1995. Mel Potter bought him when he was two-years-old. He's the son of *Sun Frost* out of *Casey's Charm*, the daughter of *Tiny Circus* by *Tiny Watch*, and a full-brother to Kristie Peterson's *Bozo* and sire of Hailey Kinsel's *Sister*. He was the senior stallion at the Potter Ranch for twenty-three years. Sherry Cervi already had two National Finals championships by the time she hauled *Dinero* to the Finals as a back-up horse in 2005. They left Las Vegas after the Finals fourth in the world, and third in the average. *Dinero* was used in team roping as well as barrel racing and won the "AQHA/PRCA Heeling Horse of the Year" in 2005. Sherry said about *Dinero*, "He was the first *Tiny Watch* horse I had ridden. He was really gritty. He always gave 110% and was tough. He was really athletic and really quick. As a performance horse I think that's what you need."[7] *Dinero* was such a versatile competitor. In Nampa, Idaho, in 2005, he was ridden by Cory Petska, a heeler in the team roping, who won fifth with header Walt Woodard; then Sherry, rode him in the barrel racing and got fifth, and they won a total $11,000 at the rodeo. Mel Potter, the owner, said "*Dinero* sired at least fifteen horses that have gone to the National Finals. Seven or eight in barrel racing, some in steer wrestling and in team roping." *Dinero* was such a versatile competitor.[8]

Dutch Watch was born in 1975 to breeders Howard and Joannie Driggers. He was a son of *Tiny Watch* out of a *Hug Bars/Three Bars* mare registered as *Bar O Dutchess*. He was to follow his sire's race career but was short-lived when a respiratory virus sidelined him. After a short time he was trained for the National Reined Cow

Horse Association's marquee event. The owner's daughter wanted to make a cutting horse out of him, but he was just too much. "He was an outlaw," announced veteran barrel racer Marlene McRae. "He was rank. He ran off, broke a kid's leg, and jumped on the daughter's shoulder and broke it. He was definitely a problem child." The daughter set up barrels to walk and trot the pattern but that is all that was done. McRae visited the Driggers' ranch to purchase a stallion when she met seven-year-old *Dutch* the first time. Instead of buying the stallion, only to geld him to make him a barrel horse, she asked about *Dutch*. They told Marlene the fine pedigree, but failed to mention how much trouble he caused. She bought him and planned to spend the first year making him a well broke barrel horse, but they discovered by June they were ranked among the top fifteen WPRA barrel racers. "When I won the world in 1983 on *Dutch* he was a very green barrel horse," admitted Marlene. In addition to the 1983 world title, she won three reserved champion titles, 1987, '88 and '89, two NFR average titles, 1983, 1988, and numerous circuit titles on him. They also won the Calgary Stampede barrel racing title an amazing five times. "I think I went to 110 rodeos and put 150,000 miles on *Dutch* that first year. I vowed I would never do that again," McRae said. Later she only took him to twenty-five to thirty rodeos a year. His last win was Salinas, Calif., in 1992 and she retired him. He died six years later. Marlene continues to use *Tiny Watch* horses including three that carry *Dash Ta Fame* which is *First Down Dash x Sudden Fame/Tinys Gay* lineage.[9]

Fire Water Flit aka Milo was born April 23, 1978, by *Flit Bar* and out of *Slash J Harletta*. He was owned by Vicki Adams, and trained by Celie Whitcomb Ray. He was a shiny Palomino and was born with barrel racing royalty in his veins. Adams first sent *Milo* to the track, where he earned an eighty-six speed index but was stopped by ulcers in his throat. He missed a futurity run due to a fractured splint bone. With limited training at the Old Fort Days Rodeo, his first rodeo, he won fourth the first night and first two nights later under Celie's saddle. He had a derby win, and then won the average at the State Fair of Texas PRCA Rodeo in Dallas. In 1984 Adams moved in to the top fifteen riding him but a fractured pelvis and groin injury gave him a six month lay-off. A fall during a run at the

Helldorado Days PRCA rodeo in Las Vegas was a career ender for *Milo*. Even with limited exposure Adams realized his talent as a great barrel horse and not wanting another injury he began siring the next generation of barrel horses. His crops of colts brought out many excellent barrel horses. Adams estimated out of 623 foaled by him, 510 were of an age to compete and 262 have been money earners. He died peacefully December 20, 2005, of natural causes, and was buried on the Adams Fire Water Creek Ranch in a specially made steel coffin, with two pillows under his head.[10]

Hell On The Red aka Reddy was born in 2012. Kylie Weast, of Comanche, Okla., trained her home-grown fiery mare for barrel racing futurities and she did quite well in 2017. In 2018 Kylie qualified for the National Finals on *Reddy*. She won the tenth round by posting the fastest time of the entire rodeo — 13.37 seconds. Kylie comes from a three-generation family that is experienced in barrel racing training and competition, so her knowledge and training is very 'matter of fact.' Kylie admitted she hadn't given *Reddy* an option, "I just stuck her in the trailer and went to rodeos." The first rodeos were in buildings and *Reddy* did well. Then the rodeo outside at Guyman, Okla., — she won it. "We've thrown her to the wolves and she's taken it, so I'm thrilled with how she is transitioning. *Reddy's* competitiveness is pure try. If anything happens that is bad it is because she tries too hard," commented Kylie. "When she goes down that alleyway, it's like that's what she's meant to do. Her ears perk up and she looks for the first barrel no matter where we are. I know she loves her job," says the owner, "with barrel racing in her genes."[11]

I Got Bugs aka Bugsy was born in 1982 and bred out of *Slash J Harlatta* and by *Bugs Alive in 75* on the ranch of Celie Whitcomb Ray near Sterling, Colo. Celie trained him and he won lots of money in futurities and derbys, but she also qualified for the National Finals on him in 1987 and 1989 and came in ninth and third in the world, respectively.[12] *Bugsy* was not a tall horse, but weighed 1,200 pounds. It has been said his frame matched his larger than life personality. Mary Cecelia Tharp, Celie's daughter, was asked what did her mother, who died in 1994 of cancer, think was her greatest accomplishment. Her answer laughingly was, "Me, and *I Got Bugs!*" But *Bugsy* and Celie had a special connection. Kenneth

Springer, photographer for all things WPRA, reported that Celie and *Bugsy* won the first futurity she ran him in at the West Texas Barrel Racing Futurity. He was smooth, he was quick and he was fast. But he was a handful. He even took the paint off the side of his trailer with his teeth and chewed the electrical wiring. He was bored easily and had so much energy. His intelligence was what made him great but also what made him so hard to handle. Celie and *Bugsy* won Rodeo Houston twice. A few years later, after Celie's death, her daughter, Mary Cecelia, competed on *Bugsy*. The transition for *Bugs* was rough, as it was for Mary Cecelia, but in time he eased up on his hard-charging style. Then as Mary Cecelia became a more seasoned racer he built his speed up again. When his health began to fail he wouldn't give up. The family had to make a decision and he was laid to rest May 21, 2018.[13]

Lucky was a 'spoiled roping' horse that was bought by Mildred Farris to be her barrel racing horse. He was also 'high-headed' and you couldn't use a tie down on him. But she found that when he started running he would put his head down and handled very well. Mildred's husband, John, said, "It was the late 1950s, before we married, and she had practiced him a few times and knew he could do well. The first rodeo they entered was an amateur rodeo in Lamesa, Texas. At the last minute the rodeo officials decided to change the pattern and run to the first barrel, then to the third barrel (the one farthest away) and back to the second barrel. Mildred was not sure just what would happen since she hadn't practiced *Lucky* that way. He'd never run this pattern before, but they finished second. After the rodeo Mildred practiced him on this new pattern several times. At the second performance the next day they finished first.[14]

Rafter W Minnie Reba aka Sister is a blue roan mare, sired by *KS Cash N Fame* and dam *Espuela Roan* ridden by Nellie Miller of Cottonwood, Calif. *Sister* was Nellie's barrel racing horse when she won the 2017 world championship. *Sister's* half-brother, *Blue Duck* was Nellie's horse when she qualified in 2010 for her first National Finals. Her dad, Sam Williams, trained *Sister*, as well as *Blue Duck*, and she calls it "good, basic old school training and he teaches them to do many things." Nellie said, "When my dad trains he does everything on them, they must be versatile as possible. She works cattle, too, and is always confident and athletic." What makes her win so special on *Sister* is that Nellie feels she isn't even in her prime yet. They only went to forty-seven rodeos to get to the Finals, and the reason was to keep *Sister* sound.[15]

Robin Flit Bar aka Billy was by *Flit Bar* and out of a mare named *Robin Hood Price* which was bought for Jimmie Gibbs from Rebecca Tyler, of Uvalde, Texas. When he was three and Jimmie was attending Sam Houston State University, she took *Billy* with her. She qualified for the 1974 College Finals, in Bozeman, Mont., and won the national all-around and the barrel racing championship on *Billy* and was a member of the national championship women's team. Jimmie and her mom stayed in the north and just kept competing until September, when she had to go back to college. Jimmie and *Billie* qualified for the National Finals also that year and went in second place, her rookie year, finishing in third place. The next year she won the college barrel racing championship again on *Billy*. Jimmie basically said, "*Billy* had a huge heart and always gave a 100%." In 1976 and 1977 he was the season high money horse in the GRA. She lost *Billy* when he was thirteen to a viral infection, they couldn't heal. But in spite of that, he won six barrel races he was in over the Fourth of July. "That is a cool way I want to remember *Billy* running as good as he ever had," said Jimmie.[15]

Star Plaudit aka Red was a big boned bay gelding with lots of potential and speed that Benny Combs, a steer wrestler, bought with his brother, Willard. Originally *Red* was to be a steer wrestling horse, used and trained by Sherry's husband, Benny. When Sherry married Benny she did not have a horse for barrels, but she had been running barrels since she was a kid. She agreed to try *Red* when the guys finished working him as a steer wrestling horse. Sherry practiced him on the barrel pattern. Sherry admits that his steer wrestling training taught him how to run hard during the barrel racing. She enlisted her sister, Florence Youree and husband, Dale, for some training advice. At the Denver National Western Stock Show and Rodeo, *Red* and Sherry won their first professional barrel race. *Red* continued to work both events. "Steer wrestlers started watching the barrel racing event just to see *Red* run," said Sherry. *Red* took Sherry to the GRA Finals in 1960 and 1961 where she won the GRA all-around world title. *Red* won two world championships in one year, 1962 — one for Sherry in barrel racing and one for their friend, Tom Nesmith, in steer wrestling. Tom also won the all around championship that year, so you might say *Red* had a hand in that as well. Sherry and Red went to the NFR from 1962 through 1967. *Red* was retired at age eighteen and he died at age twenty-two.[16]

Scamper was born in 1977 and named *Gill's Bay Boy*. He was a son of *Gills Sonny Boy* out of *Drapers Jay*. A cowboy, working for Charlie James at the Clayton (New Mexico) Cattle Feeders feed lot, was selling his horses. A colt, later named *Scamper*, was one of them for sale. The James family bought him, since Charmayne's barrel racing horse had recently broken its leg. The colt had been sold several times because he had bucked off one of the cowboys who raised him and he ended up in the hospital. The horse was suspect of all humans from then on — until he met Charmayne. She immediately started training him on the barrel pattern. In between barrel patterns, she'd take him to the feed lot and work him there, then go back to the barrels. Charmayne named him *Scamper* because of the way he handled the barrels. She quickly learned he was totally broke and would do whatever she asked of him. Charmayne said, "What people don't know about *Scamper* is that when we first started I had to wake him up before we ran or he wouldn't fire. He finally figured it out. He just wanted to run barrels." They quickly forged a strong partnership and started winning or placing in all the rodeos they entered. It was amazing and lasted from the time they went professional in 1984 to *Scamper's* retirement in 1993. They won the Houston rodeo ten times. As a team they won ten consecutive world titles at the NFR. In ten years of riding *Scamper* at the NFR, Charmayne rode *Scamper* in all but one round, making ninty-nine total runs. They placed in fifty-six rounds and got twenty firsts. They only hit three barrels in ninty-nine runs. Scamper won the AQHA "Silver Spur Award," recognized by *Sports Illustrated* magazine as one of "25 Amazing Animal Athletes in 2005." In 1996 *Scamper* was inducted into the ProRodeo Hall of Fame.[17]

Stingray aka Mp Meter My Hay was born on the Potter Ranch in 2002, a foal by *PC Frenchmans Hayday* x *Miss Meter Jet aka Dinero*. *Stingray* is a Palomino, as was her sire, *Dinero*, and she has the same talents and traits as he. In 2010 *Stingray* and Sherry Cervi won the world title, Sherry passed the $2 million mark as a barrel racer, and set a new NFR arena record in round eight with a time of 13.49 seconds.[18]

V's Sandy was born in 1948. He was a dark dun gelding with a red stripe that ran from his forelock to the root of his tail. He had a bald face and four white legs. His AQHA number was P-18304. He was bred by *Oklahoma Star, Jr.*, who was by *Oklahoma Star* by the Thoroughbred, *Dennis Reed*. His mother was *Adonna* by *Bert* by *Tommy Clegg*. Jane Mayo bought him January 18, 1958, from J.T. Walters of Tulsa, Okla. She traded a stud, a mare and some cash for him. She had only been on him one time but had tried to buy him four times before. Walters had started training him but he rode differently than Mayo. She won the barrel racing championship on *V's Sandy* in 1959, 1960 and 1961. She said it wasn't hard to get him to run her style but it takes a long time for a horse and rider to come to an understanding.[19]

Yeah Hes Firen aka Duke was sired by *Alive N Firen* and dam *Splended Discovery* and was born in 2003. Brittany Pozzi Tonozzi bought him as a four-year-old. He was trained and she brought him along and he quickly became her top barrel horse. He never slowed down once he left the gate, even around the barrels, he would run on any kind of ground, and she could just feel the talent, quickness of his feet and how he positioned himself around the barrels. He took her to her 2009 world championship and she is sure he helped her win at least $1.5 million during her career. He got hurt before the 2018 NFR, but she had taken him to the winter rodeos and he did well in 2019.

Note: Sherry Cervi, a world champion barrel racer, from a family of well-known home-trained barrel horses, said in a *Barrel Horse News* article, "It still happens. The breeding is getting so precise, and there are so many more people breeding for barrel racing, that the competition is getting tougher and tougher every year. That's what's great about the sport — everyone's trying to make it better and make better barrel horses."[20]

Some of the Important Women in Barrel Racing
This is not to exclude other important women that did outstanding things in the field of barrel racing.

Mary Ellen "Dude" Barton was born in January, 1924, and lived on Cross 6 Ranch east of Flomot, Texas. She was the youngest of nine children. The family tied her in the saddle as an infant on *Old Jim*. All the kids worked on the ranch, but during the school year they lived in Matador, Texas. She loved basketball and was the football sweetheart. She entered her first rodeo at age fifteen in Matador. She won her first saddle the next year, 1940. In Wichita Falls at Kirkwood's All Girl Rodeo in 1942 she won it all. In 1947 in Midland, Texas, she won the $1,500 saddle for barrel racing, and a $600 trailer for the cutting horse contest. She always had a great sense of humor and enjoyed having fun. She was a founding member of the GRA.[1] Her last competition was in 1953 at Colorado Springs. The responsibilities of the ranch became more demanding of her time and she had to quit competing. She was inducted to the National Cowgirl Hall of Fame in 1984.[2] She spent her later days on the ranch making bird houses and miniature outhouses. She passed away in 2019 at Matador.[3]

Kay Proctor Blandford was born August 17, 1955. Today she lives in Sutherland Springs, Texas, with husband, Robert, on the land she bought with money won with *Llave*, the bay gelding she considers her "Greatest Blessing." She stays busy teaching schools and clinics for barrel racers. Kay always trained her own horses. She started college at Howard College and graduated with a degree in elementary education from Southeastern Oklahoma State University in Durant, Okla. She qualified for the National Finals twelve times, over four decades, beginning in 1975, '77, '79, '81, '93, '95 thru '97, '99 and '02. She won the WPRA World Championship in 2007 (the only year that PRCA had the PWRA at NFR).

In 1996 she was the reserve champion and second in the average at the NFR. She also had the fastest time at the NFR with 13.97 seconds, and won the most money of any barrel racer at the Finals, $78,786. In 1997 she won the Dodge National Circuit barrel racing championship. She won the Texas Circuit championship four years, 1995, '96, '97 & 2002. In 2002 her horse *The Key Grip aka Llave* (which means key in Spanish) was chosen the "AQHA Barrel Racing Horse of the Year." *Llave* was out of *Eagles Poco Jen* by *Sierra T*. Kay retired from competition in 2005. Since then Kay has trained barrel horses and taught barrel racers. She was inducted in to the Texas Rodeo Cowboy Hall of Fame in 2010. She has two DVDs about barrel racing titled: *The Key to Success* and *The Power of Dreams*.[4]

Sammy Fancher Brackenbury was born in Kingman, Ariz., December 11, 1933. She began her rodeo career by roping calves in Las Vegas and going to amateur rodeos. She would also enter the wild cow milking and team roping. She was a versatile cowgirl. Her dad's team roping partner didn't show up and she became his partner. Bill Linderman, president of RCA, gave her permission to enter and rope at any RCA rodeo. She also got involved in barrel racing. Sammy helped form the California GRA chapter. She started holding barrel racing clinics in 1965 and held them for ten years. She taught barrel racers to switch hands when going around the right and left barrels. Her dad also trained her to lead and bear rein, which put the mounts nose where it should be, which was part of her training. She also designed a barrel racing saddle that was sold at her clinics. It was light-weight, 14" seat, and provided a Monty Forman (well known equine-clinician) balanced ride. She also designed protective boots for horses — run down boots, skid and bell boots. She qualified for the RCA National Finals eleven consecutive years (1960 through 1970) winning the world barrel racing championship in 1965. She was a strikingly beautiful woman, who was also a stuntwoman and actress in the movies. She was inducted in to the Rodeo Historical Society's Rodeo Hall of Fame in 2012, and an inductee at the 2019 ProRodeo Hall of Fame in Colorado Springs, Colo. She has also received the California Circuit "True Grit Award" and the WPRA "Pioneer Cowgirl Award."[5]

Ardith Bruce was born July 22, 1931, in Clay Center, Kan. At five, her family moved to the Ozarks, in Missouri. She favored horses, and learned to show them and helped with the work horses on the farm. She married Jim Bruce after graduating from high school and moved to Farwell, Texas, in June, 1949. The Muleshoe, Texas, Fourth of July rodeo was to hold a barrel race and Jim set barrels up in their front yard so Ardith could practice. She had never seen barrel racing before, but in spite of her lack of experience she won both days. In 1952 they moved to Colorado. Their son Dan was born the next year. Ardith continued to compete in barrel racing, in and around her area, and jockeyed on some small tracks in Colorado. She joined the GRA in 1960. She was riding *Holy Toledo*, a friend's horse, who wanted her to compete in the GRA barrel racing at the National Western Stock Show & Rodeo. In 1964 she won the world championship on her horse *Red*. She was the first title winner to win the world going to the left barrel first. By the mid-1960s she was teaching barrel racing, mainly at clinics in the East and Canada. So many girls, in distant areas, wanted to compete in barrel racing, but there was no one from their community to teach them. Ardith's photo was on the cover of the AQHA magazine and they highly recommended her. Ardith began flying to her teaching locations. Video cameras had just come out and she would video the students. She would then show them their runs plus videos of the top barrel racers of that era. She also trained a few horses for others. Ardith was still barrel racing, at age eighty-twoBruce passed away June, 27, 2022, just prior to her induction to the Pro-Rodeo Hall of Fame.[6]

Wanda Harper Bush was born October 6, 1931, in Mason, Texas. She grew up on the Harper Ranch and was doing chores on the ranch as early as she could. She rode her horse three miles to meet the school bus. Her horse was left in a pen, until she returned from school, to ride him home. Her dad made sure the horse had hay and water during his daily wait for Wanda. Winning at rodeos would mean extra money for the family. When she heard about the GRA she joined immediately. Her card number was fourteen. She was a roper, as well as a great horsewoman. She won the first barrel racing champion title in 1952 on her mare *Dee Gee*. She also competed in cutting, flag race, ribbon roping and calf roping. She won the 1953 barrel racing title the following year. From 1951 to 1969 there was only one year she didn't win a GRA world title in at least one event. She was the most decorated cowgirl in the history of GRA with 32 world championships in various events. She was truly a versatile contestant and won titles in all-around, barrel racing, ribbon roping, tie-down roping, cutting and flag events. Wanda is credited with getting the Houston rodeo to start having barrel racing. Although she had left her duties on the board of the GRA years before, she was asked to return by Jimmie Gibbs Munroe, the president, during the 1980s. They were determined to get equal monies in barrel racing and knew Wanda's relationships with important people throughout her competitive years would aid in reaching their goal. She was the Texas director on the GRA board. When that was completed she began to hold barrel racing clinics. Her daughter, Shanna, said of her mother, "Her work ethics were amazing." Wanda passed away in December 2015. She has been inducted in to the National Cowgirl Hall of Fame, the Rodeo Historical Society Hall of Fame, ProRodeo Hall of Fame, the Texas Rodeo Cowboy Hall of Fame and the Texas Cowboy Hall of Fame.[7]

Dee Watt Butterfield was raised on a cattle ranch near Big Creek, B.C., Canada. She began riding at three-years-old, and by four she was wrangling on thirty mile cattle drives. She learned about barrel racing from a book by Jane Mayo and entered her first rodeo at age twelve. She was nicknamed 'Cowboy' by the local cowboys because she could rope and ride as well as any man. She also rode English as her grandmother had the first English riding academy in western Canada. Dee qualified for the first Canadian Finals Rodeo in 1974. The following year, 1975, she moved to Alberta and qualified for the National Finals Rodeo (under the name Dee Watt). In 1975 she was named Canadian ProRodeo "Woman of the Year" during International Women's Year celebrations. In 1992 she was crowned Canadian ProRodeo (CPRA) champion barrel racer. She qualified for the Canadian Finals eleven years, with 1994 being her last. She taught clinics across Canada, the U.S. and Australia. Her students have included Lindsay Sears, Calgary Stampede champ Jill Besplug and Canadian champ Gaylene Buff. She was inducted in to the Canadian ProRodeo Hall of Fame in 2015.[8]

Sharon Camarillo was born January 8, 1948, and lived in Southern California. She had a love of horses, but just rode on occasion as a youngster. Her parents traveled, with her, and she saved her money to be able to trail ride in national parks. At age twelve she did some work at a sale yard where cattle were sold and when the sale was over, she and friends turned over the trash barrels and pretended to barrel race. At an early National Finals Rodeo she attended, she saw the women compete in barrel racing. That put dreams in her head of wearing pink western shirts and starched Wranglers and being a cowgirl. During college at Cal Poly at San Luis Obispo, she was on the rodeo team and won the national goat tying championshipin 1970. She married Leo Camarillo, world champion team roper, in 1974. He and his brother, Reg, were having roping clinics and Sharon then began her preparation to have her own clinics to teach barrel racing. She believed in goal setting and went to the National Finals in 1979 through 1982. At the 1980 Finals she tied with Donna Krening for the fastest run — 16.25 seconds. Sharon competed from 1966 to 1986. Since then she has been giving clinics and teaching in various places around the world. Sharon was a fierce competitor and realized that the mental game in barrel racing is very important. She received the "Tad Lucas Memorial Award," at the Rodeo Historical Society in the National Cowboy & Western Heritage Museum in 1997, and inducted in to the National Cowgirl Hall of Fame in 2006.[9]

Sherry Cervi was born September 17, 1975 to Mel and Wendy Potter in Tucson, Ariz. Her mother, Wendy, qualified for the National Finals Rodeo in the barrel racing in 1970, '71 and '72. Sherry started competing in barrel racing at rodeos where her dad steer roped. Sherry joined the WPRA in 1986 when she was twelve-years-old (since then they have changed the age limit for insurance reasons). "It's fun to have your family involved in something you love to do," said Sherry. Her mom traveled with her and she admits she learned so much from her, but she also said, "There are so many great horse women, I learned from a lot of them." Sherry didn't start going hard until she was eighteen-years-old. She went to nineteen PRCA National Finals Rodeos, beginning in 1994 through 2001, '03, '05, '06, 2009 through 2016. She won four world championships in barrel racing; 1995, 1999, 2010 and 2013. She also won

Martha Josey and *Cebe Reed* at Burwell, Neb., in 1977.
Photo by and courtesy of Ferrell Butler.

Mildred Farris riding *Lucky*.
Photo courtesy of Joleen Steiner and the National Cowboy & Western Heritage Center.

three NFR averages; 1999, 2009 and 2013. In 2010 she set a new WPRA record by winning two million dollars in her career. She also set another NFR record in barrel racing that year. In round eight, her time of 13.49 seconds was the fastest time up to that time at the NFR, plus she also won $120,000 at the Finals. *Stingray*, her mount, was the "AQHA Barrel Racing Horse of the Year" in 2010. When she won her fourth championship in 2013 she set another NFR record by winning the "Top Gun Award," earning $155,899 — the contestant that won the most monies at the Finals. Sherry also set a new average record with 138.15 seconds in ten rounds. Her main horses for these successes were *Hawk, Trouble, Tin Man, Stingray*, a twelve-year-old old Palomino mare, *George*, an eleven-year-old Palomino gelding and *Dinero*, a nineteen-year-old Palomino stallion, who's full name was *PC Frenchman's Hayday*. *Dinero* sired *Stingray* and *George*. She gives her horse seventy-five to eighty percent of the credit for her successes. Sherry was married to Mike Cervi, Jr., who died in a plane crash in 2001. She married Cory Petska in 2014. She watched Cory win his first world championship in team roping in 2017.[10]

Jerri Duce was born in 1953 in Canada. At the age of eleven she won her first Canadian barrel racing championship in 1964. She won additional championships in 1965, '66, '68, 1970, 1974 and 1977. She also was the first Canadian barrel racer to qualify for the National Finals Rodeo in 1973, and again in 1976 and '77. In November 1997, Jerri became the first woman to be inducted into the Canadian Rodeo Hall of Fame. She was also the first crowned Miss Rodeo Canada at the Canadian Finals Rodeo held in Edmonton, Alberta. Jerri also teamed with her sister, Joy, and became know throughout the world as the Flying Duces in trick riding with their high speed horses. They performed across Canada including Expo '67, the World's Fair, Calgary Stampede and the opening ceremonies for the 1988 Calgary Winter Olympic Games. In the US they performed from one coast to the other at significant venues and rodeos. She runs Jerri Duce Phillips Trick Riding School in Carseland, Alberta. She also trains horses and is a stunt performer in films on occasion. Jerri was also the first woman to be inducted into the Alberta Sports Hall of Fame and Museum, for the sport of rodeo.[11]

Mildred Farris was born a twin August 8, 1933 to W.B. and Blanche Cotton in Andrews, Texas. She graduated from Sul Ross State College in Alpine, Texas, with a degree in physical education in 1955, and also participated on the Sul Ross rodeo team. She married John Farris, also a rodeo contestant, on May 31 of that year. They made their home on the family ranch outside Addington, Okla. She was inducted into the Sul Ross Rodeo Hall of Fame in 1994. She also won the Texas Barrel Racers Association championship from 1955 through 1957. She joined the GRA in 1958 and served as a director, vice president, then president from 1965 to 1971. Mildred qualified as one of the top barrel racers in the country and went to the National Finals Rodeo thirteen times. She never won a championship but was runner-up to the champion three times. In 1968 she posted the fastest time at the NFR with 16.6 seconds. She was selected "WPRA Woman of the Year," in 1996. You might say her lack of a championship was because she had too many 'irons in the fire.' She served as rodeo secretary to the Women's National Finals Rodeo seven times. She was named "PRCA Secretary of the Year," nine times, and twice by the WPRA. She served on the PRCA contract personnel executive council from 1988 to 2002. For seventeen years she carried the American flag at the opening of the National Finals Rodeo in Oklahoma City. She was rodeo secretary for the Fort Worth Stock Show & Rodeo for thirty years. She was a five-time rodeo secretary for the Wrangler National Finals Rodeo, a five-time NFR assistant secretary and a NFR timer for fifteen years. She was inducted in to the National Cowgirl Hall of Fame in 2012; with husband John inducted to the Rodeo Historical Society Rodeo Hall of Fame in 2010; with John in the ProRodeo Hall of Fame in 2006; and the Texas Rodeo Cowboy Hall of Fame in 2004. She died of pancreatic cancer May 13, 2013.[12]

Isabella Haraga: At age sixteen, Isabella Miller put stock racks on her dad's grey pickup to carry her Thoroughbred horse *Misty Dawn* plus a friend's horse. They were headed to the very first barrel race at the 1957 Calgary Spring Horse Show. Before they left home her dad advised her, "Whether the judge is right or wrong, you have to accept his decision with no complaining when you get home, or the truck stays here." At that show the first Canadian Barrel Racing Association was founded. Isabella became a director and worked tirelessly, in and out of the arena, for the sport she loved. She spent long hours horseback to train and condition her horses. She even skipped rope to keep in physical shape. As president of CGRA in 1959, 1961 and 1981 through '86 she made sure things were done right. She was a team player, everyone liked her, and she liked them. She trained and sold horses, was a barrel racing and rodeo clinician, and so much more. She was a four time Canadian barrel racing champion, 1960, 1969, 1986 and 2006. Five time CGRA senior all-around champion and only the second woman to be inducted in the CPRA Cowboys Hall of Fame.[13]

Tina Sikes Hodge was born in 1940 and lived on a farm/ranch in Central Texas. She walked three miles to a one-room school with one teacher until she was in the fifth grade. She started riding when three-years-old, and always rode bareback until Santa Claus delivered a saddle on Christmas, when she was nine. She loved to be with her dad, who used horses to plow the fields. At the Fourth of July rodeo in their community, her dad took them to buck in the bronc riding. When the bronc riding was over Tina would ride one of the horses as they were taken back to the trailer. Tina was only eight and delighted in teasing the cowboys, who had bucked off of them during the event that she could ride them and they wouldn't buck. After she got her saddle she began barrel racing. She won or placed in many barrel races. She also competed in rodeo queen contests and won several. She made all her cowboy shirts from Purina feed sacks, on her grandmother's peddle sewing machine. She continued to do the same for her entire family when she married. She became Texas State Rodeo Queen in 1956. In 1958 she was invited to go to Cuba with a rodeo team, but turned it down. In 1959 she was one of six Texas girls invited to the American Royal Rodeo in Kansas City, Missouri. She won fifth in barrel racing and also got engaged to her husband while there. She sold her horse and with the money she got for him, she furnished their home. She's been inducted in to the Texas Rodeo Cowboy Hall of Fame and continues to work with them as their scholarship chairman. She and husband, John, have two boys, who competed in rodeo, and now she enjoys her four grandchildren, three still involved in rodeo.[14]

Charmayne James was born in Amarillo, Texas, on June 23, 1970, and grew up near Clayton, N.M. She began her competitive career

Some of the Important Women in Barrel Racing

Sharon Camarillo
Photo by Hilary Yantis and courtesy of Sharon Camarillo.

LaTonne Sewalt
Photo from Back in the Saddle magazine and courtesy of Dixie Reger Mosely.

Martha Josey
Photo courtesy of Josey Enterprises.

Jimmie Gibbs Munroe
Photo by Steve Gray and courtesy of the ProRodeo Hall of Fame.

at 4-H shows competing in whatever they offered. All she could think about was riding horses. Her first barrel racing horse broke his leg. As fate would have it, just at that time, a fellow was selling all his horses which included a feisty gelding that had bucked his owner off and he ended up in the hospital. The horse was named *Gills Bay Boy*, but when the James family bought him Charmayne nicknamed him *Scamper*. She commented when she was inducted in to the ProRodeo Hall of Fame in 2017, "I tell people at my barrel racing schools I saw a path around the barrels and I focused on that path. So many that run barrels focused on the barrels, not the road or path around it. I felt that set me apart." She was only thirteen when she decided to go professional in 1984. Her mother, Gloria, drove her to all those rodeos. She was only fourteen when she won her first world title, plus the "Rookie of the Year" award. Charmayne and *Scamper* went on to win ten world barrel racing titles in a row — 1984 through 1993. She won an eleventh world champion title in 2002 on her horse, *Cruiser*, who she bought for $2,000 and trained him. The win proved to her, and the world, she could win the world on a horse other than *Scamper*. She was the first barrel racer to wear the coveted number one back number at the NFR. She was also the first barrel racer to pass the million dollar mark in winnings.[15] Charmayne accomplished what no other barrel racer has done so far. It is said of her accomplishments — she cared so much for her horses, she got advice on food supplements, long before it became the thing to do. She found alternative and holistic ways of caring for her mounts. She created her own all-natural supplements; she found a more humane form of equine dentistry, and much more. In her clinics she shares this knowledge as she teaches how to be better a better barrel racer. Charmayne was inducted to the National Cowgirl Hall of Fame in 1992. She was inducted in to the ProRodeo Hall of Fame and joined her horse, *Scamper*, who had been inducted earlier, in 2017.[16]

Charlene Evetts Jespersen was born March 28, 1935. She grew up in a rodeo family in the central San Joaquin Valley in California. Her father, Hoke Evetts, was a roper. Her mother, Alma Evetts, was a barrel racer and continued until she was in her late seventies. Charlene inherited her mother's talents, as other barrel racers had tried to outrun her, for many years. She started competing by going to jackpot ropings with her dad, because they held barrel races, also. She also team roped with her dad. Charlene also traveled to barrel races with her mother and both barrel raced, although she said her mother didn't win anything, but she enjoyed competing. Charlene joined the GRA in the 1950s; her card number is thirty-two. She qualified for the California Circuit Finals once it started and was the GRA California circuit champ for several years. At that time she was riding *Lotta Dollar*, a stud, and considers him one of her best. Her dad even roped on him. She qualified for the National Finals in Dallas, on him in 1961. She qualified again for the NFR in 1965 (but did not compete). In 1966, at the NFR in Oklahoma City, she came in fifth in the world. Charlene's last NFR was in 1974. Her brother was a world champion team roper, H. P. Evetts. Her favorite rodeo is Salinas, Calif. Her favorite barrel race is the National Barrel Horse Association Super Show in Las Vegas. In 2013 at age seventy-eight, she was winning it, with over 700 contestants, until "one of them got me," she said. She was also honored that year as the California Circuit "Pioneer Cowgirl." She and her husband, David Mueller, own *NF Frenchman's Brucey*, her most recent main mount. Charlene had a stroke a few years ago while riding, and ended up on the ground. She would love to still be riding but feels her balance would not allow her to be comfortable in the saddle. She said when asked what she was most proud of, she had difficulty in choosing one thing, however, she said, "I won the 'Best Dressed Cowgirl' at the Houston rodeo one year. I always liked to wear shiny stuff." At eighty-four years 'young' she enjoyed talking about those earlier days and said, "I always rode to win!"[17] Jesperson passed away, July 10, 2023.

Sherry Price Combs Johnson was born August 16, 1938 in Duncan, Okla., to John and Lena Price. She had one older sister, Florence. Since there were no brothers, the girls worked with their dad, doing whatever ranch work was necessary. Their parents didn't really like rodeos and only allowed the girls two rodeos a year at first, but eventually gave in. Sherry was the AJRA all-around champion twice. In addition to running barrels, she also competed in the flag race and whatever else was available. She was the 1955 National High School all-around champion. She joined the GRA in 1957 and made the first National Finals Rodeo in 1959 held at Clayton N.M. She was eligible for the NFR every year through

1968, then again in 1970 and 1991, making it twleve years in four decades. She did not go to the 1961 NFR in Santa Maria, Calif., because the money to win was not enough ($2,205) to cover the cost of traveling from Oklahoma to California. In 1962 she became the world champion barrel racer held at Dallas. Her barrel racing horse was a steer wrestling horse first. Sherry feels that is why *Red* was so fast. In 1962 *Red* also won the steer wrestling world championship for Tom Nesmith. Sherry said that she trained six different horses, and they taught her to be patient. Plus she said they also had a very calming effect on her. She was inducted in to the Rodeo Historical Society Rodeo Hall of Fame in 2009 and the Texas Rodeo Cowboy Hall of Fame in 2015.[18] She was inducted into the ProRodeo Hall of Fame in July 2023, and passed away on August 2, 2023.

Martha Josey was born March 11, 1938, in Longview, Texas, to Mr. and Mrs. Henry Arthur. Her father was one of the first four directors of the National Quarter Horse Association. He collected thirty-five great mares and a stud. When he died suddenly her mother had to sell all but the stud, *Jimbo*, a *Joe Reed* bred horse. Martha was invited to a rodeo in Shreveport, La., when she was a senior in high school and the barrel racing ignited a spark in her. She wanted to be in that arena competing in barrel racing. She got *Jimbo* out of the barn and started to practice. She immediately knew barrel racing was where she wanted to be. One of her father's great mares, *Bay Canary*, was sold to C.B. Reynolds who bred her to a Thoroughbred, *Frank's Pal*. The result was *Cebe Reed*. Mr. Reynolds called Martha, in 1960 and asked her to haul the three-year-old and get him started as a barrel horse. Her mother gave her an old Buick with over 300,000 miles on it. She had to rent a horse trailer for five dollars every time she went to a rodeo or horse show. She knew *Cebe Reed* was good and she started winning on him. With help financially from her mother she bought him from Mr. Reynolds for $2,500. They traveled to the American Royal Horse Show in Kansas City, Mo., and she broke the arena record and won every go-round. They went on a fifty-two race winning streak and didn't hit a barrel all year. She joined GRA in 1968 and *Cebe Reed* took her to her first National Finals Rodeo. She went to eleven more NFRs on six different horses over four decades. Martha married R.E. Josey in 1966. He won the AQHA world champion calf roping title three times. They have held barrel racing schools and clinics since 1967 and also hold roping events at their ranch near Marshall, Texas. Martha was inducted in to the National Cowgirl Hall of Fame in 1985; the Texas Cowboy Hall of Fame 2002; Texas Rodeo Hall of Fame 2007; ARK-LA-TEX Sports Museum 2008; inducted into the the Rodeo Historical Society Rodeo Hall of Fame in 2011 and received the Tad Lucas Award in 2022. She was inducted into the ProRodeo Hall of Fame in 2020, but the induction was not held until 2021, due to covid. She won a gold medal at the 1988 Calgary Olympics on the barrel racing team, and an individual bronze medal. She has also been a futurity champion many times.[20]

Hailey Kinsel was born October 3, 1994. She lives near Cotulla, Texas, and didn't start barrel racing until she ended her gymnastic days at age eleven. She grew up on a cattle ranch and her mother, Leslie, was a former Miss Rodeo Texas. She and Hailey's dad both competed in rodeo through high school and college. Hailey began competing at age four. She also competed in the Texas High School Rodeo Association in all the girls events, plus served as state president and won the state barrel racing in 2011. She also held offices in FFA and 4H. Her parents bought *DM Sissy Hayday* called *Sister* as a two-year-old, with Leslie and Hailey training her. Hailey went to Texas A&M and graduated in agricultural economics. Hailey and *Sister* came on strong at the 2017 National Finals and ended the year as reserve champion. She set an earnings record in barrel racing at the 2017 Finals with $189,385 plus a record-setting 13.11 second run in the third round. It was not a surprise that in 2018 Hailey became the world champion barrel racer with a total won of $350,700 for the year. Her family's support and giving her an amazing work ethic has been the key. She became the world champion barrel racer again in 2019, 2020 and 2222. She also won the average in 2020 with 170.95 seconds in ten runs.[21]

Ann Lewis and and her twin sister were born in Sulphur, Okla., on June 4, 1958. She won her first barrel racing money at Atoka, Okla., when she was five. The rodeo officials asked her to sign a receipt when she picked up her winnings, but she couldn't write yet. "I can print my name if you want me to," she told the officials. In 1968 as a rookie in the GRA she signed her name for a second place win at Houston - $1,064. She just kept on winning that year.

She set an arena record at Shreveport, La., on her horse, *Charlie Bay Dan*, by running in 16 seconds and in 15.8 seconds. Traveling at night in the family pickup-camper on Highway 67 just eleven miles west of Hope, Ark., an eastbound semi-trailer truck hit two cows, jackknifed and overturned. The Lewis pickup-camper hit the overturned truck and burst into flames. It was October 2, and Ann and *Sissy* had made their first runs at Little Rock, Ark., and were headed to Waco to compete the next night. Ann, her mother, and Sissy were killed. Jan, Ann's twin sister, died five days later. The only survivors were her father and brother, Randy. Posthumously, Ann won the 1968 barrel racing championship, at age ten, with $8,649.69. Sissy Thurman, also deceased, won third place for the year. A memorial membership for Ann and *Sissy* is evident at the National Cowboy & Western Heritage Museum.[22]

Lisa Lockhart, a Montana native, was born on November 11, 1965, in Wolf Point. Today she lives in Oelrichs, S.D. She has seventeen consecutive National Finals under her belt, 2007-2023. Three reserve championships, 2014, 2015 and 2023, and she won the NFR average three times, 2014, 2016 and 2023. She won The American, presently the richest one-day rodeo twice, 2014 and 2015. At the 2017 National Finals surpassed $1 million in prize money. She won the 2018 Ram National Circuit Finals and the Calgary Stampede's $100,000 in 2019. At the end of 2023 Wrangler National Finals Rodeo, Lisa had earned $3,518,00 in her professional barrel racing, setting a record for carrer-earnings. She loves to train and compete. She has used five horses in her twelve NFR trips — *Louie, Rosa, Chisum, Sterling* and *Bugs*, she has owned them all but *Rosa*. Due to an injury to *Louie*, at the Houston rodeo in early 2019, she had to take *Cutter*, an eight-year-old gelding, to the 2018 Circuit Finals. Their runs at the Kissimmee, Fla., Circuit Finals were 15.29 seconds, 19.36 seconds, and 15.47 seconds and in the sudden-death final against another South Dakota racer, Jessica Routier, Cutter ran a 15.30 second run giving Lisa the Ram National Circuit Finals Championship. Lisa's great horse, *Chisum*, passed away in 2023. Lisa is married to a PRCA roper, Grady, and they have three children, Alyssa, Thane and Cade. Lisa admits the hardest thing about being on the barrel racing circuit is being away from her family. She tried to not go to more than thirty-five to fifty-five rodeos a year. When asked if winning the world championship was on her 'bucket list' she said, "I'm not pursuing it, if it happens, it happens."[23]

Missy Long from Duncan, Okla. was twelve-years-old in 1969. She had started riding horses at four, competing at six in Quarter Horse shows and found barrel racing a natural for her. She got her GRA permit in 1968. By May of 1969 she was in fourteenth-place, but started a streak of wins in the summer and went in to the National Finals in first place. She placed in eight out of nine rounds, won the championship and won the average, winning $1,566 at the Finals and finished the year with $9,783. She only went to fifty-two rodeos in 1969.[24]

Wanda & Wilma Ludwig (Wanda Cagliari & Wilma Hybarger): They were twins born in Auburn, Calif. in 1935. As teenagers they saw trick riding for the first time and decided that is what they wanted to do. From the age of eighteen until the early 1970s they wowed audiences across the country with their tricks and abilities on the back of their horses. Eventually they were ready to quit. They had both married and had families, but they both stayed in the horse world. Wilma gave lessons and tutored riders from many venues. Wanda trained horses and began barrel racing in Nevada and California at state associations. She won the Nevada Cowboys Association barrel racing nine consecutive years. In 1980 she joined WPRA and became the "Rookie of the Year." She also qualified for the National Finals in 1980 and 1981. She competed in WPRA for eleven years. She then joined the National Senior ProRodeo Association and barrel raced, team roped and ribbon roped. Wanda won the barrel racing title ten consecutive years, the all-around title eight years and was also the Canadian Senior ProRodeo champion barrel racer in 1993. Her daughter, Cathy Cagliari, won the 1988 NIRA barrel racing title on a horse Wanda had trained.[25] Wanda Cagliari died in December 2021 and her sister, Wilma Hybarger passed away six days later.[25]

Billie Mcbride was born in Copperas Cove, Texas, on March 4, 1927 and later lived at San Angelo, Texas. She and her sisters started competing in rodeos at an early age. Billie was a charter member of the GRA and held offices for thirteen years as president, vice president, secretary and as a director. She was instrumental in getting barrel racing to be a part of the first RCA National Finals Rodeo, at Clayton, N.M., with the steer roping and team roping finals. She and her mare, *Zombie*, won four consecutive world championships in barrel racing, 1955 through 1958. Winning four championships in a row was a record for thirty years, until Charmayne James won her fifth title in 1988. Billie was reserve champion in 1954. Her daughter, Alva Jean, also competed on *Zombie*. Billie was inducted in to the National Cowgirl Hall of Fame and the Texas Rodeo Cowboy Hall of Fame in 1981. She was inducted to the ProRodeo Hall of Fame in 2018. She worked at M.L. Leddy's, in San Angelo, for thirty years stitching boot tops and other items.[26] She passed away May 10, 2018, in San Angelo, at the age of ninety.

Gina McDougall was born in 1927 in Alabama. Her family moved to Canada and started the Bar C Ranch west of Cochrane. She and her brother, Jack, ran trap lines for extra money, she drove a team of horses, gathered wild mustangs, and rescued four-legged orphans and did most of the chores as well as breaking colts. Barrel racing became her first love, in addition to her three children. She competed on the pro rodeo circuit for four years, capturing the Alberta Circuit championship in 1961 and two Canadian barrel racing championships in 1962 and '63. Gina always gave her horse all the credit. When she counted her blessings, she counted her horse twice! Following her rodeo career she turned to sculpting and depicts the western life. Her bronzes are world famous. She did bronzes for the 1988 Calgary Olympics and was the first artist to be inducted to the Calgary Stampede Western Art Show Hall of Fame in 2007.[27]

Ruth Nelson McDougall, a daughter-in-law to Gina McDougall, from High River, Alberta. Her father had a ProRodeo Thoroughbred chuck wagon racing team on the circuit for many years. She started barrel racing in 1983. The same year ladies' barrel racing joined the CPRA. Ruth placed in the top two for eight consecutive years. Five of those years she won the championship title and in 1987 through 1989, she won three in a row. She won the 1986 Calgary Stampede barrel racing and qualified for the National Finals that year. Ruth also operated a western store in Nanton, Alberta. She divorced Bob McDougall and later partnered with Junior Garrison, a tie-down roper, from Oklahoma, where she lived until her death in 2016. She was inducted to the Canadian Pro Rodeo Hall of Fame in 2009.[28]

Marlene Eddleman Mcrae was born January 15, 1957, in Ordway, Colo. She showed Shetland ponies when she was six-years-old, and then became Colorado 4-H Champion Horseman & Showman at age nine through age twelve. For four years she qualified for the Little Britches finals entering barrel racing, pole bending, breakaway roping, team roping, goat tying and cutting. In 1980 she was drafted and competed for the Denver Stars rodeo team and was chosen most valuable player for the team. Marlene went to the National Finals ten years, 1983 through 1991 riding *Custer*. She qualified again in 2000 riding *Tender Tobian*. She was the 1983 WPRA barrel racing champion. Marlene won the NFR average twice, 1987 and 1989. In 1988 at the Olympics in Calgary, Alb. Canada, she won two gold medals. She was the Calgary Stampede champion barrel racer five times. In 2018, Marlene received the "Pioneers of the Rodeo" award from the Calgary Stampede. She was inducted in to the National Cowgirl Hall of Fame in 1995. She has been training and instructing numerous barrel racing clinics all over the world since 1982. She conducted an Australian clinic in 2019. She has ten barrel racing DVDs, and the author of *Barrel Racing 101*. She lives in Paso Robles, Calif., with her husband Doug. They also return to their property in Colorado for clinics.[29]

Jane Mayo was born in 1937 and her family had a ranch near Okemah, Okla. As a child she was diagnosed with a rare blood disease and doctors thought she would die before she reached the age of five. Her father, W.H. Mayo, bought her a gentle horse, *Old Buck*, and she learned to ride. The fresh air and sunshine helped her get her health back. At age thirteen she entered a rodeo competition at Greenwood, Ark., and won the barrel race. She also roped. She graduated from high school in 1955 and became a member of GRA. That year she won $5,794 in barrel racing and including roping and horse shows her total wins amounted to $6,473.[30] In 1957 and '58 she became the GRA team tying champion. With *V's Sandy*, a Quarter Horse champion, her barrel racing wins were amazing. She won the world title for 1959, 1960 and 1961. Jane admitted that the hardest part of professional rodeo work is the long drive between rodeos. She drove pulling her own horse more than 60,000 miles a year. She also said some months her gasoline bill was $300. Jane gives *Sandy* all the credit for her titles as well as her roping wins.[30] Jane and *V's Sandy* made the cover of the *American Quarter Horse Journal*. She wrote a book entitled, *Championship Barrel Racing*, based on how to train a horse for barrel racing. Apparently she knew what she wrote, as very few cowgirls have won three world championships in barrel racing three years in a row. Only four cowgirls have accomplished more — Charmayne James and *Scamper*, who won ten years in a row and another year nine years later, 1984 through 1993 and in 2002, and by Billie McBride and *Zombie* who won four years in a row,1955 through 1958. Krisitie Peterson won three in a row, 1996 thru 1998, and Hailey Kinsel won 2018 thru 2020[31]

Nellie Miller began riding at ten and competing at gymkhanas by roping and running barrels. In high school she competed in team roping, barrel racing, breakaway roping, pole bending and goat tying. She made the High School Rodeo Finals all four years in barrel racing, but only attended three. She knew she had a good horse for state level competition, but not at the national level. *Blue Duck* was her first good barrel horse, trained by her father, Sam Williams. Nellie went to the University of Nevada at Las Vegas and won the region and came in second at the NIRA Finals. She filled her WPRA permit in 2008 and went to her first National Finals in 2010, finishing eleventh. That year she met her soon-to-be husband, James Miller. They married the next year. He is the general manager for the Red Bluff Calif. rodeo, and they live at Cottonwood, about fifteen miles away. Nellie's entire family is involved in her barrel racing, and family is extremely important to her. Daughters, Peyton and Hadley, both travel with her as often as possible, sometimes Nellie's mom, Roxie, goes to help out, too. Even her brothers help haul her horses and are very supportive. The 2017 National Finals ended with Nellie becoming the world champ riding *Blue Duck*. She was the only lady in barrel racing to cross the $300,000 barrier in 2017. Her win for the average was in 137.32 seconds in ten rounds. She won a total of $177,962 during those ten grueling days in Vegas, and ended the year with $308,498. In 2018, Nellie finished eighth for the year, although they had a good year, their National Finals was a struggle. Nellie recognized *Sister* wasn't as strong as she had been expected. However, in 2019

Sister was doing her job. Nellie and *Sister* were leading the barrel racing event with having gone to only twenty-seven rodeos. She won Houston early in the year, then went to rodeos close to home until July when she came in fourth at Calgary and won Cheyenne in a hail storm. Nellie and *Sister* came in third at the end of the season. Nellie is a laid-back kind of girl, she has goals, but she feels like she 'goes with the flow,' keeping her horse sound and has learned a lot about going down the rodeo road. Her main "go to" is her family — they make her competition as a barrel racer a team effort.[32]

Lydia Moore lived in the St. Louis, Mo., area when she and her sister, Percyna, first learned about barrel racing. In the mid-1950s St. Louis had an outdoor RCA rodeo and barrel racing was one of the events. Wanda Bush was there to compete but there weren't many other entries, so Wanda went to Valley Mount Ranch, a prominent facility for all things western, and put out an appeal to the local horsewomen to enter. Lydia and her sister, Percyna, competed in barrel racing while living in Missouri and helped organize the Missouri Chapter of GRA. When Lydia moved to Oklahoma City in 1967 she was introduced by June Ivory to Stanley Draper of the Chamber of Commerce, who was instrumental in getting the National Finals to Oklahoma City. He hired Lydia to be the liaison between the Chamber and the GRA barrel racers that were competing taking care of their needs since this was their first year at the main National Finals. She continued in this position, plus handled the NFR press room and did many secretarial duties for them until the National Finals moved to Las Vegas. Lydia held the following offices in the GRA: calf roping director, Southern Region director, and bull riding director. She was also on the board of directors for five years. The GRA hired Lydia as awards chairman and she became the GRA executive secretary in 1973 to 1995.[33] She was inducted into the Rodeo Historical Society Hall of Fame in 2019 and lives in Wayne, Okla.

Jimmie Gibbs Munroe was born April 15, 1952 in Waco, Texas. Her mother's father was Zack Miller, one of the three brothers that owned the historic famous 101 Wild West Show and Ranch. Her dad was in the cattle business and competed in amateur calf and team roping. Her mother was raised on a ranch and competed in cutting events and local horse shows. Jimmie had a pony at three-years-old and began competing at horse shows, competing in barrel racing and roping. At age ten she joined American Junior Rodeo Association. "My love was roping before I became a barrel racer," she admitted. She attended Sam Houston State University on a rodeo scholarship. She was the national women's director for the NIRA for two years. She won the National Intercollegiate Rodeo Association all around-cowgirl and barrel racing championships in 1974, the same year she joined the GRA. Jimmie also went to the National Finals Rodeo and finished third in the world in 1974. She won the NIRA barrel racing title again in 1975 and the GRA all-around, barrel racing and tie-down roping world championship. She also won the GRA barrel racing title again in 1976 and 1977. She became the GRA president in 1978 to 1993, during which time the GRA changed their name to WPRA. She became president again in 2011 and '12. She was the main force, with her board, to get equal money in rodeo for the barrel racing contestants. She was president of the Rodeo Historical Society in 2002. She has received the "Tad Lucas Memorial Award" for being an outstanding woman in rodeo. She and husband, Bud Munroe, were inducted into the Rodeo Historical Society Rodeo Hall of Fame in Oklahoma City in 2016. She was inducted to the National Cowgirl Hall of Fame in Fort Worth in 1992. She was inducted in to the ProRodeo Hall of Fame in 2019, where her husband was all ready an honoree. She and Bud, college champion saddle bronc rider in 1975 and world champion in 1986 married in 1980. They have one daughter, Tassie, named after Jimmie's mother. Bud passed away in 2022. In 2023 she started her third reign as president of the WPRA.[34]

Kristie Peterson grew up on a ranch near Parker, Colo. Her family had horses and Kristi and her brother rode a lot, but her parents knew nothing of rodeo. The children wanted to enter Little Britches rodeos and although their parents were novices, they took them to all the Little Britches events in their area. Kristie won the Little Britches all-around world title for her age group, but barrel racing was her least favorite event. When she became an adult, Kristi went to work at the Elbert County Sheriff's Department and married Chuck, and had son, Justin, and two daughters, Jaime and Jordan. It was not until she got a horse named *Blue Whizz Bob* she got back into competition and for the first time enjoyed barrel racing. She bought another horse from a neighbor for $400 named *French Flash Hawk*, who she called "*Bozo*." After gelding *Bozo*, Chuck broke him to ride, then Kristie began working him on the barrel pattern. By summer he was running open and it was evident he loved the sport. She started competing in futurities and derbys in 1991 and 1992. She won the Barrel Futurities of America World Championship Derby and Sweepstakes in 1992. She joined WPRA in 1991 and earned her first of eleven Mountain States Circuit titles in barrel racing. She collected four Dodge National Circuit Finals wins. She went to eight consecutive NFR rodeos beginning in 1993. She won the world championship in barrel racing in 1994, 1996, '97 and '98. She was reserve champ three times — 1993, 1995 & 1999. She won the NFR average five times — 1994 through 1998.[35] Peterson and *Bozo* were inducted into the ProRodeo Hall of Fame in 2018.

Gail Petska of Norman, Okla., knew when she was in high school she wanted to be a professional barrel racer. It was sheer hard work in perfecting her skills but she never wavered. She joined the GRA in 1971, and placed well that year going in to her first National Finals Rodeo, winning one round and placing in five others. The following year, in June 1972, she married Paul Petska, a roper and horse trainer. With her marriage came a confidence she had not had before and by August she was second in the standings. During September/October she won Oklahoma City, Memphis, Abilene, Albuquerque, Pine Bluff and Little Rock, plus four other rodeos. She went to the Finals in first place and won seven go-rounds and placed second in two other go-rounds. Out of sixty-five rodeos she had won or placed at fifty. She became the world champion with $17,104 and also won the average. In 1973 she didn't slow down, she won six go-rounds and placed in two more and won the world with $19,448, adding $2,236 during the Finals.[36]

Molly Swanson Powell was born January 14, 1976, to Chuck and Julee Swanson at Pincher Creek, Alberta, Canada. Chuck was a NFR saddle bronc rider and won Calgary in 1967. Molly went professional when she was ten-years-old at Medicine Hat. The family moved to Montana when she was five and she has dual citizenship. In her barrel racing career she has won over a million dollars. She went to the College Finals two years. Then she went to the

National Finals for ten years from 1995-1998, 2000-2002, 2004-2005 and again in 2007. Her best year, 2004, she was runner-up to the champion, and won the average. She was invited to compete at the Salt Lake City Winter Olympics in 2002. As happens she flew from San Antonio, where she had been at a friend's wedding, to Salt Lake City. She was rushed when she arrived so she took a cab, in her high heels and dress, to the rodeo grounds, where she changed clothes. She ran the barrels on a horse she had never seen, riding a borrowed saddle and won the gold. The USA barrel racing team also won the gold medal. She married world champion team roper, Turtle Powell, in 2001. They have two children, Layne and Raina, and live in Stephenville, Texas.[37]

Carman Pozzobon of Aldergrove, British Columbia, received a dream box from her aunt when she was a young girl. Her aunt told her to write down her dream, put it in the box, and leave it. She wrote 'make the NFR on a horse I trained myself.' In 2018 she went in to her first National Finals Rodeo in Las Vegas in fifteenth place with $86,947. She won at fifty-eight rodeos in Canada and the U.S. She finished the NFR in fourth place, and was the only barrel racer that left all the barrels standing for ten rounds. She won the average with 139.46 in ten rounds and received $67,269.Added to her other monies won at the Finals, gave her a total of $117,884, in the city that never sleeps. Carman won a total of $204,831 for 2018. She also won the Canadian National Finals in 2017, and her seven year old *Ripn' Lady*, (aka *Ripp*) out of *French's Hula Guy* and *Bijou Betali*, won the Canadian National Finals "Horse With The Most Heart" in 2018.[38]

Betty Gayle Cooper Ratliff was born February 7, 1952, in Hobbs, N.M. to Tuffy and Betty Rose Cooper. She was a four time WPRA world champion in calf roping — 1979, 1981, 1982 and 1983. She won one world championship in goat tying, 1982, and in breakaway roping, 1989. She was the all-around cowgirl three years in a row 1981 through 1983. She was the first ever recipient of the WPRA "Pioneer Award" in 1996. She got a BA in Education from Eastern New Mexico University in 1975. While in college she was the NIRA all-around women's champion in 1972, leading the ENMU women's team to the NIRA title that year. She received the "Outstanding Female Athlete" honor at ENMU in 1973. She coached the men's and women's rodeo teams at Southeastern Oklahoma State University (SOSU) for twenty-three years, starting in 1976. She led her athletes to nine team titles, four reserve national championships and sixteen individual titles at the College National Finals (NIRA). This included Caryn Standifer Snyder who was the NIRA woman's all-around and barrel racing champion in 1996. Betty Gayle was inducted in to the National Cowgirl Hall of Fame in 1987 and the Lea County (NM) Cowboy Hall of Fame in 1998. She died of cancer while coaching at SOSU in 1999.[39]

Celie Whitcomb-Ray was born January 23, 1949, in Sterling, Colo. She started riding very early. Her dad, Milo Whitcomb, trained cutting and reining horses. He started colts but once he took the buck out of them, he turned them over to Celie. She had a knack of communicating with them like no other. The way she used her body, especially her hands and feet, when riding, were subtle but important in her ability to compete and to train. Her first competition was the show arena where she learned how to win. When she switched to barrel racing it was soon recognized by other trainers that she was unique in the way she rode. Although she obviously used her hands and feet in guiding her barrel horses, it was so subtle it could hardly be detected. She knew a top level barrel racing horse must have speed and be versatile. *Harletta (Slash J Harletta)*, a flashy, good looking Palomino, was Celie's first great horse. She earned many performance points and AQHA points and was her mount when she went to her first NFR in 1971. She finished fifth in the world. She and good friend, Vicki Adams, formed a business partnership with *Harletta's* offspring. If *Harletta* had a colt it would go to Vicki. If it was a mare it would be Celie's. Vicki got her colt first. *In 1983 Celie went to the Finals again on Free-Etta, a foal from Harletta.* In 1987 and 1989 she rode *I Got Bugs* at the Finals. Most of the horses Celie trained for others were futurity and derby horses, but her talents in training were so good she was highly respected in all areas of barrel racing horses. Her hauling partner and close friend, Dena Kirkpatrick said, "Celie had a mental connection with all of her horses. That ability to think with them was the key to her success." Celie's life was cut short due to cancer and she died at age forty-five. She had one daughter, Mary Cecilia, who continued to compete in barrel racing for a time.[40]

Deb Guelly-Renger was born October 13, 1968, in Fort St. John, B.C., Canada. She resides at Okotoks, Alberta presently. She has qualified for the Wrangler National Finals six times, won the Canadian barrel racing championship five times, won the Calgary Stampede barrel racing championship, and has qualified for the Canadian Finals twenty-two times. Deb's National Finals years were: 1995, '99, 2004, '07, '08 and 2015. She was fourth in the world in 1999, and won second in the average twice, 1999 and 2007.[41]

Latonne Sewalt was the youngest girl to win the GRA barrel racing title in 1950. She was eleven years old. Her dad, Royce Sewalt, won the world champion calf roping title in 1946. Her brother, Ronnie, and her nephew, Rusty, were calf ropers. When she competed, she was driven. It was reported in *Hoofs and Horns*, in an article about her family, that at age eleven, she won all the go-rounds and averages at eight straight rodeos in 1950, for a total win of $3,997. It started at an all-girl rodeo in Childress, then Jacksboro and Texarkana, Texas; Memphis, Tenn.; Little Rock, Ark.; Colorado Springs, Colo.; Burwell, Neb.; and an all-girl rodeo in Tulsa, Okla.[42]

Fallon Taylor was born July 18, 1982 in Tampa, Fla. Her family moved to Whitesboro, Texas, when she was a youngster. She was home-schooled so she could focus on her horseback riding. She went to her first National Finals Rodeo in 1995 at the age of thirteen. She continued to qualify for the next three years, but got tired of life on the road. The glamour of New York appealed to her and she did fashion and runway modeling there for the next ten years. However in between modeling jobs, she trained horses for other people in Texas. In 2009 a tall gelding she was training began to go wild. He bucked and threw his head back and fractured Fallon's skull in four places. She landed on her head and broke her C2 vertebrae. The right side of her face was shattered, including her eye socket and she was paralyzed for three days. The doctors gave her a two-percent chance of ever walking again. She was required to wear a halo for three months. Her frustration was constant, but she was determined to walk and overcome her injuries. Delbert Alvarado's uncle worked with Fallon's dad. Delbert Alvarado was a kicker for the Dallas Cowboys. One day her dad asked if Fallon would show this football player their ranch. Three years later they were married. Delbert encouraged Fallon to get back in the barrel racing game. In 2013 she again qualified for the National Finals on a horse that had been born on the ranch and trained by Fallon, called *Babyflo*. The full name of the horse is *Flos Heiress* sired by *Dr. Nick Bar* out of *Flowers and Money*. She didn't do as well as she had wanted. She had qualified fifth in the world and ended the year in tenth place. However, because of her outstanding outfits that are always coordinated from the top of her head to her boot toes, she was awarded the "Jerry Ann (Portwood) Taylor WPRA Best Dressed Award" by Carolynn Vietor, president of WPRA. In 2014 she went to eighty-six rodeos and was neck and neck with Lisa Lockhart all year, but at the end of the year Fallon was barrel racing world champion.[43] "We made ten amazing runs, " said Fallon, who was just the third barrel racer in WPRA history to win a world title going to the left barrel first. The gold buckle was a triumphant comeback from what had been a most devastating time in her life.[44]

Viola Thomas was raised on a ranch southwest of Calgary. She started riding at two and had her own pony by age four. Her father, George, was a staff sergeant with The Lord Strathcona Light Horse Regiment and a WWI and WWII veteran, who was also a farrier and a rancher. Viola was rambunctious and horse crazy and rode her horse to school until she had to go to the city for high school and college. As a teenager she won many trophies in competitive cross country trail and horse show events. She began barrel racing against seasoned riders, but did not let her competitors intimidate her. She quit the show ring in 1957 and began steer decorating with the horses she trained. Viola hazed on her horse, *Danny*, while the cowboys steer wrestled off her horse, *Smoky*. In her rookie year she won the 1958 Canadian barrel racing title. Then she repeated her win in 1959. In 1960 she decided to head south to the U.S. and competed the entire year there. In 1961 she again hit the Canadian rodeo trail and for a third time was the Canadian barrel racing champion. Once her rodeo days were over she became a jockey in Alberta and California. Viola was the first woman to become a jockey at "A" tracks in Alberta and soon had that distinction in B.C., Sask., and Washington state. It is said she 'kicked the doors open and blazed a trail a mile wide in her early days in a male dominated world as an accomplished horse trainer and everything she has she earned on the back of a horse.' She was inducted to the Canadian ProRodeo Hall of Fame in 2014.[45]

Brittany Pozzi Tonnozzi was born February 9, 1984. She's from Victoria, Texas, but moved to Lampasas, Texas. She began rodeoing when she was twelve, but didn't come from a rodeo family. In high school she played on the golf team and competed in high school rodeo and was the Texas High School barrel champion in 2002. She attended Texas A&M and joined the WPRA in 2003. She has been to the National Finals seventeen times beginning in 2003. Brittany won the world barrel racing title in 2007, 2009 and 2023. She won the NFR average in 2006 and 2007. She also won the National Circuit Finals in 2012 and 2013. She and her horse, *Kiss Kiss Bang Bang*, set the world record on the WPRA regular pattern with a 16.479 second run. She became the third WPRA member to cross the two-million-dollar mark in 2017. She married team roper, Garrett Tonozzi, in October, 2015 and they had daughter, Tinlee, on March 21, 2017. They travel together and Garrett does most of the entering for them both. They travel with five horses, three for Brittany and two header horses for Garrett. On occasion they must go different directions, such as Calgary that Brittany enters and there is no team roping. Brittany continued to make the NFR yearly and was reserve champion in 2020. But in 2023 she 'blew the doors open in barrel racing when she finished the season nearly $110,000 ahead of Jordan Briggs who was second. Brittany won $225,935 at the finals and not only won the world championship but ended her year with $496,498 and is the third barrel racer to pass earning over three million dollars with $3,077,597.[46]

Carolynn Vietor grew up in San Antonio, Texas, but spent much time at her grandparents' ranch near Campbelton. She knew she wanted to barrel race the minute she saw the event at the San Antonio rodeo. Her grandparents were responsible for her first horse, a Palomino gelding named *Sunny Boy*. At first she used ranch horses as her barrel horse and also competed in breakaway roping. In college at Southwest Texas State, in San Marcos, she competed on the rodeo team as a goat tyer and won the NIRA Southern Region champion goat tyer two years. In 1965 Carolynn became the NIRA Rodeo Queen, and followed that becoming Miss Rodeo Texas which put her in contention for the Miss Rodeo America honor which was her's in 1966. She met Bill Vietor, who everyone calls Willy, her senior year in college and they married six months later. Once he finished his Air Force responsibilities they moved back to his family ranch and raised commercial cattle near Phillipsburg, Mont. Carolyn stayed close to home to focus on the family, but barrel raced at local amateur rodeos. Carolynn's horse, *Promino*, a son of *Classy Bar*, was the best horse she ever owned. She bought his full sister, *Classy Julie*, which she bred to their *Doc Bar* stud, *Dee Barretta* for the foundation of every horse she has owned since the late 1970s. She got her GRA permit in 1979, and went to the Circuit Finals to barrel race eighteen times on seven different horses. She was Montana Circuit champion in 2003 riding her horse called *Bump*. In 2005 she and Willy built a home near Wickenburg, Ariz. They both continued to compete in the National Senior Pro Rodeo Association and Carolynn won the 2008 barrel racing title on *Bump*. For ten years she was a director for WPRA starting in 1985. She took the reins as president in 1995 and held the position until 2003. She was re-elected in 2013 and served until 2016. She was instrumental in improvements in WPRA including equal money. She was named "Coca Cola Woman of the Year" in 1999; "Pioneer Woman of the Year" and the WPRA "Heritage Award" in 2002. Carolyn and husband Willy spend every Tuesday night during the summer at the Ranch at Rock Creek, a luxurious dude ranch, performing during the rodeo. Carolynn barrel raced in full dress code, on one of her best horses, the only professional barrel racer to star in the rodeo. Willy meanwhile flagged timed events and competed as a team roper. Since the event stopped in 2020, Carolyn has been enjoying her 'retirement' and going to an occasional jackpot barrel race. Meanwhile, Willy is still roping. The Vietors were inducted in to the Montana ProRodeo Hall and Wall of Fame in 2017.[47]

Martha Tompkins Wright was born December 30, 1951 to Rosemary and Harry Tompkins, all-around and bull Riding champion of the world. She lives near Dublin, Texas. When she was twelve-years-old her aunt, Caroline Colborn, took her to the Youree Ranch Barrel Racing Camp and she spent two weeks. She enjoyed it so much she went back later as a counselor and then worked for Dale and Florence Youree again in the mid-seventies. "They are just like family to me," said Martha. She competed during her sophomore year at Tarleton State University and was part of the women's team that won the NIRA for 1971, plus she won the barrel racing too. When she and Ed Wright married she went to Eastern New Mexico University and was part of the women's team that won the NIRA for 1972. She qualified for the National Finals in 1971 and won six go-rounds, and came in sixth. She qualified again later for the NFR but did not go because her rodeo horse was not sound. She had a good futurity horse so she went to the Barrel Futurity of America in Oklahoma City instead. Martha said, "You can't imagine the flack I got for not going to the Finals. In fact, they put a fine on people who qualified in the top fifteen and didn't go, after that." Martha and Ed trained barrel horses and Martha competed on other people's horse in rodeos, futurities and such. By the late 1980s they began buying and training their own horses that came off the race track and trained them to be barrel horses. Martha still competes in jackpot barrel races that pay between $500 to $5,000 added money. She said "Last weekend I went to one and there were 400 entries in the barrel race." She has a client whose wife and two daughters barrel race and Martha keeps seven to eight of their horses on her ranch and keeps them keenly trained. She and Ed (deceased) have a training manual for barrel racing entitled, *Barrel Racing - Training the Wright Way*.

Florence Youree was born April 19, 1933, the older of two girls. Their folks were ranchers and since they had no boys, Florence and her sister, Sherry, worked the ranch with their dad. Their grandpa had box seats at the Fort Worth rodeo when it was still held in the coliseum in the Fort Worth Stockyards. When Florence saw the couples come out playing 'musical chairs' on horseback and barrel racing (in a straight line in those days) she thought to herself, "I can do that!" She met and married her husband, Dale, in 1950, while at Oklahoma A & M and they went to jackpot ropings and barrel races. In 1953 she joined the GRA and went to the first NFR at Clayton, N.M., 1959. She then went to eleven more NFRs. She became the president of GRA in 1960 through 1964. She resigned as president and became the secretary of GRA and started the *GRA News* magazine. She said the secretary job paid money, the president didn't! Florence was also the GRA all-around champion in 1966. In 1967 she was instrumental in getting the barrel racing moved from a separate NFR location to the main National Finals Rodeo in Oklahoma City. She convinced the 'powers that be' that beautiful girls riding fast horses would be a plus at the NFR. She and husband, Dale, trained barrel horses and had their yearly Youree Horsemanship Camp for kids. They built a dormitory large enough that 100 kids could stay during the month of June. Plus they trained at clinics all over the U.S. and Canada.[48] They started the Barrel Futurities of America, in 1970 and Florence was president for twenty years.They also started the Oklahoma Youth Rodeo Association and the world's first progressive barrel race. In 1980 Florence and Dale were invited to the Smithsonian Institute in Washington D.C. to demonstrate barrel racing skills for a Folk Life Festival. Dale has also won some barrel racing contests in futurities and the Oklahoma Senior Barrel Racing. They also give two Dale Youree scholarships yearly, to help defray costs for some lucky barrel racers. The largest barrel race in 1986 was held in Oklahoma City with a $50,000 purse, the largest ever held at that time. Florence was inducted in to the National Cowgirl Hall of Fame in 1996 and the Rodeo Historical Society Rodeo Hall of Fame in the National Cowboy & Western Heritage Museum in Oklahoma City, in 2009. Florence also received the Lifetime Achievement Award from WPRA in 2018. The Youree's daughter, Renee Ward went to the National Finals in barrel racing in 1985. Their granddaughter Janae Ward went to the National Finals in 14th place and won the World Championship in 2003 and the average, too. She made $111,908 at the Finals and finished the year with $155,792. Granddaughter, Kylie Weast qualified for her first National Finals in 2018. She won round ten, finished in 10th place and made $173,484 for the year.[49]

Appendix 1
GRA-WPRA World Champion Barrel Racers

Date	Name	Hometown
1948	Margaret Owens	Rankin, TX
1949	Amy McGilvray	Mertzon, TX
1950	LaTonne Sewalt	Brownwood, TX
1951	Margaret Owens	Rankin, TX
1952	Wanda Harper Bush	Mason, TX
1953	Wanda Harper Bush	Mason, TX
1954	LaTonne Sewalt	Brownwood, TX
1955	Billie McBride	San Angelo, TX
1956	Billie McBride	San Angelo, TX
1957	Billie McBride	San Angelo, TX
1958	Billie McBride	San Angelo, TX
1959	Jane Mayo	Okemah, OK
1960	Jane Mayo	Okemah, OK
1961	Jane Mayo	Okemah, OK
1962	Sherry Combs Johnson	Addington, OK
1963	Loretta Manual	Celeste, TX
1964	Ardith Bruce	Fountain, CO
1965	Sammie Thurman Brackenbury	Lobec, CA
1966	Norita Krause Henderson	O'Fallon, MO
1967	Loretta Manual	Celeste, TX
1968	Ann Lewis	Sulphur, OK
1969	Missy Long	Duncan, OK
1970	Joyce Burk Loomis	Duncan, OK
1971	Donna Patterson	Tecumseh, OK
1972	Gail Petska	Norman, OK
1973	Gail Petska	Norman, OK
1974	Jeana Day Felts	Woodward, OK
1975	Jimmie Gibbs Munroe	Valley Mills, TX
1976	Connie Combs Kirby	Comanche, OK
1977	Jackie Jo Perrin	Antlers, OK
1978	Lynn McKenzie	Shreveport, LA
1979	Carol Goostree	Perryton, TX
1980	Martha Josey	Karmack, TX
1981	Lynn McKenzie	Shreveport, LA
1982	Jan Hansen Smith	Tucson, AZ
1983	Marlene Eddleman	Ordway, CO
1984	Charmayne James	Clayton, NM
1985	Charmayne James	Clayton, NM
1986	Charmayne James	Clayton, NM
1987	Charmayne James	Clayton, NM
1988	Charmayne James	Clayton, NM
1989	Charmayne James	Clayton, NM

Year	Champion	Hometown
1990	Charmayne James	Galt, CA
1991	Charmayne James	Galt, CA
1992	Charmayne James	Galt, CA
1993	Charmayne James	Galt, CA
1994	Kristie Peterson	Elbert, CO
1995	Sherry Cervi	Marana, AZ
1996	Kristie Peterson	Elbert, CO
1997	Kristie Peterson	Elbert, CO
1998	Kristie Peterson	Elbert, CO
1999	Sherry Cervi	Marana, AZ
2000	Kappy Allen	Austin, TX
2001	Janet Stover	Rusk, TX
2002	Charmayne James	Grand Prairie, TX
2003	Janae Ward	Addington, OK
2004	Kelly Kaminski	Bellville, TX
2005	Kelly Kaminski	Bellville, TX
2006	Mary Burger	Pauls Valley, OK
2007	Kay Blandford (WPRA)	Sutherland Springs, TX
2007	Brittany Pozzi (PWBR)	Victoria, TX
2008	Lindsay Sears	Nanton, Alberta, CA
2009	Brittany Pozzi	Victoria, TX
2010	Sherry Cervi	Marana, AZ
2011	Lindsay Sears	Nanton, Alberta, CA
2012	Mary Walker	Fort Worth, TX
2013	Sherry Cervi	Marana, AZ
2014	Fallon Taylor	Collinsville, TX
2015	Callie duPerier	Boerne, TX
2016	Mary Burger	Pauls Valley, OK
2017	Nellie Miller	Cottonwood, CA
2018	Hailey Kinsel	Cotulla, TX
2019	Hailey Kinsel	Cotulla, TX
2020	Hailey Kinsel	Cotulla, TX
2021	Jordan Briggs	Tolar, TX
2022	Hailey Kinsel	Cotulla, TX
2023	Brittany Pozzi-Tonozzi	Lampasas, TX

Appendix 2
Year-End & Finals
The 1958 Finals were held at the GRA Finals, prior to the first National Finals Rodeo

	Name	Season Total
1.	Billie McBride	$6,498
2.	Wanda Harper Bush	$4,808
3.	Janet Dudley	$3,269
4.	Jane Mayo	$2,455
5.	LaTonne Sewalt	$2,067
6.	Norita Kraus	$1,828
7.	Fay Ann Horton	$1,370
8.	Manuelita Mitchell	$1,238
9.	D'Ann Young	$959

National Finals Rodeo 1959 to Present Top 15 Barrel Racers

1959
Clayton, N.M. - Four Go-Rounds - $1,950 Prize Money

Name	NFR Earnings	Season Total	Average
1. Jane Mayo	$663	$5,814	1-59.7/3
2. Mildred Farris	$19	$5,264	12/13
3. Janet Dudley	$507	$2,950	3
4. Jo Ann Crosby	0	$2,850	10
5. Sissy Thurman	$39	$2,093	6
6. Wanda Bush	$546	$1,975	2
7. Billie McBride	0	$1,899	5
8. Norita Kraus		$1,755	*Did Not Compete at Finals*
9. Fay Ann Horton	$13	$1,752	7
10. Sis Armstrong	$71	$1,665	4
11. Sherry Combs	0	$1,459	8
12. Dottye Kraus		$1,214	*Did Not Compete at Finals*
13. LaTonne Sewalt		$1,178	*Did Not Compete at Finals*
14. Melinda Bartlett		$1,122	*Did Not Compete at Finals*
15. Martha Ann Symons	0	$875	14
Billie Ann Evans*	$91		12/13
Manuelita Mitchell*	0		11
Betty Ray*	0		9
Florence Youree*	0		15

Fastest time at the Finals 19.2 seconds by Jane Mayo
*Replaced qualifiers who did not compete at the Finals.

1960
Clayton, N.M. - Six Go-Rounds - $1,950 Prize Money

Name	NFR Earnings	Season Total	Average
1. Jane Mayo	$746	$7,833	1/2-107.0/6
2. Mildred Farris	$52	$7,034	
3. Sherry Combs	$207	$3,850	

Year-End & Finals

Name	NFR Earnings	Season Total	Average
4. Sammy Thurman	$739	$3,777	1/2-107.0/6
5. Billie Ann Evans	0	$2,834	
6. Charlene Jespersen		$1,493	*Did Not Compete at Finals*
7. Fay Ann Horton		$1,636	*Did Not Compete at Finals*
8. Phyllis Bryant		$1,574	*Did Not Compete at Finals*
9. Pat Marr	$52	$1,561	3/4-107.9
10. Norita Kraus		$1,531	*Did Not Compete at Finals*
11. Florence Youree	$13	$1,484	
12. Wanda Bush	0	$1,415	3/4-107.9
13. Janet Dudley		$1,383	*Did Not Compete at Finals*
14. Melinda Meek		$1,358	*Did Not Compete at Finals*
15. Sissy Thurman		$1,115	*Did Not Compete at Finals*
Nancy Farquhar*	$78		
Jody Thomas*	$87		
Sis Armstrong*	$67		
Tana White*	$9		
Frances Moates*	$13		
Florence Youree	0		
Jo Ann Crosby	0		

Fastest time at the Finals 17.6 seconds by Jane Mayo (twice) and Sammy Thurman.
Replaced qualifiers who did not compete at the Finals.

1961
Santa Maria, Calif - Six Go-Rounds - $2,205 Prize Money

Name	NFR Earnings	Season Total	Average
1. Jane Mayo	$429	$8,356	
2. Sammy Thurman	$605	$7,042	2
3. Mildred Farris		$5,733	*Did Not Compete at Finals*
4. Sherry Combs		$4,833	*Did Not Compete at Finals*
5. Fay Ann Horton		$2,983	*Did Not Compete at Finals*
6. Boots Tucker	$761	$2,793	1-109.2/6
7. JoAnn Crosby		$2,321	*Did Not Compete at Finals*
8. Pat Marr	$332	$2,107	3
9. Florence Youree		$1,484	*Did Not Compete at Finals*
10. Judy Marshall	$39	$1,928	4
11. Kay Sublette	$98	$1,269	
12. Diane Chapman	0	$1,048	
13. Tokie Wood	0	$971	
14. Phyllis Teague	0		*Did Not Compete at Finals*
15. Charlene Jespersen	$293	$646	
Jean Sharp*	$39		
Sally Kennedy*	0		
Marion Roddy*	0		

Fastest time at the Finals 17.9 seconds by Sammy Thurman
Replaced qualifiers who did not compete at the Finals.

1962
Dallas, Texas - Seven Go-Rounds - $3,226 Prize Money

Name	NFR Earnings	Season Total	Average
1. Sherry Combs	$202	$7,899	
2. Wanda Bush	$324	$6,942	2
3. Fay Ann Horton	$383	$5,878	
4. Mildred Farris	$10	$4,718	
5. Loretta Manual	$232	$4,406	3
6. Janet Dudley	$504	$3,045	
7. Sissy Thurman	$988	$2,944	1 125.4/7
8. Diana Chapman	$242	$2,880	
9. Boots Tucker	$60	$2,741	4
10. Sammy Thurman	0	$2,473	
11. Mary Sanders	$71	$2,161	
12. Jeanette Day Smith	$10	$1,487	
13. Sue Roberts*		$1,299	*Did Not Compete at Finals*
14. Jean Roberts Sharp*		$1,091	*Did Not Compete at Finals*
15. Florence Youree	0	$995	

Fastest time at the Finals was 17.6 seconds by Sissy Thurman

1963
Dallas, Texas - Seven Go-Rounds - $3,208 Prize Money

Name	NFR Earnings	Season Total	Average
1. Loretta Manual		$7,600	3-127.2/7
2. Wanda Bush		$6,750	2-126.8/7
3. Sherry Combs		$5,526	
4. Sissy Thurman		$5,378	1-125.4/7
5. Fay Ann Horton		$4,814	
6. Diana Chapman		$4,069	
7. Sammy Thurman		$3,120	
8. Boots Tucker		$2,855	
9. Mildred Farris		$2,160	
10. Ardith Bruce		$2,032	
11. Sis Armstrong		$1,979	
12. Norita Henderson		$1,978	
13. Janet Dudley		$1,919	
14. Donna Mullins		$1,873	
15. Billie Edwards		$1,825	

Fastest time at the Finals not available

1964
Dallas, Texas - Seven Go-Rounds - $2,822 Prize Money

Name	NFR Earnings	Season Total	Average
1. Ardith Bruce	$361	$6,510	2-120.2/7
2. Sissy Thurman	$279	$6,099	
3. Wanda Bush	$522	$5,472	
4. Sammy Thurman	$191	$5,220	
5. Loretta Manual		$4.463	*Did Not Compete at Finals*
6. Sis Armstrong	$545	$3,582	

Name	NFR Earnings	Season Total	Average
7. Dorothy Snow	$192	$3,558	4-121.1/7
8. Dottye Goodspeed	$190	$3,539	
9. Sherry Combs		$3,307	*Did Not Compete at Finals*
10. Allene Gayler	$479	$3,278	1-119.0/7
11. Fay Ann Horton	$72	$3,041	
12. Pat Marr	$319	$2,822	3-120.3/7
13. Mildred Farris		$2,789	*Did Not Compete at Finals*
14. Donna Shaw		$2,423	*Did Not Compete at Finals*
15. Frances Glenwinkle	$67	$2,380	

Fastest time at the Finals was 16.6 seconds by Sissy Thurman.

1965
Dallas, Texas - Seven Go-Rounds - $3,225 Prize Money

Name	NFR Earnings	Season Total	Average
1. Sammy Thurman	$332	$6,096	3
2. Loretta Manual	$335	$5,253	
3. Pat Marr	$663	$5,004	1-117.73/7
4. Sherry Combs	$36	$4,061	
5. Dottye Goodspeed	$112	$3,773	
6. Wanda Bush	$117	$2,948	
7. Allene Gayler	$564	$2,887	2
8. Diana Chapman		$2,876	*Did Not Compete at Finals*
9. Sissy Thurman	$306	$2,765	
10. Fay Ann Horton	$77	$2,752	
11. Ardith Bruce	0	$2,517	
12. Sis Armstrong	$551	$2,380	
13. Dorothy Snow		$2,052	*Did Not Compete at Finals*
14. Charlene Jespersen		$2,007	
15. Roxy Curtis		$1,627	*Did Not Compete at Finals*
16. Florence Youree	$132		4-120.22/7

Fastest time at the Finals was 16.46 by Pat Marr.

1966
Fort Worth, Texas - Four Go-Rounds - $1,750 Prize Money

Name	NFR Earnings	Season Total	Average
1. Norita Henderson	$ 70	$7,157	3-75.24/4
2. Pat Marr	$140	$5,906	
3. Ardith Bruce	$350	$4,567	
4. Sissy Thurman	$280	$ 4,423	
5. Charlene Jespersen	$105	$4,262	
6. Sammy Thurman	$123	$3,974	
7. Judy Marshall	0	$3,877	
8. Fay Ann Horton	0	$3,339	
9. Allene Gayler	$298	$3,134	1-74.55/4
10. Sherry Combs	$140	$3,004	
11. Loretta Manual	$70	$2,731	4-75.46/4
12. Florence Youree	$175	$2,108	2-75.17/4
13. Connie Stinson	0	$1,941	

Name	NFR Earnings	Season Total	Average
14. Mildred Farris	0	$1,923	
15. Margaret Clemons	0	$1,887	

Fastest time at the Finals was 18.06 by Sissy Thurman

1967
The first year all of the rodeo events were held in one location.
Oklahoma City, Okla. - Nine Go-Rounds - $4,144 Prize Money

Name	NFR Earnings	Season Total	Average
1. Loretta Manual	$103	$6,050	
2. Sissy Thurman	$636	$5,838	
3. Judy Marshall	$13	$4,743	
4. Ardith Bruce	$600	$4,659	
5. Patti Mack	$397	$4,409	3-155.6/9
6. Florence Youree	$172	$3,905	4-158.4/9
7. Sherry Combs	$46	$3,575	
8. Frances Smith	$745	$3,477	1-155.0/9
9. Allene Gayler	$109	$3,410	
10. Sammy Thurman	$145	$3,405	
11. Sis Armstrong	$339	$3,214	
12. Fay Ann Leach	$609	$2,827	2-155.3/9
13. Mildred Farris	$109	$2,821	
14. Kay Whitaker	$109	$2,360	
15. Roxy McFarland	$12	$2,280	

Fastest time at the Finals was 16.06 seconds by Sissy Thurman.

1968
Oklahoma City, Okla. - Nine Go-Rounds - $4,009 Prize Money

Name	NFR Earnings	Season Total	Average
1. Ann Lewis		$9,783	*Killed in car crash prior to NFR.*
2. Kay Whitaker	$518	$8,271	2
3. Sissy Thurman		$6,311	*Killed in car crash prior to NFR.*
4. Mildred Farris	$403	$5,090	7
5. Kathie O'Brien	$800	$5,055	1-153.8/9
6. Ardith Bruce	$655	$4,449	4
7. Sammy Thurman	$349	$4,381	6
8. Donna Kincade	$463	$4,196	8
9. Faye Faulin	$200	$4,083	12
10. Rosie Johnson	$36	$4,009	13
11. Martha Josey	$172	$3,917	15
12. Kay Newman	0	$3,422	14
13. Allene Gayler	$131	$2,962	9
14. Connie Stinson	0	$2,769	5
15. Sherry Combs	$209	$2,827	3
16. Patti Prather	$73	$2,302	11
17. Roxi McFarlane	0	$2,119	10

Fastest time at the Finals was 16.6 seconds by Mildred Farris.
Patti Prather and Roxy McFarlane replaced Ann Lewis and Sissy Thurman after they were killed in a car crash in October.

1969
Oklahoma City, Okla. - Nine Go-Rounds - $6,504 Prize Money

Name	NFR Earnings	Season Total	Average
1. Missy Long	$1,566	$9,783	1-152.65/9
2. Mildred Farris	$798	$8,537	3
3. Barbara Baer	$650	$5,793	6
4. Martha Josey	$473	$5,387	5
5. Joyce Burk	$651	$5,194	11
6. Kay Vamvoras	0	$5,051	10
7. Sammy Thurman	0	$4,994	7
8. Ardith Bruce	$769	$4,600	8
9. Frances Smith	$207	$4,220	9
10. Kathie O'Brien	$946	$4,127	2-153.82/9
11. Judy Arnold	$207	$3,462	4
12. Roxy McFarlane	$237	$3,302	14
13. Lee Natale	0	$3,229	12
14. Allene Gayler	0	$3,201	13
15. Loretta Manual	0	$3,039	15

Fastest time at the Finals was 16.64 seconds by Roxy McFarlane.

1970
Oklahoma City, Okla. - Nine Go-Rounds - $6,659 Prize Money

Name	NFR Earnings	Season Total	Average
1. Joyce Burk	$822	$10,629	1-170.38/10
2. Jeana Day	$55	$9,006	
3. Sammy Thurman	0	$6,607	
4. Terry Lewis	$55	$5,993	
5. Loretta Manual	$1,302	$5,217	
6. Barbara Baer	$1,030	$5,093	
7. Joleen Hurst	$921	$5,079	
8. Anita Kilgore	$461	$5,011	
9. Diana Morris	$155	$4,958	
10. Mildred Farris	$339	$4,885	3-171.37/10
11. Missy Long	$109	$4,825	
12. Sherry Combs-Thurman	$218	$4,332	4-171.62/10
13. Kathie O'Brien	$135	$4,118	
14. Wendy Potter	$515	$3,935	2-171.21/10
15. Dottye Goodspeed	$542	$3,907	

Fastest time at the Finals was 16.60 seconds by Dottye Goodspeed.

1971
Oklahoma City, Okla. - Ten Go-Rounds - $7,309 Prize Money

Name	NFR Earnings	Season Total	Average
1. Donna Patterson	$935	$11,952	1-168.79/10
2. Jeana Day	$1,405	$11,801	4-173.91/10
3. Joleen Hurst	$1,155	$11,549	3-172.71/10
4. Karen Greenough	$529	$11,063	10
5. Celie Whitcomb	0	$6,514	8
6. Martha Tompkins	$2,019	$6,456	2-169.96/10
7. Marion Witcher	$195	$6,397	6

Name	NFR Earnings	Season Total	Average
8. Diana Morris		$5,441	*Did Not Compete at Finals*
9. Gail Barrett	$809	$5,138	11
10. Marilyn Jolly	$150	$4,001	5
11. Barbara Baer	0	$3,841	15
12. Bonnie Lemaire	$56	$3,431	14
13. Barbi Scott	0	$3,428	12
14. Loretta Manual	0	$3,339	9
15. Lee Natale	0	$3,266	7
16. Wendy Potter	$56	$3,231	13

Fastest time at the Finals was 16.33 seconds by Martha Tompkins.

1972
Oklahoma City, Okla. - Ten Go-Rounds - $6,933 Prize Money

Name	NFR Earnings	Season Total	Average
1. Gail Petska	$$2,503	$17,104	1-167.41/10
2. Jeana Day	$850	$14,740	6
3. Karen Greenough	$352	$9,852	12
4. Allene Gayler	$1,477	$9,597	2-169.72/10
5. Barbara Bell	$334	$7,290	3-171.34/10
6. Jo Russell	$294	$6,857	7
7. Kay Vamvoras	$158	$5,927	8
8. Terri Himes	$323	$5,605	11
9. Kathie O'Brien	0	$5,317	9
10. Ruth Sanders	0	$5,192	14
11. Jan Kremling	0	$5,111	13
12. Julie Benson	$158	$5,073	5
13. Marion Gramith	0	$5,007	10
14. Marilyn Jolly	$249	$4,681	4-172.28/10
15. Wendy Potter	$235	$4,244	15

Fastest time at the Finals was 16.54 seconds by Jeana Day.

1973
Oklahoma City, Okla. - Ten Go-Rounds - $10,399 Prize Money

Name	NFR Earnings	Season Total	Average
1. Gail Petska	$2,236	$19,448	7
2. Jeana Day	$1,335	$15,032	11
3. Carol O'Rourke	$314	$10,109	15
4. Marilyn Jolly	$981	$9,678	13
5. Allene Gayler	$496	$9,197	8
6. Cherry Sanchez	$566	$6,957	4-169.38/10
7. Becky Carson	$1,625	$6,890	1-166/52/10
8. Dixie Pring	$683	$6,433	3-167.47/10
9. Gayle Brannon	$157	$5,784	9
10. Lila Mae Stewart	$879	$5,674	2-167.25/10
11. Terri Himes	$550	$5,578	12
12. Rogenia Clayman	$118	$5,415	6
13. Kay Vamvoras	$79	$4,937	14
14. Jerri Duce	$380	$4,848	5
15. Julie Benson	0	$4,799	10

Fastest time at the Finals was 16.37 seconds by Becky Carson and Marilyn Jolly.

1974
Oklahoma City, Okla. - Ten Go-Rounds - $10,411 Prize Money

Name	NFR Earnings	Season Total	Average
1. Jeana Day Felts	$783	$14,384	3-173.24/10
2. Colette Graves	$2,883	$12,055	1-171.18/10
3. Jimmie Gibbs	$1,010	$11,893	12
4. Julie Benson	$283	$7,850	10
5. Karen Abercrombie	$404	$7,738	8
6. Dixie Pring	$162	$7,609	9
7. Marilyn Jolly Camarillo	$218	$7,555	5
8. DeLyssa Trotter		$7,524	*Did Not Compete at Finals*
9. Deb Beck	$1,349	$7,496	2-173.20/10
10. Allene Gayler	$1,010	$7,269	7
11. Becky Carson	0	$7,244	15
12. Gayle Ann Brannon	$379	$6,966	4-174.38/10
13. Charlene Jepersen	$1,010	$6,770	6
14. Lila Mae Stewart	$718	$6,478	11
15. Wanda Bush	0	$5,580	13
16. Barbara Day	0	$5,484	14

Fastest time at the Finals was 16.90 seconds by Lila Mae Stewart.

1975
Oklahoma City, Okla. - Ten Go-Rounds - $14,033 Prize Money

Name	NFR Earnings	Season Total	Average
1. Jimmie Gibbs	$1,781	$22,769	6
2. Becky Carson	$685	$18,209	15
3. Connie Combs	$2,867	$17,228	1-164.66/10
4. Gail Petska	$843	$13,358	9
5. Colette Avery	$1,707	$10,061	2-165.72/10
6. Kay Proctor	$1,423	$9,214	14
7. Jeana Day Felts	$1,444	$9,061	5
8. Dammy Johnson	$653	$8,764	3-166.50/10
9. June Evetts	$685	$7,971	11
10. Marilyn Jolly Camarillo	$952	$6,726	10
11. Deb Beck	$653	$6,095	4-167.57/10
12. Lynn Mays	$100	$5,938	8
13. Thay Lewis	$210	$5,821	7
14. Diane Sleeter	0	$5,311	13
15. Dee Watt	0	$4,905	12

Fastest time at the Finals was 16.15 by Connie Combs.

Note: For the first time, in 1976, '77 and '78 each event's world champion was determined not by earnings throughout the year, but solely by the winnings at the National Finals Rodeo. As always, regular season money counted toward qualifying for the NFR. This was designed to make a true "World Series" of rodeo.

1976
Oklahoma City, Okla. - Ten Go-Rounds - $16,517 Prize Money

Name	NFR Earnings	Average
1. Connie Combs	$3,665	1-166.66/10
2. Colette Graves	$2,696	5
3. Jimmie Gibbs	$2,108	2-168.08/10
4. Kay Vamvoras	$1,995	11
5/6. Dammy Johnson	$1,353	9
5/6. Marion Gramith	$1,353	3-169.75/10
7. Gail Petska	$1,382	7
8. Dottye Goodspeed	$855	8
9. Marilyn Camarillo	$498	15
10. Lila Glade	$315	4-171.51/10
11. Cindy Witcher	$185	13
12. Darla Higgins	$112	6
13. Renee Sutherland	0	14
14. Pam Ross	0	12
15. Lorraine Alexander	0	10

Fastest time at the Finals was 16.30 seconds by Connie Combs.

Name	1976 Season Earnings
1. Jimmie Gibbs	$22,557
2. Connie Combs	$21.528
3. Gail Petska	$16,284
4. Kay Vamvoras	$10,464
5. Dammy Johnson	$8,305
6. Jerri Duce (injured)	$7,708
7. Darla Higgins	$7,579
8. Renee Sutherland	$7,364
9. Dottye Goodspeed	$7,216
10. Cindy Witcher	$6.505
11. Marilyn Jolly Camarillo	$6,403
12. Pam Ross	$6,188
13. Colette Graves	$6,111
14. Lila Glade	$5,881
15. Marion Gramith	$5,866

1977
Oklahoma City, Okla. - Ten Go-Rounds - $19,000 Prize Money

Name	NFR Earnings	No Average
1. Jackie Jo Perrin	$3,610	
2. Becky Carson	$3,420	
3. Connie Combs	$2,280	
4. Karen Farris	$2,090	
5. Jimmie Gibbs	$1,900	

Name	NFR Earnings
6. Colette Graves	$1,520
7/8. Gail Tyson	$1,140
7/8. Donna Saul	$1,140
9. Kay Vamvoras	$950
10/11. Anne Bateson	$380
10/11. Renee Sutherland	$380
12. June Hipple	$190
13. Vicki Adams	0
14. Kay Bland	0
15. Gail Petska	0

Fastest time at the Finals was 16.32 seconds by Karen Farris. No average money was paid, but Jackie Jo Perrin had the fastest total time 181.47/10 seconds.

Name	1977 Season Earnings
1. Jimmie Gibbs	$21,894
2. Kay Vamvoras	$16,880
3. Connie Combs	$16,831
4. Colette Graves	$13,662
5. Gail Tyson	$13,147
6. Jackie Jo Perrin	$12,200
7. Ann Bateson	$10,943
8. Gail Petska	$9,307
9. June Hipple	$9,029
10. Kay Blandford	$8,762
11. Jerri Duce	$8,537
12. Vickie Adams	$8,408
13. Renee Sutherland	$7,972
14. Dammy Johnson	$7,966
15. Becky Carson	$7,749

1978
Oklahoma City, Okla. - Eleven Go-Rounds - $24,500 Prize Money

Name	NFR Earnings	Average
1. Lynn McKenzie	$6,500	1-185.69/11
2. Carol Goostree	$4,300	5
3. Becky Carson	$3,200	2-187,69/11
4. Jackie Jo Perrin	$2,200	9
5. Martha Josey	$1,700	3-187.92/11
6. Connie Combs	$1,500	7
7. Lorraine Alexander	$1,200	4-189.58/11
8. Marilyn Duplissey	$1,000	10
9. Janie Riemer	$800	12
10. Becky Fullerton	$600	11
11. Gail Tyson	$500	14
12. Shari Korff	$400	12
13. Heidi Indermuhle	$300	8
14. Anne Bateson	$200	13
15. Jimmie Gibbs	$100	15

Fastest time at the Finals was 16.47 seconds by Lynn McKenzie.

Name	1978 Season Earnings
1. Carol Goostree	$29,651
2. Jimmie Gibbs	$23,268
3. Gail Tyson	$16,949
4. Connie Combs	$16,627
5. Shari Korff	$13,123
6. Janie Reimer	$13,058
7. Martha Josey	$11,699
8. Ann Bateson	$11,588
9/10. Jackie Jo Perrin	$10,261
9/10. Lorraine Alexander	$10,261
11. Becky Fulleton	$9,565
12. Marilyn Duplissey	$9,314
13. Heidi Indermuhle	$9,245
14. Becky Carson	$9,105
15. Lynn McKenzie	$9,013

Fastest time at the Finals was 16.32 seconds by Lynn McKenzie.

PRCA restored the traditional method of determining its champions in 1979.

1979
Oklahoma City, Okla. - Ten Go-Rounds - $34,720 Prize Money

Name	NFR Earnings	Season Total	Average
1. Carol Goostree	$6,000	$43,100	7
2. Lynn McKenzie	$10,000	$36,134	1-165.36/10
3. Martha Josey	$1,200	$27,933	12
4. Jerri Mann	$700	$19,049	13
5. Sharon Camarillo	$1,600	$17,681	4-168.85/10
6. Gail Tyson	$1,800	$17,473	5
7. Shari Korff	$800	$17,140	6
8. Connie Combs	$3,500	$16,774	2-167.57/10
9. Kay Garrison	$2,000	$16,445	3-168.64/10
10. Anne Bateson	$820	$15,719	11
11. Lynn Manning	$2,500	$14,933	8
12. Jimmie Gibbs	$1,400	$14,358	9
13. Becky Fulleton	$1,000	$13,881	10
14. Kelly Miller	$900	$10,683	14
15. Kay Bland	$500	$10,063	15

1980
Oklahoma City, Okla. - Ten Go-Rounds - $44,500 Prize Money

Name	NFR Earnings	Season Total	Average
1. Martha Josey	$6,000	$45,883	2-166.98/10
2. Lynn McKenzie	$8,000	$44,678	1-166.43/10
3. Carol Goostree	$3,500	$34,569	15
4. Donna Krening	$10,000	$27,159	6
5. Wanda Cagliari	$4,250	$22,756	3-167.59/10
6. Lynda Gordon	$2,500	$18,912	14
7. Shayne Mason	$1,100	$18,426	4-168.59/10
8. Sharon Youngblood	$2,000	$17,912	8

Name	NFR Earnings	Season Total	Average
9. Sharon Camarillo	$1,500	$15,742	13
10. Connie Combs	$1,000	$14,550	7
11. Linda Kay	$1,750	$14,325	5
12. Lynn Manning	$750	$13,550	10
13. Kay Davis	$965	$13,107	11
14. Jerri Mann	$500	$12,256	12
15. Jeanne Davis	$625	$12,216	9

Fastest time at the Finals was 16.25 seconds by Donna Krening and Sharon Camarillo.

1981
Oklahoma City, Okla. - Ten Go-Rounds - $45,314 Prize Money

Name	NFR Earnings	Season Total	Average
1. Lynn McKenzie	$2,000	$45,314	5
2. Jan Hansen	$6,500	$44,510	3-164.26/10
3. Martha Josey	$1,500	$35,708	14
4. Donna Krening	$12,000	$29,974	1-162.73/10
5. Lee Ann Guilkey	$9,500	$27,587	2-163.68/10
6. Shayne Mason	$4,000	$27,400	4-164.55/10
7. Lynda Gordon	$3,500	$25,760	7
8. Wanda Cagliari	$1,400	$25,500	8
9. Jerri Mann	$1,300	$24,245	12
10. Debbie Miller	$2,500	$21,734	11
11. Jimmie Gibbs Munroe	$5,000	$20,328	10
12. Paula Fortner	$3,000	$18,345	6
13. Sharon Camarillo	$1,200	$18,096	15
14. Bonnie Lemaire	$1,100	$16,424	9
15. Kay Blandford	$1,000	$15,517	13

Fastest time at the Finals was 16.03 seconds by Lee Ann Guilkey.

1982
Oklahoma City, Okla. - Ten Go-Rounds - $58,173 Prize Money

Name	NFR Earnings	Season Total	Average
1. Jan Hansen	$2,905	$40,965	5
2. Donna Krening	$12,963	$36,751	3-168.58/10
3. Lee Ann Guilkey	$895	$35,778	7
4. Lynn McKenzie	$6,929	$33,382	4-169.26/10
5. Paula Fortner	$9,834	$29,533	1-164.47/10
6. Julie Doering	$4,470	$29,200	10
7. Jacque Woolman	$3,800	$27,237	12
8. Sherry Altizer	$3,800	$25,129	6
9. Jerri Mann	0	$24,202	8
10. Dixie Thomas	$2,235	$22,778	9
11. Shayne Mason	$1,401	$22,771	11
12. Lynn Manning-Flynn	$2,012	$22,072	13
13. Lisa Davis	$2,459	$21,750	15
14. Sharon Camarillo	$4,470	$20,988	2-167.21/10
15. Kathy Spears	0	$19,670	14

Fastest time at the Finals was 15.95 seconds by Sherry Altizer.

1983
Oklahoma City, Okla. - Ten Go-Rounds - $66,042 Prize Money

Name	NFR Earnings	Season Total	Average
1. Marlene Eddleman	$17,120	$51,840	1-163.96/10
2. Sherry Elms	$8,738	$45,746	3-165.38/10
3. Jimmie Munroe	$10,008	$30,182	2-165.12/10
4. Kathy Spears	$3,048	$28,617	14
5. Lee Ann Guilkey	$2,032	$26,885	10
6. Shauna Wright	$8,636	$26,293	7
7. Celie Whitcomb	$4,572	$25,045	8
8. Jerri Mann	0	$24,181	12
9. Susan Whyte	$4,165	$23,295	4-166.16/10
10. Donna Krening	$2,032	$22,179	9
11. Vickie Maker	$3,404	$21,806	5
12. Nancy Mayes	$1,017	$20,998	15
13. Didi Taylor	$508	$20,890	11
14. Jyme Beth Hammonds	$762	$19,850	6
15. Christy Fryar	0	$17,923	13

Fastest time at the Finals was 16.10 seconds by Marlene Eddleman.

1984
Oklahoma City, Okla. - Ten Go-Rounds - $72,800 Prize Money

Name	NFR Earnings	Season Total	Average
1. Charmayne James	$14,112	$53,499	1-166.22/10
2. Lee Ann Guilkey	$4,872	$48,709	3-167.95/10
3. Jimmie Munroe	$15,792	$39,836	4-170.72/10
4. Brenda Tyler	$6,719	$36,745	9
5. Kathy Spears	$7,560	$36,253	7
6. Marlene Eddleman	$7,392	$30,360	2-167.27/10
7. Pam Ross	$3,639	$27,064	8
8. Trudy Freeman	$3,919	$25,841	15
9. Twila Haller	$839	$22,353	6
10. Shauna Wright	$5,151	$22,107	5
11. Peggy Reiter	$1,120	$21,340	13
12. Lori Whiting	0	$21,075	12
13. Kelly Yates	$1,680	$17,681	14
14. Lauren Belcher	0	$17,306	11
15. Shanna Bush	00	$15,475	10

Fastest time at the Finals was 16.29 by Charmayne James.

1985
Las Vegas, Nev. - Ten Go-Rounds - $164,126 Prize Money

Name	NFR Earnings	Season Total	Average
1. Charmayne James	$31,562	$91,847	7
2. Janet Stover	$40,021	$84,356	1-145.38/10
3. Rose Webb	$19,190	$60,752	2-147.06/10
4. Tacy Lynn Cates	$13,256	$47,213	6
5. Trudy Freeman	$9,090	$41,527	4-148.46/10

Name	NFR Earnings	Season Total	Average
6. Brenda Tyler	0	$39,830	13
7. Marlene Eddleman	$3,409	$38,487	5
8. Martha Josey	$11,994	$37,939	8
9. Renee Ward	$11,615	$33,098	3-147.68/10
10. Danna Cogburn	$3,788	$32,177	15
11. Suzanne Fausett	$5,050	$31,250	14
12. Jimmie Munroe	$1,263	$31,206	12
13. Kathy Spears	$7,575	$30,203	10
14. Barb Lucas	$6,313	$26,564	9
15. Sherry Altizer	0	$22,155	11

Fastest time at the Finals was 14.26 seconds by Kathy Spears.

1986
Las Vegas Nev. - Ten Go-Rounds - $171,596 Prize Money

Name	NFR Earnings	Season Total	Average
1. Charmayne James	$45,144	$151,969	1-138.93/10
2. Janet Stover	$29,304	$66,160	2-139.97/10
3. Marlene Eddleman	$22,704	$63,941	4-145.27/10
4. Rose Webb	$2,640	$45,458	12
5. Ginny Pat Smith	$18,084	$41,523	3-141.61/10
6. Jimmie Munroe	$7,919	$39,215	10
7. Tamara Hammons	$9,900	$36,720	14
8. Deb Mohon	$10,560	$35,767	13
9. Danna Cogburn-Jandreau	$3,960	$34,636	15
10. Suzanne Fausett	$6,599	$30,211	11
11. Jackie Bob Cox	$3,959	$28,226	8
12. Karen Galemba	$4,884	$27,797	5
13. Ruth McDougal	$3,299	$27,604	6
14. Joyce Jackson	$2,640	$26,550	7
15. Kathy Spears	0	$21,481	9

Fastest time at the Finals was 13.58 seconds by Janet Stover.

1987
Las Vegas, Nev. - Ten Go-Rounds - $355,321 Prize Money

Name	NFR Earnings	Season Total	Average
1. Charmayne James	$37,855	$120,002	1-143.51/10
2. Marlene Eddleman	$33,756	$54,064	2-144.14/10
3. Deb Mohon	$23,233	$50,184	7
4. Lana Merrick	$9,567	$40,888	11
5. Betty Roper	$11,207	$39,451	3-145.53/10
6. Trish Brown	$18,039	$38,158	4-145.72/10
7. Tamara Hammons	$14,350	$36,128	12
8. Suzanne Fausett	$5,467	$31,967	13
9. Celie Whitcomb-Ray	$5,467	$31,610	10
10. Kappy Nelson	$8,883	$31,030	8
11. Martha Josey	$7,790	$28,933	5
12. Gale Beebe	0	$26,498	14
13. Nancy Wells	0	$25,517	15

Name	NFR Earnings	Season Total	Average
14. Cathy Felts	$2,050	$24,715	6
15. Rose Webb	0	$24,673	9

Fastest time at the Finals was 14.11 seconds by Charmayne James.

1988
Las Vegas Nev. - Ten Go-Rounds - $187,986 Prize Money

Name	NFR Earnings	Season Total	Average
1. Charmayne James	$44,772	$130,540	2-142.98/10
2. Marlene Eddleman	$44,772	$87,045	1-142.85/10
3. Beth Baudrick	$15,355	$52,123	3-144.53/10
4. Twila Haller	$16,072	$44,114	5
5. Cheryl Lynn Mann	$11,480	$40,781	8
6. Vana Beissinger	$15,875	$39,588	7
7. Rose Webb	$6,027	$37,971	4-150.96/10
8. Deb Mohon	$10,763	$35,946	6
9. Rachael Myllymaki	$5,740	$33,444	10
10. Vickie Vickers	$8,610	$31,651	12
11. Kappy Nelson	0	$30,692	15
12. Gale Beebe	$4,305	$29,483	9
13. Suzanne Fausett	$1,435	$27,269	11
14. Janeen Johnson	$2,870	$26,084	14
15. Martee Lien	0	$22,907	13

Fastest time at the Finals was 14.05 seconds by Marlene Eddleman.

1989
Las Vegas Nev. - Ten Go-Rounds - $201,496 Prize Money

Name	NFR Earnings	Season Total	Average
1. Charmayne James	$26,816	$96,651	1-146/33/10
2. Marlene Eddleman	$22,725	$92,645	7
3. Celie Whitcomb-Ray	$21,210	$63,141	9
4. Martha Josey	$15,908	$59,926	6
5. Deb Mohon	$19,998	$56,831	4-151.12/10
6. Charlotte Schmidt	$19,998	$43,548	2-146.79/10
7. Vickie Vickers	$18,180	$41,216	11
8. Tracey Crosby	$13,180	$38,463	5
9. Lana Merrick Hemsted	$14,696	$37,466	3-148.39/10
10. Martee Meter	$10,605	$34,465	13
11. Colette Baier	$10,605	$32,777	8
12. Gale Beebe	0	$31,944	15
13. Cheryl Luman	$3,030	$27,723	14
14. Cheryl Lynn Mann	$4,545	$27,233	12
15. Martha Wright		$26,052	*Did Not Compete at Finals*
16. Beth Braudrick	0	$23,858	10

Fastest time at the Finals was 14.25 seconds by Vickie Vickers.
Beth Braudrick replaced Martha Wright at the Finals.

1990
Las Vegas Nev. - Ten Go-Rounds - $210,873 Prize Money

Name	NFR Earnings	Season Total	Average
1. Charmayne James	$44,250	$130,328	1-145.39/10
2. Deb Mohon	$23,217	$64,779	4-151.31/10
3. Marlene Eddleman	32,369	$60,873	2-148.27/10
4. Angie Meadors	$13,581	$49,437	8
5. Vana Beissinger	$21,885	$45,939	5
6. Charlotte Schmidt	$7,189	$45,614	6
7. Martha Josey	$13,899	$44,535	3-148.57/10
8. Rachael Myllymaki	$17,574	$42,075	7
9. Janet Stover	$12,780	$37,867	10
10. Rose Webb	$4,793	$35,921	14
11. Terri Tackett	$6,390	$30,441	15
12. Colette Baier	$6,922	$28,786	11
13. Kelli Fletcher	$2,397	$27,338	12
14. Cheryl Luman	$3,727	$25,489	9
15. Vickie Vickers	0	$22,860	13

Fastest time at the Finals was 14.27 by Vana Beissinger.

1991
Las Vegas Nev. - Ten Go-Rounds - $221,310 Prize Money

Name	NFR Earnings	Season Total	Average
1. Charmayne James	$13,818	$92,403	4-150.02/10
2. Vana Beissinger	$33,194	$87,736	2-144.94/10
3. Twila Haller	$47,180	$87,400	6
4. Deb Mohon	$13,481	$79,924	8
5. Kim West	$38,249	$70,084	1-144.01/10
6. Angie Meadors	$32,857	$58,243	7
7. Donna Kennedy	$3,370	$42,078	11
8. Rayel Robinson	$8,426	$41,585	12
9. Lita Scott-Price	$3,370	$38,652	14
10. Mary Salmond	$14,660	$37,827	3-148.13/10
11. Marlene Eddleman	$6,470	$33,286	15
12. Charlotte Schmidt	$4,550	$29,983	5
13. Kelli Currin	0	$27,163	13
14. Shelley Bird-Matthews	0	$25,575	10
15. Sherry Combs Johnson	$1,685	$24,178	9

Fastest time at the Finals was 13.94 seconds by Marlene Eddleman.

1992
Las Vegas Nev. - Ten Go-Rounds - $231,075 Prize Money

Name	NFR Earnings	Season Total	Average
1. Charmayne James	$29,684	$110,868	2-143.77/10
2. Twila Haller	$46,571	$104,099	4-147.37/10
3. Vana Beissinger	$36,498	$78,099	1-143.33/10
4. Deb Mohon	$14,220	$89,428	10
5. Lita Scott-Price	$14,220	$65,384	8

Name	NFR Earnings	Season Total	Average
6. Kim West	$22,279	$55,818	5
7. Donna Kennedy	$24,885	$54,069	6
8. Marilyn Camarillo	$14,221	$48,296	7
9. Barbara Merrill	$10,132	$46,438	3-144.70/10
10. Sharon Smith	$593	$45,005	15
11. Rayel Robinson	$2,667	$44,757	14
12. Martee Pruitt	$7,999	$42,312	13
13. Toni Hagen	0	$36,516	11
14. Corley Cox	$5,333	$34,285	12
15. Lindsey Hayes	0	$29,051	9

Fastest time at the Finals was 14.02 seconds by Deb Mohon.

1993
Las Vegas Nev. - Ten Go-Rounds - $240,817 Prize Money

Name	NFR Earnings	Season Total	Average
1. Charmayne James	$21,934	$103,610	1-145.15/10
2. Kristie Peterson	$36,948	$84,120	5
3. Deb Mohon	$8,440	$73,561	6
4. Twila Haller	$31,884	$71,761	15
5. Sharon Kobold	$18,755	$63,808	10
6. Kim West	$7,502	$60,941	9
7. Lanita Powers	$25,508	$59,121	2-145.26/10
8. Charlotte Schmidt	$19,693	$56,458	7
9. Lita Scott-Price	$21,006	$54,607	4-146.06/10
10. Susie Seppala	$22,881	$54,062	3-145.85/10
11. Angie Meadors	$16,879	$48,894	8
12. Barbara Merrill	0	$46,354	11
13. JoAnn Middleton	$5,627	$36,961	12
14. Kay Blandford	$3,751	$36,717	13
15. Donna Napier	0	$32,207	14

Fastest time at the Finals was 14.02 seconds by Lita Scott-Price.

1994
Las Vegas Nev. - Ten Go-Rounds - $257,400 Prize Money

Name	NFR Earnings	Season Total	Average
1. Kristie Peterson	$50,886	$110,341	1-143.83/10
2. Sherry Potter	$50,866	$105,022	3-147.23/10
3. Sharon Kobold	$40,986	$94,618	5
4. Deb Mohon	$2,970	$69,757	7
5. Sue Miller	$15,840	$67,697	12
6. Charmayne James	0	$67,170	14
7. Lindsey Hayes	$13,860	$62,170	6
8. Tye Petska	$22,176	$59,758	2-145.37/10
9. Rachael Myllymaki	$13,860	$57,211	13
10. Mindy Schueneman	$7,920	$51,191	15
11. Sharon Smith	$13,860	$47,996	8
12. Vana Beissinger	$7,920	$46,935	10
13. Felicia Otis	$8,316	$42,056	4-147.43/10

Name	NFR Earnings	Season Total	Average
14. Charlotte Schmidt	$990	$38,813	9
15. Mardee Hollenbeck	0	$35,181	11

Fastest time at the Finals was 13.80 by Sherry Potter.

1995
Las Vegas Nev. - Ten Go-Rounds - $271,700 Prize Money

Name	NFR Earnings	Season Total	Average
1. Sherry Potter-Cervi	$27,588	$157,172	4-149.99/10
2. Kristie Petereson	$61,208	$149,780	1-142.22/10
3. Vana Beissinger	$21.945	$75,454	15
4. Kay Blandford	$37,620	$73,944	11
5. Donna Napier	$27,588	$69,529	3-149.52/10
6. Fallon Taylor	$17,138	$62,414	2-145.34/10
7. Sharon Smith	$2,560	$59,802	6
8. Sue Miller	$4,180	$58,737	7
9. Lindsey Hayes	$13,585	$53,668	14
10. Deb Mohon	$14,630	$53,084	8
11. Angie Meadors	$12,540	$51,486	9
12. Charmayne James	$10,868	$50,345	5
13. Molly Swanson	$5,225	$44,179	10
14. Danyelle Campbell	0	$42,085	13
15. Debbie Guelly	0	$35,966	12

Fastest time at the Finals was 13.91 by Kristie Peterson.

1996
Las Vegas Nev. - Ten Go-Rounds - $286,936 Prize Money

Name	NFR Earnings	Season Total	Average
1. Kristie Peterson	$77,793	$170,083	1-141.89/10
2. Kay Blandford	$78,786	$152,895	2-142.00/10
3. Sherry Cervi	$24,732	$109,271	8
4. Sharon Kobold	$26,707	$76,237	9
5. Molly Swanson	$10,440	$72,891	14
6. Deb Mohon	$5,849	$61,511	7
7. Tacy Lynn Johnson	$15,097	$61,223	13
8. Charlotte Schmidt	$11,919	$59,925	3-147.17/10
9. Fallon Taylor	$1,876	$59,925	12
10. Sharon Smith	$10,528	$59,907	5
11. Shandi Metzinger	$2,560	$54,992	15
12. Sandi Emond	$8,807	$53,265	4-147.58/10
13. Charmayne James	$4,878	$49,995	10
14. Angie Meadors	$3,852	$48,158	11
15. Melissa Hubier	$3,112	$47,357	6

Fastest time at the Finals was 13.97 seconds by Kay Blandford.

1997
Las Vegas Nev. - Ten Go-Rounds - $303,082 Prize Money

Name	NFR Earnings	Season Total	Average
1. Kristie Peterson	$67,925	$165,238	1-143.28/10
2. Sherry Cervi	$50,626	$157,238	4-153.54/10

Name	NFR Earnings	Season Total	Average
3. Kay Blandford	$37,920	$121,100	8
4. Ember Givens	$36,486	$72,651	5
5. Cheyenne Wimberley	$19,852	$66,843	6
6. Peyton Raney	$16,716	$60,782	9
7. Fallon Taylor	0	$56,556	12
8. Sandi Emond	$13,336	$55,674	3-152.34/10
9. Charmayne James	$10,072	$54,442	14
10. Leslie Schlosser	$15,877	$53,657	2-1148.02/10
11. Nina Binder	$11,797	$51,255	11
12. Sharon Smith	$3,963	$47,709	15
13. Terri Tackett	$8,113	$46,074	10
14. Molly Swanson	$2,145	$42,339	13
15. Tacy Lynn Johnson	$8,253	$42,255	7

Fastest time at the Finals was 14.10 seconds by Charmayne James.

1998
Las Vegas Nev. - Ten Go-Rounds - $512,034 Prize Money

Name	NFR Earnings	Season Total	Average
1. Kristie Peterson	$99,091	$212,998	1-141.58/10
2. Janet Stover	$89,555	$153,465	6
3. Sherry Cervi	$36,531	$148,511	10
4. Ruth Haislip	$81,791	$119,745	2-141.98/10
5. Charmayne James	$58,534	$116,325	7
6. Melissa Hubier	$50,909	$91,164	3-143.77/10
7. Gail Hillman	$27,329	$65,660	8
8. Martha Josey	$16,197	$59,113	11
9. Sue Miller	$16,965	$57,822	4-144.06/10
10. Judy Myllymaki	$18,364	$57,647	5
11. Kim West	$9,123	$50,123	12
12. Fallon Taylor	$5,412	$47,277	9
13. Molly Swanson	$1,241	$45,853	13
14. Cheyenne Wimberley	$1,261	$45,627	14
15. Lisa Ogden	0	$39,587	15

Fastest time at the Finals was 13.75 by Janet Stover.

1999
Las Vegas Nev. - Ten Go-Rounds - $541,333 Prize Money

Name	NFR Earnings	Season Total	Average
1.Sherry Cervi	$114,374	$245,369	1-141.56/10
2. Kristie Peterson	$71,518	$148,063	7
3. Janet Stover	$47,471	$102,300	11
4. Debbie Renger	$60,379	$101,937	2-143.36/10
5. Kay Blandford	$40,045	$91,549	5
6. Charmayne James	$40,253	$88,520	3-143.44/10
7. Rachael Myllymaki	$11,035	$87,091	14
8. Ruth Haislip	$36,852	$85,267	15
9. Kappy Allen	$35,915	$84,377	4-143.56/10
10. Gail Hillman	$9,577	$74,001	13

Name	NFR Earnings	Season Total	Average
11. Tona Wright	$20,890	$72,505	9
12. Melissa Hubier	$20,821	$63,538	5
13. Sue Miller	$16,379	$63,170	10
14. Sherrylynn Adams	$7,704	$51,865	12
15. Katie McCoin	$8,120	$49,174	6

Fastest time at the Finals was 13.93 seconds by Sherry Cervi.

2000
Las Vegas Nev. - Ten Go-Rounds - $550,758 Prize Money

Name	NFR Earnings	Season Total	Average
1. Kappy Allen	$95,112	$145,204	1-140.0/10
2. Charmayne James	$45,332	$142,348	7
3. Kristie Peterson	$67,009	$134,499	2-140.73/10
4. Kelly Yates	$60,160	$131,863	12
5. Tona Wright	$55,923	$110,443	8
6. Sherry Cervi	$16,168	$101,646	13
7. Molly Swanson	$46,073	$92,047	3-141.53/10
8. Marlene McRae	$44,802	$89,833	6
9. Ruth Haislip	$33,469	$79,899	5
10. Rachael Sproul	$28,173	$76,152	4-141.86/10
11. Jamie Richards	$22,242	$69,132	14
12. Sherrylynn Adams	$13,345	$65,918	9
13. Kay Blandford	$11,015	$64,988	10
14. Gloria Freeman	$3,672	$64,914	15
15. Kristin Weaver	$8,261	$54,202	11

Fastest time at the Finals was 13.74 by Tona Wright.

2001
Las Vegas Nev. - Ten Go-Rounds - $567,060 Prize Money

Name	NFR Earnings	Season Total	Average
1. Janet Stover	$126,934	$186,812	2-144.13/10
2. Kelly Yates	$29,771	$138,427	15
3. Charmayne James	$50,163	$129,270	8
4. Tona Wright	$41,875	$107,208	6
5. Kappy Allen	$62,013	$107,147	1-142.20/10
6. Gloria Freeman	$42,929	$100,417	3-147.70/10
7. Jennifer Wilson	$44,492	$91,688	5
8. Janae Ward	$25,627	$88,568	10
9. Tami Fontenot	$32,133	$88,231	9
10. Rachael Sproul	$30,752	$85,288	7
11. Delores Toole	$27,044	$85,157	4-147.71/10
12. Sherry Cervi	$19,520	$83,265	11
13. Kay Blandford	$27,044	$77,024	12
14. Molly Swanson-Powell	$6,761	$60,393	14
15. Rayna Prewitt	0	$44,838	13

Fastest time at the Finals was 13.76 seconds by Charmayne James.

2002
Las Vegas Nev. - Ten Go-Rounds - $583,856 Prize Money

Name	NFR Earnings	Season Total	Average
1. Charmayne James	$66,582	$186,483	1-141.75/10
2. Kelly Kaminski	$82,189	$161,196	6
3. Tammy Key	$80,617	$158,897	10
4. Rachael Sproul	$59,845	$121,266	2-141.92/10
5. Brandie Halls	$63,550	$112,717	5
6. Carol Barr	$53,445	$100,809	3-142.21/10
7. Melanie Southard-White	$33,225	$90,162	15
8. Delores Toole	$27,845	$86,295	4-144.30/10
9. Tami Fontenot	$26,386	$83,817	7
10. Janae Ward	$22,007	$81,990	11
11. Danyelle Campbell	$24,477	$80,216	8
12. Jolee Lautaret	$26,835	$78,527	12
13. Molly Powell	$13,249	$71,515	13
14. Kay Blandford	$3,593	$67,597	9
15. Amy Dale	0	$42,921	14

Fastest time at the Finals was 13.63 seconds by Tammy Key.

2003
Las Vegas Nev. - Ten Go-Rounds - $601,159 Prize Money

Name	NFR Earnings	Season Total	Average
1. Janae Ward	$111,908	$155,792	1-140.50/10
2. Kelly Kaminski	$53,179	$127,152	12
3. Jackie Dube	$74,451	$120,690	8
4. McKenzie Brower	$68,864	$114,455	3-151.14/10
5. Sherry Cervi	$64,817	$113,362	5
6. Kappy Allen	$59,731	$108,819	2-141.33/10
7. Brittany Pozzi	$9,942	$89,003	7
8. Melanie Southard	$23,122	$87,440	10
9. Kelly Maben	$32,447	$84,324	9
10. Brandie Halls	$31,561	$83,722	6
11. Darlene Kasper	$11,252	$82,893	13
12. Kelly Yates	$17,341	$76,004	4-153.53/10
13. Jolee Lautaret	$25,665	$71,207	11
14. Tammy Key	$10,867	$58,240	14
15. Terri Kay Kirkland	$6,012	$48,466	15

Fastest time at the Finals was 13.67 seconds by Jackie Dube

2004
Las Vegas Nev. - Ten Go-Rounds - $612,743 Prize Money

Name	NFR Earnings	Season Total	Average
1. Kelly Kaminski	$82,707	$179,373	2-141.34/10
2. Molly Powell	$99,869	$156,820	1-140.93/10
3. Liz Pinkston	$66,738	$128,271	6
4. Jackie Dube	$72,578	$127,768	12
5. Paula Seay	$26,457	$118,663	15
6. Sheri Sinor Estrada	$33,488	$114,799	9

Name	NFR Earnings	Season Total	Average
7. Kelly Maben	$56,846	$114,041	13
8. Terri Kaye Kirkland	$32,892	$98,704	3-144.00/10
9. Denise Adams Fea	$28,364	$94,619	11
10. Amanda Clayman	$32,654	$91,849	8
11. Janet Stover	$26,338	$87,334	7
12. Deb Renger	$9,772	$82,373	14
13. Delores Toole	$24,550	$78,398	5
14. Jolee Lautaret	$20,260	$76,592	4-146.63/10
15. Darlene Kasper	$6,197	$73,648	10

Fastest time at the Finals was 13.67 seconds by Kelly Maben.

2005
Las Vegas Nev. - Ten Go-Rounds - $638,053 Prize Money

Name	NFR Earnings	Season Total	Average
1. Kelly Kaminski	$107,091	$191,702	4-146.08/10
2. Linda Vick	$47,704	$158,570	12
3. Shali Lord	$70,799	$143,348	9
4. Sherry Cervi	$38,365	$142,258	3-143.47/10
5. Denise Adams Fea	$61,587	$135,740	10
6. Sheri Sinor Estrada	$70,421	$131,194	5
7. Liz Pinkston	$65,373	$127,121	1-142.65/10
8. Molly Powell	$60,829	$110,214	2-143.03/10
9. Terri Kaye Kirkland	$82,687	$109,442	15
10. Brittany Pozzi	$35,463	$106,568	11
11. Talina Bird	$35,841	$88,794	6
12. June Holeman	$13,377	$77,246	7
13. Melanie Southard	$12,368	$65,928	13
14. Kassie Mowry	$10,349	$62,309	8
15. Paula Seay	0	$61,264	14

Fastest time at the Finals was 13.77 seconds by Sheri Sinor Estrada.

2006
Las Vegas Nev. - Ten Go-Rounds - $671,875 Prize Money

Name	NFR Earnings	Season Total	Average
1. Mary Burger	$78,558	$189,185	3-143.96/10
2. Brittany Pozzi	$57,239	$186,618	1-141.12/10
3. Kelly Maben	$102,332	$173,692	6
4. Brandie Halls	$73,648	$129,176	7
5. Shelly Anzick	$59,047	$128,293	12
6. Denise Adams	$71,839	$127,728	5
7. Codi Baucom	$53,750	$123,343	2-141.40/10
8. Tana Poppino	$39,925	$114,097	8
9. Sherry Cervi	$40,571	$102,525	9
10. Terra Bynum	$38,762	$96,829	4-147.92/10
11. Tammy Key	$17,701	$81,843	13
12. Lindsay Sears	$12,662	$78,993	15
13. Kelly Kaminski	$13,954	$74,278	14

Name	NFR Earnings	Season Total	Average
14. Layna Kight	$2,584	$74,175	11
15. Terri Kaye Kirkland	$9,303	$64,663	10

Fastest time at the Finals was 13.52 seconds by Brandie Halls.

Professional Women's Barrel Race was a subsidiary of the PRCA and these were individuals that competed at the NFR. This was the ONLY year this was done.

2007
Las Vegas Nev. - Ten Go-Rounds - $687,500 Prize Money

Name	NFR Earnings	Season Total	Average
1. Brittany Pozzi-Pharr	$95,192	$259,713	1-140.18/10
2. Lindsay Sears	$19,255	$230,797	6
3. Jill Moody	$83,690	$169,099	11
4. Terra Bynum	$62,139	$130.787	4-141.52/10
5. Lisa Lockhart	$58,173	$125,492	9
6. Maegan Reichert	$53,942	$111,411	3-141.31/10
7. Deb Renger	$53,942	$110,367	2-141.00/10
8. Vicki Solmonsen	$23,534	$107,096	12
9. Brenda Mays	$29,615	$99,197	10
10. Codi Baucom	$10,841	$97,262	8
11. Molly Powell	$38,738	$95,897	7
12. Brandie Halls	$20,889	$85,171	15
13. Sherrylynn Johnson	0	$79,312	14
14. Tana Poppino	$20,625	$71,901	5
15. Brittany Hofstetter	$16,923	$70,379	13

Fastest time at the Finals was 13.64 seconds by Jill Moody and Lindsay Sears.

2008
Las Vegas Nev. - Ten Go-Rounds - $709,185 Prize Money

Name	NFR Earnings	Season Total	Average
1. Lindsay Sears	$139,002	$323,570	3-143.25/10
2. Jill Moody	$104,117	$218,880	1-140.11/10
3. Brittany Pozzi-Pharr	$61,118	$196,346	13
4. Cassie Moseley	$96,544	$156,298	4-149.40/10
5. Maegan Reichert	$89,513	$155,337	2-140.42/10
6. Annesa Self	$28,395	$126,514	11
7. Mary Burger	$30,018	$116,518	5
8. Brenda Mays	$19,201	$108,250	6
9. Shelley Murphy	$4,327	$107,219	14
10. Terra Bynum	$41,106	$102,348	8
11. Tammy Key Fischer	$28,666	$97,448	12
12. Lisa Lockhart	$24,069	$95,751	9
13. Stephanie Fryar	$27,043	$88,156	10
14. Traci Dawson	$2,704	$73,347	15
15. Deb Renger	$7,302	$66,284	7

Fastest time and the Finals was 13.53 seconds by Lindsay Sears.

2009
Las Vegas Nev. - Ten Go-Rounds - $718,750 Prize Money

Name	NFR Earnings	Season Total	Average
1. Brittany Pozzi	$123,569	$279,434	3-144.29/10
2. Lindsay Sears	$131,125	$272,343	2-139.06/10
3. Sherry Cervi	$145,199	$219,628	1-139.01/10
4. Mary Burger	$33,865	$156,153	6-146.77/10
5. Sue Smith	$63,399	$130,209	4-145.32/10
6. Jordon Peterson	$34,002	$126,051	12
7. Tiffany Fox	$23,220	$123,457	14
8. Lisa Lockhart	$47,547	$120,246	5-145.82/10
9. Cassie Moseley	$39,070	$109,110	10
10. Shelley Morgan	$44,508	$103.960	9
11. Sheena Robbins	$14,651	$85,658	7-152.27/10
12. Brenda Mays	$4,147	$81,523	8-152.74/10
13. Tammy Fischer	$6,358	$73,198	13
14. Danyelle Campbell	$2,764	$69,523	11
15. P. J. Burger	$4,423	$61,484	15

Fastest time at the Finals was 13.60 seconds by Sherry Cervi.

2010
Las Vegas Nev. - Ten Go-Rounds - $734,381 Prize Money

Name	NFR Earnings	Season Total	Average
1. Sherry Cervi	$137,555	$299,894	2-143.29/10
2. Jill Moody	$133,035	$219,686	1-138.26/10
3. Lindsay Sears	$55,449	$189,407	6-150.05/10
4. Lisa Lockhart	$89,915	$188,027	3-144.09/10
5. Brittany Pozzi	$51,548	$165,999	4-145.25/10
6. Brenda Mays	$44,345	$144,593	5-149.63/10
7. Kelli Tolbert	$59,879	$123,240	11
8. Angie Meadors	$50,700	$103,173	13
9. Sydni Blanchard	$40,109	$90,012	12
10. Christina Richman	$21,332	$88,418	7-150.54/10
11. Nellie Williams	$13,840	$86,473	10
12. Jeanne Anderson	$11,863	$69,406	14
13. Tana Poppino	$11,863	$67,445	15
14. Sherrylynn Johnson	$5,649	$66,395	8-150.64/10
15. Benette Barrington	$7,344	$58,927	9

Fastest time at the Finals was 13.49 seconds by Sherry Cervi.

2011
Las Vegas Nev. - Ten Go-Rounds - $750,000 Prize Money

Name	NFR Earnings	Season Total	Average
1. Lindsay Sears	$133,560	$238,864	1-139.50/10
2. Brittany Pozzi	$77,452	$192,725	
3. Sherry Cervi	$$93,320	$183,838	4-145.29/10
4. Lisa Lockhart	$79,040	$159,710	
5. Carlee Pierce	$50,770	$136,274	
6. Jane Melby	$59,713	$129,994	

Name	NFR Earnings	Season Total	Average
7. Brenda Mays	$32,308	$120,269	3-142.95/10
8. Jody Sheffield	$49,903	$118,218	6-150.15/10
9. Christina Richman	$52,212	$113,926	2-142.20/10
10. Angie Meadors	$46,298	$112,892	7-151.24/10
11. Jeanne Anderson	$30,577	$97,761	5-146.68/10
12. Sue Smith	$15,000	$94,752	
13. Tammy Fischer	$13,414	$84,676	8-151.40/10
14. Britany Fleck	$2,885	$66,005	
15. Jill Moody	0	$61,421	

Fastest time at the Finals was 13.46 seconds by Carlee Pierce.

2012
Las Vegas Nev. - Ten Go-Rounds - $765,625 Prize Money

Name	NFR Earnings	Season Total	Average
1. Mary Walker	$146,941	$247,233	2-143.52/10
2. Carlee Pierce	$79,801	$204,322	
3. Brittany Pozzi	$23,264	$194,224	
4. Lindsay Sears	$53,739	$190,062	8-158.97/10
5. Lisa Lockhart	$107,873	$180,336	3-143.96/10
6. Kaley Bass	$68,022	$154,306	4-144.69/10
7. Brenda Mays	$55,950	$137,748	1-141.79/10
8. Sherry Cervi	$37,201	$130,263	
9. Nikki Steffes	$23,558	$110,279	5-147.19/10
10. Kelli Tolbert	$42,698	$109,324	
11. Lee Ann Rust	$42,255	$103,844	
12. Benette Barrington-Little	$24,245	$92,638	
13. Trula Churchill	$23,853	$84,629	
14. Christina Richman	$14,429	$75,301	6-156.32/10
15. Christy Loflin	$18,847	$73,698	7-158.41/10

Fastest time at the Finals was 13.51 seconds by Carlee Pierce.

2013
Las Vegas Nev. - Ten Go-Rounds - $781,250 Prize Money

Name	NFR Earnings	Season Total	Average
1. Sherry Cervi	$155,899	$303,317	1-138.15/10
2. Mary Walker	$92,250	$229,363	6-153.21/10
3. Lisa Lockhart	$91,665	$184,201	2-143.71/10
4. Taylor Jacob	$82,433	$164,484	
5. Michele McLeod	$41,768	$151,347	8-158.08/10
6. Kaley Bass	$69,112	$148,512	3-145.21/10
7. Christy Loflin	$43,370	$148,412	5-150.74/10
8. Shada Brazile	$42,669	$130,278	4-149.70/10
9. Jane Melby	$48,379	$124,642	7-154.41/10
10. Sabrina Ketcham	$18,931	$119,147	
11. Fallon Taylor	$27,144	$116,785	
12. Brittany Pozzi	$18,931	$113,156	
13. Trula Churchill	$23,588	$90,313	
14. Sydni Blanchard	$14,724	$82,867	

Name	NFR Earnings	Season Total	Average
15. Jean Winters	0	$69,847	

Fastest time at the Finals was 13.37 seconds by Taylor Jacob.

2014
Las Vegas Nev. - Ten Go-Rounds - $796,874 Prize Money

Name	NFR Earnings	Season Total	Average
1. Fallon Taylor	$144,969	$276,441	2-145.10/10
2. Lisa Lockhart	$143,896	$265,514	1-144.93/10
3. Kaley Bass	$59,153	$214,432	3-147.15/10
4. Michele McLeod	$62,830	$163,476	5-151.06/10
5. Britany Diaz	$51,643	$154,590	4-147.37/10
6. Carlee Pierce	$63,750	$154,181	6-151.61/10
7. Mary Walker	$45,973	$145,686	
8. Trula Churchill	$66,201	$142,076	8-154.84/10
9. Nancy Hunter	$32,488	$136,777	
10. Kassidy Dennison	$34,020	$126,072	
11. Sherry Cervi	$29,117	$122,165	
12. Christy Loflin	$21,148	$112,884	
13. Jana Bean	$30,343	$100,758	7-151.97/10
14. Christine Laughlin	0	$93,135	
15. Samantha Lyne	$11,340	$1,917	

Fastest time at the Finals was 13.66 seconds by Michele McLeod.

2015
Las Vegas Nev. - Ten Go-Rounds - $1,374,995 Prize Money

Name	NFR Earnings	Season Total	Average
1. Callie duPerier	$126,922	$303,846	1-140.41/10
2. Lisa Lockhart	$123,538	$285,059	7-148.54/10
3. Sara Rose McDonald	$139,827	$284,426	6-148.50/10
4. Michele McLeod	$138,347	$218,744	4-145.19/10
5. Cassidy Kruse	$126,077	$217,423	3-144.84/10
6. Fallon Taylor	$90,750	$187,578	
7. Taylor Jacob	$87,365	$177,874	
8. Jackie Ganter	$69,808	$164,780	2-141.07/10
9. Sherry Cervi	$22,846	$163,821	5-146.04/10
10. Nancy Hunter	$40,615	$147,301	
11. Mary Walker	$15,654	$135,759	
12. Jana Bean	$41,462	$111,624	
13. Carley Richardson	$13,327	$107,493	
14. Vickie Carter	$17,346	$83,768	8-152.81/10
15. Deb Guelly	$4,231	$74,000	

Fastest time at the Finals was 13.55 seconds by Sherry Cervi.

2016
Las Vegas Nev. - Ten Go-Rounds - $1,374,995 Prize Money

Name	NFR Earnings	Season Total	Average
1. Mary Burger	$76,578	$277,554	8-153.40/10
2. Amberleigh Moore	$187,692	$266,760	2-141.53/10
3. Lisa Lockhart	$141,751	$251,975	1-137.98/10
4. Sherry Cervi	$154,635	$248,313	3-142.95/10
5. Kimmie Wall	$124,809	$242,603	4-144.67/10
6. Pamela Capper	$74,462	$171,966	5-148.07/10
7. Jackie Ganter	$45,154	$169,541	6-149.88/10
8. Ivy Conrado	$40,616	$161,775	
9. Jana Bean	$68,751	$159,086	
10. Sara Rose McDonald	$59,654	$159,018	7-152.88/10
11. Stevi Hillman	$41,885	$156,528	
12. Michele McLeod	$46,962	$144,707	
13. Cayla Melby Small	$35,962	$133,698	
14. Mary Walker	0	$122,816	
15. Carley Richardson	$13,116	$103,991	

Fastest time at the Finals was 13.37 seconds by Amberleigh Moore.

2017
Las Vegas Nev. - Ten Go-Rounds - $1,374,995 Prize Money

Name	NFR Earnings	Season Total	Average
1. Nellie Miller	$177,962	$308,498	1-137.32/10
2. Hailey Kinsel	$189,385	$288,092	6-144.95/10
3. Tiany Schuster	$24,962	$285,339	
4. Amberleigh Moore	$110,001	$240,806	
5. Ivy Conrado	$89,763	$232,521	2-137.40/10
6. Tilar Murray	$76,154	$203,904	4-142.89/10
7. Lisa Lockhart	$53,943	$203,550	3-138.12/10
8. Stevi Hillman	$3,667	$199,619	
9. Kassie Mowry	$63,886	$189,047	
10. Taci Bettis	$55,423	$162,446	
11. Brittany Pozzi Tonozzi	$35,398	$161,173	5-144.01/10
12. Kathy Grimes	$17,769	$150,978	7-149.55/10
13. Sydni Blanchard	$43,154	$144,516	
14. Kellie Collier	$8,462	$108,146	8-153.08/10
15. Kimmie Wall	0	$86,294	

Fastest time at the Finals was 13.11 seconds by Hailey Kinsel – a Thomas & Mack Arena record at the time.

2018
Las Vegas Nev. - Ten Go-Rounds - $1,374,995 Prize Money

Name	NFR Earnings	Season Total	Average
1. Hailey Kinsel	$157,865	$350,700	7-147.61/10
2. Jessica Routier	$142,701	$251,704	2-142.60/10
3. Amberleigh Moore	$147,232	$246,357	6-146.71/10
4. Carman Pozzobon	$107,885	$204,831	1-139.46/10

Name	NFR Earnings	Season Total	Average
5. Jessica Telford	$103,231	$201,573	3-143.13/10
6. Ivy Conrado	$88,001	$196,385	8-148.30/10
7. Tacy Bettis	$77,846	$191,538	
8. Nellie Miller	$31,307	$188,133	
9. Stevi Hillman	$60,289	$184,751	4-143.84/10
10. Kylie Weast	$61,770	$173,484	
11. Lisa Lockhart	$37,321	$170,746	
12. Brittany Pozzi Tonozzi	$15,653	$162,920	
13. Tammy Fischer	$29,615	$130,892	5-144.64/10
14. Kelly Bruner	$29,192	$129,708	
15. Tracy Nowlin	$15,654	$116,150	

Fastest time at the Finals was 13.37 seconds by Kylie Weast.

2019
Las Vegas Nev. - Ten Go-Rounds - $1,374,995 Prize Money

Name	NFR Earnings	Season Total	Average
1. Hailey Kinsel	$148,866	$290,020	8-147.42
2. Ivy Conrado-Saebens	$171,404	$264,673	1-138.44
3. Emily Miller	$157,654	$255,799	2-143.25
4. Lisa Lockhart	$104,346	$250,698	3-133.47
5. Nellie Miller	$81,288	$235,899	4-144.63
6. Amberleigh Moore	$114,923	$207,982	12-167.51
7. Dona Kay Rule	$95,885	$192,392	10-148.84
8. Jessica Routier	$94,615	$191,197	9-148.45
9. Shali Lord	$61,615	$173,391	5-144.73
10. Stevi Hillman	$51,885	$157,219	15-154.30
11. Brittany Pozzi Tonozzi	$46,596	$152,100	6-144.77
12. Lacinda Rose	$49,981	$138,917	7-145.17
13. Cheyenne Wimberley	$37,500	$127,861	13-175.22
14. Jennifer Sharp	$22,269	$114,024	11-165.38
15. Ericka Nelson	$18,885	$112,318	14-175.45

Fastest time at the Finals was 13.53 seconds by Stevi Hillman.

2020
Arlington, Texas - Ten Go-Rounds - $1,100,006 Prize Money

Name	NFR Earnings	Season Total	Average
1. Hailey Kinsel	$270,615	$349,076	1-170.95
2. Brittany Tonozzi	$114,500	$201,224	4-175.23
3. Jill Wilson	$112,384	$165,755	2-174.10
4. Emily Miller Beisel	$117,038	$159,426	5-177.72
5. Jimmie Smith	$88,269	$153,291	7-180.00
6. Stevi Hillman	$84,884	$137,273	13-191.18
7. Jessica Routier	$82,346	$133,717	3-174.59
8. Lisa Lockhart	$78,961	$119,865	15-221.85
9. Shelley Morgan	$63,307	$116,382	11-189.66
10. Tiany Schuster	$54,423	$109,483	10-185.72
11. Cheyenne Wimberley	$47,653	$94,693	9-185.47

Name	NFR Earnings	Season Total	Average
12. Wenda Johnson	$50,615	$90,568	8-184.92
13. Dona Kay Rule		$77,453	Did Not Compete at Finals
14. Ryann Pedone	$33,269	$75,849	6-177.78
15. Brittany Barnett	$30,730	$70,296	12-191.18
16. Jessie Telford	$21,000	$59,477	14-195.29

Fastest time at the Finals was 16.56 seconds by Hailey Kinsel.

2021
Las Vegas, Nev. - Ten Go-Rounds - $1,132,131 Prize Money

Name	NFR Earnings	Season Total	Average
1. Jordon Briggs	$194,842	$297,460	1-136.83
2. Hailey Kinsel	$167,627	$281,156	3-146.41
3. Emily Miller-Beisel	$129,091	$202,564	4/5-146.83
4. Shelley Morgan	$107,973	$202,202	7-147.19
5. Dona Kay Rule	$110,585	$195,575	6-147.09
6. Stevi Hillman	$111,892	$183,070	4/5-146.83
7. Amanda Welsh	$78,145	$155,065	8-148.01
8. Ivy Saebens	$68,784	$139,590	12-152.69
9. Wenda Johnson	$70,960	$138,345	15-167.41
10. Molly Otto	$70,525	$134,698	2-145.11
11. Brittany Pozzi Tonozzi	$54,414	$128,200	9-148.80
12. Lisa Lockhart	$51,801	$116,845	13-159.00
13. Cheyenne Wimberley	$34,166	$111,299	14-162.93
14. Jessica Routier	$21,321	$100,169	10-148.76
15. Nellie Miller	$10,000	$85,519	11-148.80

Fastest time at the Finals was 13.43 seconds by Ivy Saebbens and Emily Miller-Beisel.

2022
Las Vegas, Nev. - Ten Go-Rounds - $1,200,000 Prize Money

Name	NFR Earnings	Season Total	Average
1. Hailey Kinsel	$170,658	$302,172	8-146.06/10
2. Jordon Briggs	$96,741	$274,520	4-142.41/10
3. Shelley Morgan	$144,755	$265,030	1-137.28/10
4. Lisa Lockhart	$168,326	$253,197	3-141.66/10
5. Wenda Johnson	$100,265	$231,860	5-142.76/10
6. Emily Beisel	$127,753	$221,718	11-155.50/10
7. Margo Crowther	$87,880	$184,751	9-146.98/10
8. Bayleigh Choate	$92,078	$182,971	2-138.98/10
9. Dona Kay Rule	$43,577	$171,019	13-159.34/10
10. Leslie Smalygo	$73,890	$158,343	15-144.69/9
11. Brittany Pozzi Tonozzi	$65,729	$154,161	6-143.1/10
12. Kassie Mowry	$57,658	$150,121	10-152.33/10
13. Sissy Winn	$47,308	$149,156	7-144.03/10
14. Stevi Hillman	$17,462	$138,064	14-164.56/10
15. Jessica Routier	$36,582	$123,197	12-158.19/10

Fastest time at the Finals was 13.34 seconds by Hailey Kinsel.

2023
Las Vegas, Nev. - Ten Go-Rounds - $1,200,000 Prize Money

Name	NFREarnings	Season Total	Average
1. Brittany Pozzi-Tonozzi	$225,935.40	$496,498.82	2-141.18/10
2. Lisa Lockhart	$209,096.39	$343,688.04	1-137.18/10
3. Kassie Mowry	$188,790.54	$322,592.71	3-141.2/10
4. Jordan Briggs	$111,694.33	$272,518.53	5-142.43/10
5. Emily Beisel	$87,921.63	$246,674.04	13-161.48/10
6. Sissy Winn	$120,939.28	$229,961.77	11-156.64/10
7. Summer Kosel	$113,015.04	$228,696.65	10-152.66/10
8. Paige Jones	$114,170.65	$217,138.87	4-142.21/10
9. Jessica Routier	$75,870.19	$217,138.87	6-142.76/10
10. Stevi Hillman	$64,974.38	$173,989.82	12-158.09/10
11. Taycie Matthews	$10,000.00	$154,161.40	15-154.88/10
12. Ilyssa Riley	$28,324.79	$139,798.16	7-144.54/9
13. Hailey Kinsel	$48,630.64	$154,406.41	8-148.67/10
14. Sue Smith	$28,324.79	$133,968.73	9-149.00/10
15. Wenda Johnson	$10,000.00	$130,505.57	14-163.64/10

Appendix 3
Barrel Racing
Rookies of the Year

Year	Name	Year	Name
1967	Patti Mack-Prather	1997	Peyton Raney
1968	Ann Lewis	1998	Shelle Shaw
1969	Lee Natalie	1999	Jodi Hollingworth
1970	Joleen Hurst Steiner	2000	Gloria Freeman
1971	Martha Tompkins-Wright	2001	Connie Morris
1972	Jann Kremling	2002	Jill Besplug
1973	Cheryl Luman	2003	Brittany Pozzi
1974	Colette Graves-Baier	2004	Sabrina Lay
1975	Lynne Mayes	2005	Chani Payne
1976	Darla Higgins	2006	Audrey Ridgeway
1977	Jackie Jo Perrin	2007	Julie Erkamaa
1978	Carol Goostree	2008	Sydni Blanchard
1979	Lynn Manning-Flynn	2009	Kelli Tolbert
1980	Wanda Cagliari	2010	Lindsey Ewin
1981	Lee Ann Guilkey	2011	Lee Ann Rust
1982	Kathy Spears	2012	Emily Efurd
1983	Sherry Elms	2013	Taylor Jacob
1984	Charmayne James	2014	Sara Rose McDonald
1985	Tacy Cates-Johnson	2015	Jackie Ganter
1986	Laura Farley	2016	Cayla Melby Small
1987	Lana Merrick Hemsted	2017	Taci Bettis
1988	Vana Beissinger	2018	Jimmie Smith
1989	Charlotte Schmidt	2019	Carly Taylor
1990	Melody Smith	2020	Paige Jones
1991	Donna Kennedy	2021	Kylee Scribner
1992	Sharon Smith	2022	Bayleigh Choate
1993	JoAnn Middleton	2023	Kalli McCall
1994	Mindy Schueneman		
1995	Ramona Scott		
1996	Trula Truitt		

Jackie Ganter rookie record for most money won with $164,780 in 2015.

Appendix 4
AQHA Horse of the Year

The AQHA/WPRA/PURINA annually honor the top equine partners that carry WPRA members to the winners circle. The award is for barrel horses and is voted on by the top 30. This list represents those that have won the award through the years.

Year	Nickname	Registered Name	Owner	Rider
1989	Scamper	Gills Bay Boy	Charmayne James	Charmayne James
1990	Scamper	Gills Bay Boy	Charmayne James	Charmayne James
1991	Scamper	Gills Bay Boy	Charmayne James	Charmayne James
1992	Scamper	Gills Bay Boy	Charmayne James	Charmayne James
1993	Scamper	Gills Bay Boy	Charmayne James	Charmayne James
1994	Brown	Special Agreement	Bubba & Deb Mohon	Deb Mohon
1995	Bozo	French Flash Hawk	Kristie Peterson	Kristie Peterson
1996	Bozo	French Flash Hawk	Kristie Peterson	Kristie Peterson
1997	Bozo	French Flash Hawk	Kristie Peterson	Kristie Peterson
1998	Bozo	French Flash Hawk	Kristie Peterson	Kristie Peterson
1999	Bozo	French Flash Haw	Kristie Peterson	Kristie Peterson
2000	Fiesta	Firewater Fiesta	Kelly Yates	Kelly Yates
2001	Fiesta	Firewater Fiesta	Kelly Yates	Kelly Yates
2002	Llave	The Key Grip	Robert & Kay Blandford	Kay Blandford
2003	Tally	Top Tally	Nathan Williams	Darlene Kasper
2004	Elmer	Krimps Ready to Go	Paula Seay	Paula Seay
2005	Sparky	Sparky Impression	June & Donnell Holeman	June Holeman
2006	Fred	Rare Fred	Ron Martin	Mary Burger
2007	Stitch	Sixth Vision	Randy & Brittany Pozzi	Brittany Pozzi
2008	Martha	Sugar Moon Express	Lindsay Sears	Lindsay Sears
2009	Fred	Rare Fred	Ron Martin	Mary Burger
2010	Jethro	Judge Buy Cash	Frank & Lynn Mays	Brenda Mays
2011	Stingray	MP Meter My Hay	Mel Potter & Sherry Cervi	Sherry Cervi
(tie)	Duke	Yeah Hes Firen	Brittany Pozzi	Brittany Pozzi
2012	Latte	Perculatin	Walker & Cogburn LLC	Mary Walker
2013	Baby Flo	Flo's Heiress	Dian Taylor	Fallon Taylor
2014	Cowboy	Wonders Cowboy Dan	H. Q. Bass	Kaley Bass
2015	Custer	French First Watch	Jill Welch	Jill Welch
2016	Tibbie	CFour Tibbie Stinson	Kelly & Ivy Conrado	Ivy Conrado
2017	Sister	Rafter W Minnie	Reba Sam Williams	Nellie Miller
2018	Sister	DM Sissy Hayday	Dan & Leslie Kinsel	Hailey Kinsel
2019	Valor	High Valor	Dona Kay Rule	Dona Kay Rule
2020	Valor	High Valor	Dona Kay Rule	Dona Kay Rule
2021	Rollo	Famous Lil Jet	Jordan & Justin Briggs	Jordan Briggs
2022	Rollo	Famous Lil Jet	Jordan & Justin Briggs	Jordan Briggs
2023	Pop Rocks	Flame Fire Rocks	Mission Ranch LLC	Taycie Matthews

Appendix 5
Barrel Racing World Records

Youngest NFR Qualifiers
Ann Lewis, age 10, 1968
Rachael Myllymaki, age 11, 1988
Jackie Jo Perrin, age 13, 1977
Fallon Taylor, age 13, 1995
Sherry Potter Cervi, age 14, 1988

Oldest NFR Qualifiers
Mary Burger, 68-years-old, 2016
Dona Kay Rule, 64-years old, 2022
June Holeman, 62-years-old, 2005
Martha Josey, 60-years-old, 1998
Vickie Carter, 60-years old, 2015
Linda Vick, 58-years-old, 2005
Mary Burger 58-years old, 2006
Mary Walker, 57-years old, 2016

Youngest World Champion
Ann Lewis, age 10, 1968*
LaTonne Sewalt, age 11, 1950
Jackie Jo Perrin, age 13, 1977
Charmayne James, age 14, 1984
(*Ann was killed, a car accident just prior to the 1968 NFR but maintained her lead, the world standings and was awarded the championship posthumously.)

Oldest World Champions
Mary Burger, age 69, 2016
Mary Burger, age 60, 2006
Mary Walker, age 53, 2012
Janet Stover, age 47, 2001
Kristie Peterson, age 43, 1998
Kappy Allen, age 42, 2000
Martha Josey, age 42, 1980

Highest Single-Year Earnings
$496,499 by Brittany Pozzi Tonnozzi, 2023
$350,700 by Hailey Kinsel, 2018
$349,076 by Hailey Kinsel, 2020
$323,570 by Lindsay Sears, 2008
$308,498 by Nellie Miller, 2017
$303,846 by Callie dePerier, 2015
$303,894 by Sherry Cervi, 2013

Most Money Won at the NFR
$270,615 by Hailey Kinsel, 2020
$225,935 by Brittany Pozzi Tonozzi, 2023
$20,096 by Lisa Lockhart, 2023
$189,385 by Hailey Kinsel, 2017
$188,791 by Kassie Mowery, 2023
$187,692 by Amberleigh Moore, 2016
$164,635 by Sherry Cervi, 2016
$157,864 by Hailey Kinsel, 2018

Placed in Ten Consecutive Rounds at NFR
Colette Graves Baier, 1974
Lynn McKenzie, 1978
Charmayne James, 1986
Kristie Peterson, 1996-97
Sherry Cervi, 2013

WPRA Career Earning Leaders
1. Lisa Lockhart, $3,518,066
2. Sherry Cervi, $3,380,095
3. Brittany Pozzi, $3,077,597
4. Hailey Kinsel, $2,032,213
5. Charmayne James, $1,842,506
6. Lindsay Sears, $1,576,606
7. Stevi Hillman, $1,357,754
8. Kristie Peterson, $1,346,861
9. Mary Walker, $1,144,561
10. Ivy Saebens, $1,121,467

Back to Back World Champions
Hailey Kinsel 2018-2020
Kelly Kaminski 2004-2005
Kristie Peterson 1996-1998
Charmayne James 1984-1993
Gail Petska 1972-1973
Jane Mayo 1959-1961
Billie McBride 1955-1958
Wanda Harper Bush 1952-1953

Appendix 6
Scoti Flit Bar Rising Star Award

The Rising Star Award, given in memory of Scoti Flit Bar, was created by past NFR qualifier, Lana Merrick, as a way of recognizing the year-long achievements of a horse that is making its first appearance at the National Finals Rodeo. This award is voted on by the top fifteen barrel racers prior to the National Finals. Clint Orms designs and handcrafts the trophy buckle.

Winners

- 2000 *Firewater Fiesta* / Kelly Yates
- 2001 *Elected Official* / Tami Fontenot
- 2002 *I Am Not Te* / Brandi Halls
- 2003 *Top Dally* / Darlene Kasper
- 2004 *Krimps Read To Go* / Paula Seay
- 2005 *Running Episode* / Linda Vick
- 2006 *Hempen Streak* / Terra Bynum
- 2007 *Gonna Be Famous* / Vickie Solmonsen
- 2008 *Rare Dillon* / Annesa Self
- 2009 *Frenchman's Jester* / Jordan Peterson
- 2010 *FR Firefly* / Kelli Tolbert
- 2011 *RC Black in Black* / Jane Melby
- 2012 *Dash Ta Vanila* / Nikki Steffes
- 2013 *Slick By Design* / Michelle McLeod
- 2014 *Sierra Hall of Fame* / Kassidy Dennison
- 2015 *Fame Fling and Bling* / Sarah Rose McDonald
- 2016 *Sadiefamouslastwords* / Mary Burger
- 2017 *DM Sissy Hayday* / Hailey Kinsel
- 2018 *Hell On The Red* / Kylie Weast
- 2019 *Ima Famous Babe* / Brittany Pozzi-Tonozzi
- 2020 *Chicks Keen O Pocopoo* / Brittany Barnett
- 2021 *Teasin Dat Guy* / Molly Otto
- 2022 *Famous Ladies Man* / Kassie Mowry
- 2023 *Apollo* / Summer Kosel

Appendix 7
ProRodeo Hall of Fame Inductees

1996
Gills Bay Boy "Scamper" (livestock)

2017
Charmayne James (barrel racing)
Wanda Harper Bush (barrel racing)
Star Plaudit "Red" (livestock)

2019
Jimme Munroe (barrel racing)
Sammy Thurman (barrel racing)
Florence Youree (notable)

2018
Billie McBride (barrel racing)
Krisitie Peterson & *Bozo* (barrel racing)

2020
Martha Josey (barrel racing)

2022
Ardith Bruce (barrel racing)
Cindy Rosser (notable)

2023
Sherry Combs Johnson (barrel racing)
Fay Ann Horton Leach (notable)

Appendix 8
Additional Barrel Racing Records

The youngest qualifier in WPRA history is Ann Lewis, who earned a spot in the NFR, but was tragically killed in an automobile accident prior to NFR. Her earnings held to make her the 1968 world champion in spite of not competing at the NFR.

Rachel Myllymaki is the youngest to compete in the NFR. She was just eleven-years-old at her first NFR in 1988.

Mary Burger holds the record for the oldest NFR qualifier. She was sixty-nine in 2016 and also won the world championship that year.

Lee Ann Rust holds the title of the oldest Rookie. She was fifty-three when she earned the title in 2011. She qualified for the Wrangler NFR the following year.

Circuit Titles

Kristie Peterson and *Bozo* are the undisputed champions at the Ram National Circuit Finals Rodeo (RNCFR) with four titles (1992, 1994-'95 & 1998). Only Charmayne James, Brittany Pozzi-Tonozzi and Rachel Myllymaki have earned more than one.

On the individual circuit level, Kristie Peterson also holds the record with eleven titles, all won while competing in the Mountain States Circuit. Lisa Lockhart is right behind her with ten circuit titles, nine earned in the Badlands and one in Montana, making her one of just three ladies to earn circuit championships in more than one circuit. (Pozzi-Tonozzi has won titles in Texas and Mountain States circuits, while James earned titles in both California and Turquoise circuits.

Rachel Myllymaki, Sherry Cervi and Twila Haller come next on the list of circuit titles with nine apiece.

Placing at the National Finals Rodeo

Five cowgirls share the record for placing in ten consecutive go-rounds at the NFR: Colette Baier (1974), Lynn McKenzie (1978), Charmayne James (1986), Kristie Peterson (1996-1997) and Sherry Cervi (2013).

In earlier years when the National Finals held fewer rounds several girls placed in all the available rounds for those years. Jane Mayo placed in ten straight rounds over two years of the Finals, winning the average outright in 1959 and sharing the title with Sammy Thurman in 1960. Likewise, Thurman placed in twelve straight rounds in 1960 and '61. Sissy Thurman repeated the feat in 1962, earning seven checks in seven go-rounds, and Pat Marr matched that in 1965.

The WPRA launched its youth development programs in 2006 and 2007 — the futurity/derby recognizes young horses while the WPRA juniors offers titles to human competitors under the age of seventeen.

Two WPRA juniors have won more than one title. Kylar Terlip claimed her second championship in 2013, two years after earning the first title. In 2016-17 Laney Robinson became the first junior to win back-to-back Junior World Championships.

Two former WPRA junior world champions have gone on to compete at the Wrangler NFR, Callie dePerrier and Jackie Ganter. Ganter won the junior title in 2014 and competed at the 2015 and 2016 Wrangler NFRs. DuPerrier won the WPRA junior world title in 2010 and won the WPRA world championship in her only Wrangler NFR appearance to date in 2015.

Appendix 9
College Barrel Racing National Champions

Year	Champion	University or College
1955	Kathlyn Younger Knox	McNeese State
1956	Kathlyn Younger Knox	Colorado A&M
1957	Betty Sims Solt	New Mexico A&M
1958	Betty Sims Solt	New Mexico A&M
1959	Mike Reid Settles	West Texas State
1960	Mike Reid Settles	West Texas State
1961	Mike Reid Settles	West Texas State
1962	Lorraine Taylor	Northern Montana College
1963	Linda Kinkaid	New Mexico State University
1964	Carlee Obervy	South Dakota State University
1965	Becky Berggren	Sam Houston State University
1966	Cleonne Skinner Steinmiller	Colorado State University
1967	Barbara Baer	Cal Poly-SLO
1968	Donna Kinkaid	Eastern New Mexico University
1969	Barbara Baer	Cal Poly-SLO
1970	Connie Wilkinson Wood	Tarleton State University
1971	Martha Tompkins	Tarleton State University
1972	Becky Fullerton	Blue Mtn Community College
1973	Colette Graves Baier	Fort Hays State University
1974	Jimmie Gibbs Munroe	Sam Houston State
1975	Jimmie Gibbs Munroe	Sam Houston State
1976	Chris A. Helker	Eastern New Mexico University
1977	Joann Whitehead	Western Texas College
1978	Julie Doering	Oregon State University
1979	Bana J. Perry	SW Oklahoma State University
1980	Lori McNeil	Utah State University
1981	Kendra Bennett	Labette Community College
1982	Lori McNeil	Utah State University
1983	Tammy King Engle	New Mexico State University
1984	Lynn McCafferty	Sam Houston State University
1985	Lisa Scheffer	University of Montana
1986	Dana Lynn McCafferty	Sam Houston State University
1987	Holly Foster	McNeese State University
1988	Cathy Cagliari	West Hills College
1989	Holly Foster	Cal Poly-SLO
1990	Elisa Nielsen	Utah Valley Community College
1991	Annesa Musil	SW Oklahoma State University
1992	Mindy Morris	Texas A&M University
1993	Marilee McGraw	Garden City Community College
1994	Shane Hooks	McNeese State University
1995	Molly Swanson Powell	Vernon College
1996	Caryn Standifer Snyder	SE Oklahoma State University
1997	Rachel Myllmaki Sproul	University of Montana

College Barrel Racing National Champions ... Continued

Year	Champion	University or College
1998	Tona Wright	Western Texas College
1999	Jennifer Smith	Tarleton State University
2000	Amanda Marrett	Texas A&M University
2001	Janae Ward	Oklahoma State University
2002	McKenzie Miller	Ricks College
2003	Jessica Mueller	National American University
2004	Josie Busk	Salt Lake Community College
2005	Natalie Tatone	University of Nevada@Las Vegas
2006	Adriane M. Kochie	University of Wisconsin
2007	Alicia Sandoval	New Mexico Junior College
2008	Bailey Gow	New Mexico State University
2009	Rachel Tiedeman	South Dakota State University
2010	Sydni Blanchard	Mesalands Community College
2011	Elizabeth Combs	Sam Houston State University
2012	Elizabeth Combs	Sam Houston State University
2013	Timmi Ward	College of Southern Idaho
2014	Taylor Engesser	Gillette College
2015	Callahan Crossley	Blue Mountain Community College
2016	Kristi Steffes	Black Hills State University
2017	Hailey Kinsel	Texas A&M University
2018	Kynzie McNeill	Texas Tech University
2019	Ashlyn Carlson	College of Southern Idaho
2020	No champion – cancelled due to covid	
2021	Taylor Moeykens	Montana State University
2022	Sadie Wolaver	SW Oklahoma State University
2023	Taycie Matthews	University of West Alabama

Appendix 10
Girls Rodeo Association (GRA)
First Officers/Directors & Founding Members – 1948

Margaret Owens Montgomery – President
Dude Barton – Vice President
Mrs. Katherine Pearson – Secretary-Treasurer
Sug Owens Bloxom – Publicity Agent
Jackie Worthington – Bareback Riding Director
Marlene Harlan – Bull Riding Director
Betty Barron Dusek – Calf Roping Director
Vivian White – Saddle Bronc Director
Blanche Altizer Smith – Team Tying/Cow Milking Director
Fern Sawyer – Cutting Horse Director
Helen Barron Green – Flag Race/Barrel Race/Line Reining Director
Dixie Reger – Contract Representative

Additional Founding Members

Bebe Green, Mary Green, Ann Young
Mrs. Ted Powers, Mrs. Curtis Barron, Izora Young
June Probst, Virginia Probst, Nancy Bragg
Nancy Binford, Thena Mae Farr, Mrs. Allen
Sissy Allen, Mitzi Lucas Riley, Tad Lucas
Ora Altizer Grigg, Sally Taylor, Sally Hardin
Manuelita Mitchell, Fay Ann Horton, Doris Reed
Mary Ellen Sellers, Josephine Willis, Jesse Myers
Iris Dorsett, Frances Gist, Frances Wegg

February 28, 1948 the Association started with a group of Texas ranch women who wanted to add a little color and femininity to the rough-and-tumble sport of rodeo. A major move at the time, 38 women met in a hotel in San Angelo, Texas, to change the way they were being treated in the male-dominated world of rodeo. These women banded together to create the very first professional sports association created solely for women by women – the Girls Rodeo Association (GRA).

May 1948 the rules and regulations were drafted and approved, and a point system was enacted to crown world champions. GRA board members went to work, persuading rodeo committees and producers to hold women's contests according to GRA rules. Committees were given the option of choosing which event they would hold (bronc riding, cutting or barrel racing), and most picked barrel racing. In its inaugural year, the GRA had 74 members and they held 60 events with a total payout of $29,000.

Appendix 11
Girls Rodeo Association
Women's Professional Rodeo Association Presidents

Year	Name
1948-1949	Margaret Owens
1950	Nancy Binford
1951	Thena Mae Farr
1952-1953	Billye Burk Gamblin
1954-1956	Jackie Worthington
1957-1959	Billie McBride
1960-1964	Florence Youree
1965-1971	Mildred Farris
1972-1974	Margaret Clemons
1975	Sammie Fancher Thurman
1976	Kay Vamvoras
1977-1993	Jimmie Gibbs Munroe
1994-1995	Carol Lake
1996	Carolynn Vietor (acting)
1997-2002	Carolynn Vietor
2003-2004	Patti Davis
2005-2009	Jymmy Kay Davis
2009-2010	Kathi Myers
2011-2012	Jimmie Munroe
2013-2015	Carolynn Vietor
2016-2021	Doreen Wintermute
2021-2024	Jimmie Munroe

Thanks To The Following People
For Their Help In Putting This History Together

There is never a book, especially a history book, which is written without the help of many people. As an author, I have come to realize that if anyone thinks they can write a history book by themselves, it is because they have never tried. This book has been a challenge, and yet the more challenging it is, the more an author comes to enjoy it. You never know where your sources can be found until you get totally involved in the history.

My Thanks Goes To These People

First, I thank my husband, Cliff, who has supported me through all of my many hours on the phone, being away from home or in front of my computer, or when I had my head in a book or a musty old magazine searching for information to include that I felt was important to tell this story and he has also provided so much editorial input.

Next were all the cowgirls and cowboys that I have bothered and questioned and phoned, sometimes more than once: Jimmie Gibbs Munroe, Ann Bleiker, Linda Clark, Lydia Moore, Donna Clark, Peggy Robinson, Ardith Bruce, Billie McBride, Dude Barton, Dixie Reger Mosley, Teresa Burleson of the North Fort Worth Historical Society & Museum, Kelly Riley, Sammy Thurman Brackenbury, Kay Blandford, Siri Stevens, Steve Corey, Darin Chick, Sharon Camarillo, Jerri Duce, Wani Ellis, Shirley Edge, Mary Jo Franks, John Farris, Sherry Johnson, Florence Youree, Martha Josey, Liz Kesler, Gail Gandolfi, Kay Gay, Nelda Patton, Marguerite Happy, Betsy Harris, Irene Harris, Billy Huckaby, Tina Hodge, Billy Jordan, Brenda Michaels, Louise Knoefel, Lisa Michelle, Marlene McRae, Sylvia Mahoney, Jean McJunkin Livingston, Molly Swanson Powell, Kent Sturman & Megan Wintersfeldt from the ProRodeo Hall of Fame & Museum of the American Cowboy, Sherry Cervi, Barbara Smith, Chuck Cummings, Mary Cecelia Tharp, Lynn Stokes, Rollie Gibbs, Carolynn Vietor, Pat Tackett, Peggy Walker of the West of Pecos Rodeo Committee, Jim Bainbridge – Media PRCA, Ruth Quinn, Bobby Steiner, Joleen Steiner, Jon Mattson, Jack Shaw- Pendleton RoundUp Director, Mildred Farris, Dr. Charles "Bud" Townsend, Charlene Jespersen, Rhonda

Sedgewick Stearns, Jan Tackett, Kay Blandford, Martha Tompkins Wright, Steve Mellon, Luci Wedeking of the Cowboy Country Museum, Jan Youren, Doreen Wintermute, Connie & Gary Sandstead.

And the photographers and individuals which have let me use their photos to improve the history ten-fold: Ferrell Butler, Kenneth Springer, Siri Stevens, Craig and Gordon Cathey, Dan Hubbell, The Potter family, Kera Newby, Karen Spilman and Kimberly Roblin of the Dickinson Research Center at the National Cowboy and Western Heritage Museum. Plus all those I have forgotten to mention in my years of putting this book together.

Thanks to everyone, regardless of how large or small your input was, for all your help. It's been a great ride!

Endnotes

Chapter One
1. *50 Years A Living Legend – Texas Cowboy Reunion and Old Timers Association* by Hooper Shelton, 1979, published by Hooper Shelton in collaboration with the Texas Cowboy Reunion Old Timers Association.
2. *Ibid.*
3. *Ibid.*
4. *Fort Worth Star Telegram*, 3-16-1935

Chapter Two
1. Madison Square Garden Rodeo Program 1939.
2. Phone call with Jimmie Gibbs Munroe re: WPRA drug testing, sponsors.
3. *The Cowboy's Turtle Association, The Birth of Professional Rodeo*, by Gail Hughbanks Woerner, published in 2011 by Wild Horse Press.
4. *Ibid.*
5. Madison Square Garden Rodeo Program 1940.
6. *Ibid.*
7. *Ibid.*
8. *Cowgirls of the Rodeo* by Mary Lou LeCompte, 1993, University of Illinois Press.

Chapter Three
1. Encyclopedia of Women in the American West, published 2003 by Sage by Gordon Moris & Brenda Farrington, Section on All Girl Rodeos, page 4 through 10, by Renee M. Laegreid.
2. *Cowgirls of the Rodeo* by Mary Lou LeCompte, 1993 University of Illinois Press.
3. Fay Kirkwood Presents World's Only All Girl Rodeo Program, Wichita Falls, TX, 1942.
4. *Cowgirls of the Rodeo* by Mary Lou LeCompte, 1993 University of Illinois Press.
5. 50th Anniversary West of The Pecos Rodeo Program.
6. email: Needleworks, Peggy Walker, West of the Pecos Rodeo Committee member, 2011.
7. 50th Anniversary West of The Pecos Rodeo Program.
8. Letter from Nelda Patton, April 2016.
9. Information on Frances Crane Smith from Dickinson Research Center, Rodeo Historical Society, National Cowboy & Western Heritage Museum.
10. Phone conversation with Dr. Charles 'Bud' Townsend, 2-25-2019.
11. Phone conversation with Barbara Smith re: Fort Worth and first barrel race there, plus Celie Whitcomb Ray.
12. *Hoofs and Horns*, April 1952, "Wilma Standard" by Stew Bean.
13. *Cowgirls of the Rodeo* by Mary Lou LeCompte, 1993 University of Illinois Press.

14. Fay Kirkwood Presents World's Only All Girl Rodeo Program, Wichita Falls, TX, 1942.

Chapter Four
1. *WPRA News*, August 2018 "The Fight for Equal Money in the Barrel Racing, Part I.
2. WPRA DVD 1948 – 2008, *Sixty Years*.
3. The Girls Rodeo Association, 1949 Articles of Association, By-Laws & Rules.
4. *Cowgirls of the Rodeo* by Mary Lou LeCompte, 1993 University of Illinois Press
5. TriState All-Girl Rodeo Prize List, 1948.
6. WPRA 2005 Media Guide.
7. *Ibid.*
8. *Ibid.*

Chapter Five
1. *Fifty Years of Nebraska's Big Rodeo*, by Board of Directors, Burwell Rodeo, published by Rodeo Book Co., Burwell, 1975.
2. Phone conversation with Pat Tackett, Sidney, Iowa, 3-7-2016.
3. *Powder Puff & Spurs* magazine, Feb. 1950 issue.
4. *Ibid.*
5. Information on Frances Crane Smith from Dickinson Research Center, Rodeo Historical Society, National Cowboy & Western Heritage Museum.
6. *Powder Puff & Spurs* magazine, Feb. 1950 issue.
7. *Powder Puff & Spurs* magazine, March 1950 issue.
8. *Powder Puff & Spurs* magazine, April 1950 issue.
9. *Western Horseman* magazine, August 1950, page 10, Picked Up In The Rodeo Arena – by Jerry Armstrong.
10. *Ibid.*
11. *Powder Puff & Spurs* magazine, June 1950 issue.
12. *Powder Puff & Spurs* magazine, January 1951 issue.
13. *Powder Puff & Spurs* magazine, July 1950 issue.
14. *Powder Puff & Spurs* magazine, January 1951 issue.
15. *Powder Puff & Spurs* magazine, May 1950 issue.
16. *Pikes Peak or Bust Rodeo: The First Fifty Years*, edited by Steve Fleming and Judi Lakin, published 1990 by the ProRodeo Hall of Fame and Museum of the American Cowboy.
17. Conversations with Faye Blackstone many years ago.
18. Letter and articles from on Mattson from Days of '76 Museum, 11-6-2017.
19. Telephone conversation with John Korrey 2-7-2019 re: Logan County Fair.
20. *Cowgirls of the Rodeo* by Mary Lou LeCompte, 1993 University of Illinois Press.

Chapter Six
1. *Hoofs and Horns*, Dec. 1948 "All-Girl Rodeo – October, Amarillo, TX."
2. *Back in the Saddle* magazine, "LaTonne Sewalt – World's Youngest

Champion Cowgirl" by James Cathey, Dec. 1950.
3. *Powder Puff & Spurs* magazine, November 1950.
4. *Hoofs and Horns*, Jan. 1951, GRA Column, re: 1950 Champs.
5. *Rodeo History & Records* by Foghorn Clancy, 1952 Edition. "All-Girl Rodeo Finals of 1951."
6. *Powder Puff & Spurs* magazine, May/June 1951 issue.
7. *This Month in San Antonio,* "San Antonio Sports . . . Parade" by Harold Scherwitz.
8. *Powder Puff & Spurs* magazine, July1951 issue.
9. *Ibid.*
10. *Powder Puff & Spurs* magazine, Sept/Oct. 1951 issue.
11. *Rodeo History & Records,* by Foghorn Clancy, 1953 Edition, "All-Girls Finals of 1952"
12. *Rodeo 100 – Looking Back* compiled by Dr. Bruce Claussen in a souvenir progam for the 100th Anniversary of the North Platte, NE, 1982 Rodeo.
13. *Hoofs and Horns*, April & May 1953, GRA column.
14. "Women's Pro Rodeo Association, 69 Years of Women in Rodeo" listed in Pro Rodeo Hall of Fame & Museum of the American Cowboy, Colorado Springs, CO.
15. Phone call to Barbara Smith re: TLBA 10-7-19.
16. *Ibid.*
17. *Fifty Years at the San Angelo Stock Show & Rodeo* published by San Angelo Stock Show & Rodeo Foundation, 1982. Printed by The Talley Press, San Angelo.
18. *World's Oldest Rodeo* by Danny Freeman, 1988, published by Prescott Frontier Days, Inc.
19. *The Silver State Stampede 100 Years of Rodeo History in Elko* by Jan Peterson and Susan Abel. 2012 published by Silver State Stampede Committee.

Chapter Seven
1. "Women of the West – Jan Youren" by Jennifer Zehnder, WesternHorseman.com, 6-4-2019.
2. *College Rodeo, From Show to Sport* by Sylvia Gann Mahoney, published 2004 by Texas A & M Press.
3. *Ibid.*
4. *Ibid.*
5. *Back When They Bucked* with Betty Sims Solt, 6-15-2017.
6. *Hoofs and Horns*, Dec. 1967 'Racing through College' by Jim Hurley.
7. *College Rodeo, From Show to Sport* by Sylvia Gann Mahoney, published 2004 by Texas A & M Press.
8. Phone call to Liz Kesler re: Martha Tompkins at NIRA Finals.
9. Information sent from Sylvia Mahoney, author of "College Rodeo" book.
10. *Ibid.*

Chapter Eight
1. *Hoofs and Horns* magazine, July 1952, GRA News, Barrel Race at Killeen, TX
2. *Hoofs and Horns* magazine, August 1952, GRA News, Cloverleaf pattern,
3. *Hoofs and Horns* magazine, October 1952, GRA News

4. *Hoofs and Horns* magazine, GRA column 1953.
5. *Rodeo 100 – Looking Back* compiled by Dr. Bruce Claussen in a souvenir program for the 100th Anniversary of the North Platte, NE, 1982 Rodeo.
6. *Hoofs and Horns* magazine, February 1954.
7. Conversation with Jan Youren.
8. *1956 Rodeo Sports News Annual*, "The Girls Rodeo Association" by B. Kalland — distributed by the Rodeo Information Commission Inc. News Bureau, Kansas City, MO.

Chapter Nine
1. *Cowgirls of the Rodeo* by Mary Lou LeCompte, 1993 University of Illinois Press.
2. *The Billboard* magazine, 9-11-1954 issue, article "Bally Drums Roll For Shorter New York Rodeo"
3. *The Billboard*, 9-10-1955 issue, article "Rodeo Talent Repeats for New York Garden Run."
4. *A Hundred Years of Heroes, A History of the Southwestern Exposition & Livestock Show,* by Clay Reynolds, 1995 published by Texas Christian University Press
5. *Ibid.*
6. Telephone conversations with Gene McJunkin Livingston, 4-3-2019.
7. Notes given to author by Clay Reynolds, author of *A Hundred Years of Heroes, A History of the Southwestern Exposition and Livestock Show.*
8. Telephone conversations with Gene McJunkin Livingston, 4-3-2019.
9. Shanna Weaver, Publicity Manager, Southwest Exposition & Livestock Show, via Teresa Burleson.
10. *WPRA News*, July 2018, "Evolution of Professionalism."

Chapter Ten
1. Canadian Barrel Racers in CPRA Hall of Fame, via email from Ruth Quinn.
2. "50th Anniversary, 2007, Canadian Girls Rodeo Association. Women in Professional Rodeo booklet.
3. Canadian Barrel Racers in CPRA Hall of Fame, via email from Ruth Quinn.
4. Information send by Ruth Quinn re: Canadian Barrel Racing, Feb, 2019 to Include CGRA 60th Anniversary Program.
5. *Ibid.*
6. *Ibid.*
7. *Ibid.*
8. "50th Anniversary, 2007, Canadian Girls Rodeo Association. Women in Professional Rodeo booklet.
9. Information send by Ruth Quinn re: Canadian Barrel Racing, Feb, 2019 to include CGRA 60th Anniversary Program.
10. Emails from Ruth Quinn, Canada Finals, 5-20-2019.
11. *Ibid.*
12. Phone call to Lisa Lockhart, 8-24-2019.
13. Emails from Ruth Quinn, Canada Finals, 5-20-2019.
14. *Ibid.*

15. *WPRA News*, Online, January 2021 Article on Hailey Kinsel.

Chapter Eleven
1. "Sage Hens & Cow Ponies" and more, *Hoofs & Horns*, April 1960.
2. *Ibid.*
3. *Hoofs and Horns*, Jan. 1960, 'Sage Hens & Cow Ponies' by Sue Ann Hubbard.
4. *Reno Rodeo: A History - The First 80 Years* by Guy Clifton, 2000, published by the Reno Rodeo Foundation.
5. *World's Oldest Rodeo* by Danny Freeman, 1988, published by Prescott Frontier Days, Inc.
6. *Hoofs and Horns*, Jan. 1960 issue.
7. Information from Lydia Moore, former WPRA Secretary from 1973 to 1995, and daughter, Linda Clark.
8. *Hoofs and Horns*, Jan. 1960, 'Sage Hens & Cow Ponies' by Sue Ann Hubbard.
9. Information from Lydia Moore, former WPRA Secretary from 1973 to 1995, and daughter, Linda Clark.
10. *Hoofs and Horns*, March 1960.
11. *Hoofs and Horns*, Jan. 1960, 'Sage Hens & Cow Ponies' by Sue Ann Hubbard.
12. Interview with John & Mildred Farris for Rodeo Historical Society, Dickinson Research Center, National Cowboy & Western Heritage Museum, 10-2010.
13. Rodeo Cowboys Association 1960 Articles of Association, By-Laws & Rules.
14. *Hoofs and Horns*, Jan. 1960 issue.
15. *Hoofs and Horns*, Feb. 1962.
16. *Hoofs and Horns*, May 1962 "Sage Hens" column.
17. GRA column, *The Quarter Horse Journal*, Dec. 1963.
18. Conversation with Sherry Combs..
19. *Cowtown Rodeo, Images of America* book by Angela Speakman, published by Arcadia Publishing.
20. *Hoofs and Horns*, June 1968 "The Clinic for Barrel Racing" by Robert Freedheim.
21. *Hoofs and Horns*, August 1968.
22. *Hoofs and Horns*, Sept. 1968.
23. "Oklahoma–Land of the Barrel Racers", by Al Long, *Hoofs and Horns*, Mar-April 1973.

Chapter Twelve
1. *The Finals, A Complete History of the First 50 Years of The Wrangler National Finals, 1959 – 2008.* published by the Professional Rodeo Cowboys Association.
2. *Ibid.*
3. *Ibid.*
4. *Ibid.*
5. Oral History Interview for Rodeo Historical Society with Florence Youree, 8-24-2009.

6. "Women's Pro Rodeo Association, 69 Years of Women in Rodeo" listed in Pro Rodeo Hall of Fame & Museum of the American Cowboy, Colorado Springs, Colo.
7. Information from Lydia Moore, former WPRA Secretary from 1973 to 1995, and daughter, Linda Clark.

Chapter Thirteen
1. *Hoofs and Horns*, Jan. 1969 'One Girl Style Show.'
2. "What Are They Wearing – Barrel Racing Styles", by Robert Freedheim, *Hoofs & Horns*, Nov. 1970.
3. Conversation with Judie Fields.
4. Conversation with Loretta Manual Shuler, 2-2021.
5. Interview with Joleen Hurst Steiner, July 2018.
6. *The Western Horseman*, April 1972, "Barrel Racing at the National Finals Rodeo" by Ray Davis.
7. Email from Jim Bainbridge, PRCA Media, re: Gail Petska.
8. *WPRA News*, Jan. 2018 issue.
9. Telephone call with Mel Potter, 8-7-2019.
10. Jimmie Gibbs Munroe, Oral History, Rodeo Historical Society, Dickinson Research Center, National Cowboy & Western Heritage Museum.
11. Conversation with Bobby Steiner, 9-18-2018.
12. Conversation with John Farris, 9-18-2018.
13. Phone conversation with Ardith Bruce, 1-28-2019.
14. *WPRA News*, July 2018 "Evolution of Professionalism."
15. Phone conversations with Jimmie Gibbs Munroe re: electric timers, equal money.
16. *WPRA News*, July 2018 Evolution of Professionalism."
17. "Women's Pro Rodeo Association, 69 Years of Women in Rodeo" listed in Pro Rodeo Hall of Fame & Museum of the American Cowboy, Colorado Springs, Colo.
18. 1975 Phoenix Jaycees Rodeo of Rodeos Program.
19. "The Finals, A Complete History of the First 50 Years of The Wrangler National Finals, 1959 – 2008. published by the Professional Rodeo Cowboys Association.
20. WPRA 2017 Barrel Racing Records.
21. *WPRA News*, July 2018 "Evolution of Professionalism."
22. Information from Lydia Moore, former WPRA Secretary from 1973 to 1995, and daughter, Linda Clark.

Chapter Fourteen
1. Jimmie Gibbs Munroe, Oral History, Rodeo Historical Society, Dickinson Research Center, National Cowboy & Western Heritage Museum.
2. *WPRA News*, April 2018 "Impact of Barrel Racing Bloodlines."
3. *Ibid*.
4. *Hoof and Horns*, March 1960, article "Jane Mayo, in an Exclusive Interview discussing *V's Sandy*."
5. *Hoofs and Horns*, June, July, Aug. & Oct. 1969,'articles by Jimmie Hurley.
6. *Ibid*.
7. *Ibid*.

8. *Ibid.*
9. "Sammy Thurman Describes the Ideal Barrel Horse", by Jimmie Hurley, *Western Horseman,* January 1972.
10. "Ride to the Top'" by Sharon Camarillo and Donna Irwin, in *Rodeo News* 7-1-2018.
11. Oral History Interview, Rodeo Historical Society, with Amberley Snyder 10-1-16
12. "The Secrets of Celie" by Amber Arnold, barrelhorseworld.com.
13. Youree Ranch Barrel Horse Training – online.

Chapter Fifteen
1. Interview with Joleen Hurst Steiner, July 2018.
2. *WPRA News,* July 2018 "Evolution of Professionalism."
3. Conversatiuon with Rollie Gibbs.
4. *WPRA News,* Jan. 2018 Results of 2017 NFR, Best Footing Award.
5. Telephone visit with Louise Knoefel re: Abbeyville, Kansas Frontier Days Rodeo.
6. Abbeyville Rodeo Advertising – online.
7. *Hoofs and Horns,* Oct 1969, 'Sammy Thurman 'How to Handle Problem Grounds' by Jimmie Hurley
8. *WPRA News,* July 2018 "Evolution of Professionalism."
9. Conversation with Mel Clark re: dirt.

Chapter Sixteen
1. Information from Lydia Moore, former WPRA Secretary from 1973 to 1995, and daughter, Linda Clark.
2. *The Ketch Pen,* Sept. 1985, Volume One Number Two 'Florence Youree' page 9.
3. "Women's Pro Rodeo Association, 69 Years of Women in Rodeo" listed in Pro Rodeo Hall of Fame & Museum of the American Cowboy, Colorado Springs, Colo.
4. *The Wild Bunch,* Volume Ten Number Two Dec. 1988
5. "Women's Pro Rodeo Association, 69 Years of Women in Rodeo" listed in Pro Rodeo Hall of Fame & Museum of the American Cowboy, Colorado Springs, Colo.

Chapter Seventeen
1. *WPRA News,* Aug. 2018 "The Fight for Equal Money in the Barrel Racing, Part I.
2. Phone conversations with Jimmie Gibbs Munroe re: electric timers, equal money.
3. Jimmie Gibbs Munroe, Oral History, Rodeo Historical Society, Dickinson Research Center, National Cowboy & Western Heritage Museum.
4. *WPRA News,* Aug. 2018 "The Fight for Equal Money in the Barrel Racing, Part I.
5. "Women's Pro Rodeo Association, 69 Years of Women in Rodeo" listed in Pro Rodeo Hall of Fame & Museum of the American Cowboy, Colorado Springs, Colo.
6. *WPRA News,* Aug. 2018 "The Fight for Equal Money in the Barrel Racing,

Part I.
7. Phone conversations with Jimmie Gibbs Munroe re: electric timers, equal money.
8. *WPRA News*, Aug. 2018 "The Fight for Equal Money in the Barrel Racing, Part I.
9. *The Ketch Pen*, Volume 1 Number Three Dec. 1985
10. Phone conversations with Jimmie Gibbs Munroe re: electric timers, equal money.
11. *WPRA News*, Sept. 2019, "The Fight for Equal Money in the Barrel Racing, Part II.
12. *Ibid.*
13. Phone call with Jimmie Gibbs Munroe re: WPRA drug testing, sponsors.
14. Papers and letters re: drug testing, equal money, sponsors from Jimmie Munroe.
15. *Ibid.*

Chapter Eighteen
1. Phone conversation with Ardith Bruce, 1-28-2019.
2. Phone conversation with Sherry Johnson, 5-23-2019 re: sponsors.
3. Phone call with Jimmie Gibbs Munroe re: WPRA drug testing, sponsors.
4. Papers and letters re: drug testing, equal money, sponsors from Jimmie Munroe.
5. *The Fence Post* "June Holeman – A Rodeo Inspiration," 5-10-2010.
6. Phone conversation with Carolynn Vietor, 5-2019.
7. Phone conversation with Sherry Cervi Petska, 5-22-2019.
8. *WPRA News*, July 15, 2019, Sponsor Spotlight, page 20 & 21.

Chapter Nineteen
1. *The Finals, A Complete History of the First 50 Years of The Wrangler National Finals, 1959 – 2008.* published by the Professional Rodeo Cowboys Association.
2. Phone conversation with Mary Cecelia Tharp, Celie Ray's daughter, 3-4-2019.Phone call with Jimmie Gibbs Munroe re: WPRA drug testing, sponsors.
3. 1995 NFR Program, page 94, Sherry Potter-Cervi, Back #1
4. "Women's Pro Rodeo Association, 69 Years of Women in Rodeo" listed in Pro Rodeo Hall of Fame & Museum of the American Cowboy, Colorado Springs, Colo.
5. 1998 NFR Program, page 12, Steve Hatchell, Commissioner, letter to Fans & Contestants.
6. 1998 NFR Program, Breakdown of the total dollars for the Finals.
7. *WPRA News*, Jan. 2018 Results of 2017 NFR, Saddle Rotation Program
8. *The Finals, A Complete History of the First 50 Years of The Wrangler National Finals, 1959 – 2008.* published by the Professional Rodeo Cowboys Association.

Chapter Twenty
1. *The Finals, A Complete History of the First 50 Years of The Wrangler National Finals, 1959 – 2008.* published by the Professional Rodeo Cowboys

Association.
2. *Pendleton RoundUp at 100, Oregon's Legendary Rodeo* by Michael Bales and Ann Terry Hill, published by East Oregonian Publishing Co, 2010.
3. *Let 'er Buck, The History of Pendleton Round-Up* by Virgil Rupp published in 1985.
4. Phone conversation with Steve Corey re: 2000 Barrel Racing at Round-Up.
5. Telephone conversation with Jack Shaw, Pendleton Round-Up director, 10-29-18.
6. *Ibid.*
7. *WPRA News*, Oct. 2018.
8. *The Finals, A Complete History of the First 50 Years of The Wrangler National Finals, 1959-2008*. Published by the Professional Rodeo Cowboys Association.
9. *Ibid.*
10. *Ibid.*
11. WPRA 2005 Media Book, article "Professional Barrel Racing" by Julia Wells.
12. WPRA 2017 Barrel Racing Records.
13. Information from PRCA & WPRA members active at the time of 2007 PRWA event, including Jimmie Munroe.
14. *The Finals, A Complete History of the First 50 Years of The Wrangler National Finals, 1959 – 2008.* published by the Professional Rodeo Cowboys Association.
15. Information from PRCA & WPRA members active at the time of 2007 PRWA event, including Jimmie Munroe.
16. *The Fence Post* "June Holeman – A Rodeo Inspiration," 5-10-2010.
17. Emails from Ruth Quinn, Canada Finals, 5-20-2019.
18. WPRA 2017 Barrel Racing Records.
19. *Rodeo News*, March 2015, "On the Trail with Fallon Taylor."
20. WPRA 2017 Barrel Racing Records.
21. *Ibid.*
22. *WPRA News*, Jan. 2018 Results of 2017 NFR.
23. *Ibid.*
24. "Resistol Rookie Taci Bettis", *Rodeo News*, 4-2018.
25. "Unexpected Win, Lisa Lockhart", *WPRA News*, May 2019.

Chapter Twenty-One
1. *The Quarter Horse Journal*, Oct. 1959, column "Girls Rodeo Association Highlights" by Billie McBride.
2. *GRA News*, Nov. 1968 "Collision Deaths Shock GRA."
3. GRA News, June 1969, "From the Editor's Desk . . . "
4. *San Antonio Express News*, May 27, 2002, "Two Texas Rodeo Women Killed In Oklahoma Bridge Collapse"
5. *The Finals, A Complete History of the First 50 Years of The Wrangler National Finals, 1959 – 2008*, published by the Professional Rodeo Cowboys Association.
6. Material from Tina Hodge, 4-5-2019.

7. *Hoofs and Horns*, March-April, 1973 "No Time For Braille."
8. Phone call to Nellie Miller, 9-9-19.
9. Phone conversation with Wanie Ellis, Tina Ellis' mother.
10. "Tina Ellis, A Tiger to Remember" by Chuck Kelly, *The Belton Journal*, 7-23-2009.

Chapter Twenty-Two
1. *PRCA Sports News*, 4-14-2017 "Inductees to the Hall of Fame."
2. *WPRA Magazine*, June 2018, "McBride Among 2018 ProRodeo Hall of Fame Inductees."
3. *WPRA Magazine*, Sept. 2018 "McBride, Peterson & Bozo Join the ProRodeo Hall of Fame."
4. *ProRodeo Sports News*, August 2019.
5. *WPRA News*, July 2018, "Evolution of Professionalism."

Chapter Twenty-Three
1. Phone conversation with Jacqueline McEntire 9-23-19.
2. Information from Mary Jo Franks, 5-18-2019.
3. Conversations with Lynn Stokes, 5-18-2019.
4. *Rodeo News*, Sept. 2019, "Back When They Bucked."
5. *Rodeo News*, Sept., 2019, "Back When They Bucked."
6. "World Champion Barrel Racer, Mickey Brown", *Rodeo News*, 10-2017.

Chapter Twenty-Four
1. 2018 Wrangler National Finals Rodeo Program.
2. *WPRA News*, Jan. 2019 issue.
3. *Ibid*.
4. *Rodeo News*, Profile: Jessica Routier, Feb. 2019.
5. Phone call to Florence Youree, 8-26-19.

Chapter Twenty-Five
1. WPRA-PRCA Agreement Report – Revision 11-30-19.

Chapter Twenty-Six
1. *Barrel Horse News*, "Hailey Kinsel Clinches 3rd WPRA World Champion – Online: 12-13-2020.
2. *WPRA News*, Online, Jan. 2021 article on Hailey Kinsel.
3. *Barrel Horse News*, Aug. 2019, "Between the Reins With Hell on The Red," by Blanche Schaefer.
4. Ann Bleiker, WPRA.
5. *Ibid*.

Some Outstanding Barrel Horses to Remember
1. Phone call to Lisa Lockhart, 8-24-2019.
2. "The Impact of Tiny Watch" by Jennifer Zehnder in barrelhorsenews.com.
3. Oklahoma Quarter Horse Association article on *Bugs Alive in 75*.
4. "Martha Josey and Cebe Reed," by Breanne Hill, *Barrel Horse News*, July, 2010.
5. WPRA Story "An Unforgettable Story of a Girl and Her Horse." Jill

Welsh's 'Custer' Named AQHA Horse of the Year.
6. *WPRA News*, January 2019 issue.
7. "The Impact of Tiny Watch" by Jennifer Zehnder in barrelhorsenews.com.
8. Phone conversation with Sherry Cervi Petska, 5-22-2019.
9. "The Impact of Tiny Watch" by Jennifer Zehnder in barrelhorsenews.com.
10. *WPRA News*, Feb. 2006, page 9, *Firewater Flit*.
11. *Barrel Horse News*, Aug. 2019, "Between the Reins With Hell on The Red," by Blanche Schaefer.
12. Phone conversation with Mary Cecelia Tharp, Celie Ray's daughter, 3-4-2019.
13. "Unforgettable" by Jolee Lautaret-Jordan, I Got Bugs, *Barrel Horse News*, Aug. 2018.
14. Conversation with John Farris, 9-18-2018.
15. Phone call to Nellie Miller, 9-9-19.
16. Phone call with Jimmie Gibbs Munroe.
17. *WPRA News*, May 2017.
18. Text to Sherry Cervi re: *Stingray*.
19. *Hoof and Horns*, March 1960, article "Jane Mayo, in an Exclusive Interview discussing *V's Sandy*.
20. Talk with Sherry Cervi.

Some of the Most Important Women in Barrel Racing
1. Conversation with Dude Barton.
2. Conversation with Dixie Reger Mosley re: Dude Barton, 4-2019.
3. *Ibid*.
4. Conversation with Kay Blandford, 5-1-2019.
5. *Hoofs and Horns*, March 1960.
6. Phone conversation with Ardith Bruce, 1-28-2019.
7. *WPRA News*, June 2017.
8. Canadian Pro Rodeo Hall of Fame.org – Dee Butterfield, 2015 Inductee.
9. Phone conversation with Sharon Camarillo, 4-30-2019.
10. Sherry Cervi Oral History, Rodeo Historical Society, Dickinson Research Center, National Cowboy & Western Heritage Museum.
11. Information via email from Ruth Quinn re: Jerri Duce.
12. Interview with John & Mildred Farris for Rodeo Historical Society, Dickinson Research Center, National Cowboy & Western Heritage Museum, 10-2010.
13. Information via email from Ruth Quinn re: Canadian barrel racing history.
14. Material from Tina Hodge, 4-5-2019.
15. *WPRA News*, May 2017.
16. www.westernhorseriding.org/Charmayne James - "Just How Good Was She?" Author and publisher – *Western Range Rider*.
17. Phone Conversation with Charlene Jespersen, 4-10-2019.
18. Telephone conversation with Sherry Combs Johnson, 3-17-2019.
19. Phone conversation with Martha Tompkins Wright, 5-21-2019.

20. Martha Josey information provided by family.
21. *Rodeo News*, June 1, 2016 "Hailey Kinsel."
22. *The Oklahoman*, 9-28-1986, "Annie the Okie, Never Forgotten" by Willard Porter.
23. "Unexpected Win, Lisa Lockhart", *WPRA News*, May 2019.
24. *Hoofs and Horns*, March-April 1973 ,"Oklahoma Barrel Racers."
25. "The Ludwig Twins", *Rodeo News*, 5-2019.
26. Phone conversation with Billie McBride, 2016.
27. Information provided by Ruth Quinn re: Canadian barrel racing, Feb, 2019 to include CGRA 60th Anniversary Program.
28. *Ibid.*
29. Phone conversation with Marlene McRae, 4-10-2019.
30. *Tulsa Tribune*, 6-29-1961 "Once Ailing Cowgirl Saddled With Success", by Joseph Carter.
31. *Ibid.*
32. Phone call to Nellie Miller, 9-9-19.
33. Information from Lydia Moore, former WPRA Secretary from 1973 to 1995, and daughter, Linda Clark.
34. Phone call to Jimmie Gibbs Munroe, 9-27-19.
35. *WPRA* magazine, July 2018, "Peterson and Bozo."
36. Email from Jim Bainbridge, PRCA Media, re: Gail Petska.
37. Phone interview with Molly Swanson Powell, 2-7-2019.
38. Email – Ruth Quinn, Carman Pozzobon, 4-7-2019.
39. *College Rodeo, From Show to Sport* by Sylvia Gann Mahoney, published 2004 by Texas A&M Press.
40. "The Secrets of Celie" by Amber Arnold, barrelhorseworld.com.
41. Information provided by Ruth Quinn re: Canadian Barrel Racing, Feb, 2019 to Include CGRA 60th Anniversary Program.
42. *Hoofs and Horns*, Nov. 1970 "A Talented Rodeo Family."
43. *Rodeo News*, March 2015, "On the Trail with Fallon Taylor."
44. 2015 WPRA Barrel Racing Records.
45. Canadian Pro Rodeo Hall of Fame, 10-23-2014.
46. Phone call to Brittany Pozzi Tonozzi, 8-27-2019, 2-24-2024 & WPRA web page.
47. Phone conversation with Carolynn Vietor, 5-2019.
48. Youree Ranch Barrel Horse Training – online.
49. WPRA News, July 15, 2019, re: Yourees.

Index

Symbols

50 Years of A Living Legend – Texas Cowboy Reunion and Old Timers Association 3
101 Wild West Show and Ranch 205
707 Vitamins 111

A

Abbeyville, Kan. 97
Abbeyville PRCA Frontier Days 97
Abilene, Kansas 24
Abilene, Texas 1, 10, 154
Acton, Mary 61
Adams, Alice 11
Adams, Loraine 36, 71
Adams, Pete 11
Adams, Vicki 78, 81, 180, 209, 227
Addington, Okla. 4, 59, 93, 150, 193
Aldergrove, B.C. 148, 208
All American Futurity 176
Allan, Cheyenne 121
Allen, Kappy 119, 122, 217, 236-238, 250
Allen, Paulette 71
Allen, Sissy 26, 257
Alley, Sterling 46
Alpine, Texas 193
Altizer, Blanche 13, 17, 20, 29, 35, 257
Alvord, Fred 11
Amarillo, Texas 15, 20, 29, 194
Amarillo Tri-State All Girl Rodeo 17
Ambrose, Cassie Ward 93, 151
American Airlines 112
American Legion 22
American Quarter Horse Association 3, 61, 82, 125, 137, 143, 171
Andersonville, Tenn. 154
Angelone, Martha 74
Angermiller, Merrill Adams 42
Ann Lewis Memorial Trophy 76
An Oakie With Cash 175
Apodaca, Tim 62
Appleton, Dave 112
AQHA Barrel Horse of the Year 123
Arcadia, Neb. 124
Arizona GRA 57
Arizona (state of) 10, 36-37, 43, 57, 103
Arkansas Barrel Racing Association 61
Arkansas River 130
Arkansas State Barrel Racing 50
Arlington, Texas 98, 127, 147, 159, 245
Armstrong, Jerry 25, 262
Armstrong, Sis 62, 66-67, 69, 70, 218-222
Arnold, Carl 66
AT&T Stadium 127
Australia 112, 189, 293
Autry, Gene 10, 13

B

Baby Doll 116
Back in the Saddle 29, 195, 263
Bailey, Delbert 50
Baird, Texas 3
Baja 178
Baldy 116
Bangart, Teri 154
Barnett, Britanny 54, 161-163, 246, 251
Barnett, Wynona 26
Bar O Dutchess 179
Barrel Futurities of America 103, 207, 215
Barrel Racing, Completely Revised, The A.R.T. of Barrel Racing, Applied Riding Techniques for Work, Play and Competition 90
Barron, Betty 29, 257
Barton, Dude 15, 17, 29, 257, 259, 271
Bastrop, Texas 26
Baton Rouge, La. 24, 44
Baucom, Codi 123, 239-240
Bay Canary 176-177, 198
Bay City, Texas 24
Baylor University 40
Beach, Rae 34
Beebe, Willa 51
Belle Fourche, S.D. 28
Belmont, Mont. 32
Belton, Texas 24, 25-26, 132, 133, 270
Benbenek, Gretchen 42
Besplug, Jill 189, 248
Bethany, Conn. 64
Bettis, Taci 54, 126, 147, 244, 248, 269
Bexar County Coliseum 31
Bierbers Oakie 175
Big Lake, Texas 17

Big Regards 143
Big Spring, Texas 10
Big Valley, B.C., Canada 54
Billy Bob's Texas 159-160
Billy 73, 79, 83
Binford, Nancy 15, 17, 31, 257, 258
Blackfoot, Ida. 172
Black Hills Stock Show & Rodeo 124
Black, Mary 26, 35
Blackstone, Faye 27, 262
Blackstone, Vic 27
Blandford, Kay 130-131, 186, 217, 227, 229, 23- 238, 259-260, 271
Blandford, Robert 186
Blazing With My Dude 167
Blue Bell (see Wrangler) 112
Blue Duck 132
Blue Mountain Community College 42, 256
Blue Whizz Bob 175, 206
Bluffton, Alb. 56
Bob 48, 97, 114, 130, 159, 160, 175-176, 202, 206, 231
Bonham, Texas 11
Borgal, Pearl 51
Bostian, Bonnie 78
Boston Garden 8
Bozeman, Mont. 41, 183
Bozo 106, 114, 137, 175-176, 179, 206, 252-253, 270
Brackenbury, Sammy Thurman 139, 259
Bragg, Nancy 26, 257
Brainard, Jack 76
Bray, Texas 17
Brenneman, Ev 104
Brewster, Wash. 61
Briggs, Bexeley 166
Briggs, Justin 96-97, 113, 166-167, 206
Brodoway, Lynette 56
Brooks, Alb. 56
Brown, Beulah 26
Brownfield, Texas 10, 26
Brown, Mickey 145, 270
Brown, Rose Garrett 34
Bruce, Ardith 47, 64, 70, 79, 102, 104, 111, 167, 188, 216, 220-223, 252, 259, 266, 268, 271
Bruner, Kelly 147, 245
Brunswick, Ga. 54
Bryan, Texas 129

Bryant, Phyllis 57, 219
Buffalo, S.D. 54-55, 147
Buff, Gaylene 189
Bugs Alive In 75 176
Bugsy 181-182
Bullet 116
Burger, Mary 123, 125, 217, 239-241, 244, 250-251, 253
Burk, Joyce Shelley 72
Burnet, Texas 24
Burton, Kathy 129
Burwell, Neb. 8, 22, 24, 26, 44, 191, 210
Busby, Andrea 167
Bush, Stanley 107
Bush, Wanda 37, 58-59, 62, 67-69, 100, 106, 118, 136-137, 144, 188, 205, 216, 218-221, 225, 250, 252
Butler, Ferrell 47, 70, 102, 191, 260
Butte Falls, Ore. 131
Butterfield, Dee 52, 271
Butterfield, Dee Watt 189
Bynum, James 131
Bynum, Terra 123, 239-240, 251

C

Cagliari, Wanda 201, 228-229, 248
Caldwell, Ida. 54-55, 154, 160, 163
Caldwell, Idaho 40, 147
Calgary, Alb. 51, 53-55, 164, 167, 171, 180, 189, 192-193, 199-200, 202-204, 207, 209, 211-212
Calgary Spring Horse Show 51, 193
Calgary Stampede 53-55, 167, 171, 180, 189, 192, 200, 202-203, 209
California Barrel Racing Association 57
California Open Barrel Racing Association 57
California (state of) 6, 10, 15, 38, 44, 57, 61, 63, 69, 98, 139, 187, 189, 196-198, 201, 211, 253
Camarillo, Leo 190
Camarillo, Reg 190
Camarillo, Sharon 88-89, 142-143, 189, 195, 228-229, 259, 267, 271
Campbell, Janette 17
Canadian Girls Rodeo Association 51, 264
Canadian Ladies Barrel Racers 52
Canadian National Finals Rodeo 51, 125

Canadian Professional Rodeo Association 52, 124, 148
Canadian, Texas 3, 10, 51-56, 103, 124-125, 148, 189, 192-194, 201-202, 208-209, 211, 264, 271-272
Carrollton, Texas 26
Cartwright, Carolyn 71
Casement, Julia 33
Casement, Sandra 33
Casey's Charm 176, 179
Casper, Wyo. 42
Cassidy, Joe 25
Cathey, James 22, 29, 33, 44, 263-264
Cebe Reed 176-177, 191, 198, 271
Century, Fla. 153, 156
Cervi Championship Rodeo 158
Cervi, Mike 95, 192
Cervi, Mike Jr. 192
Cervi, Sherry 76, 112-113, 115, 118, 120, 122, 125, 168, 174, 179, 185, 190, 217, 235-236, 237-239, 241-244, 250, 253, 259, 268, 271
Chamberlin, Margaret 36, 44
Champion, Megan 154
Championship Barrel Racing 61, 203
Chapman, Diana 220-221
Chapman Ranch, Texas 172
Cheyenne Frontier Days 8, 89, 99, 167
Chicago, Illinois 2
Chicks Keen O Pocopoo 162, 251
China 158
Choate, Bayleigh 167-169, 246, 248
Chocolate 146
Chongo 164
Clark, Gene 148
Clark, Mel 98, 267
Claude, Texas 17
Clayton 123
Clayton, N.M. 66, 194, 201, 214, 218
Clemons, Margaret 64, 222, 258
Clifton, Texas 71
Coca Cola Woman of the Year 100
Cody, Wyo. 171
Coffee, Leon 103
Colborn, Everett 9
Coleman, Texas 6, 25-26
Cole, Sam Fancher 57-58
Cole, Sammy 57
College National Finals Rodeo 150

College Rodeo, From Show to Sport 42, 263, 272
Colorado A&M 38, 255
Colorado Professional Rodeo Association 175
Colorado Springs, Colo. 25-26, 31-32, 65, 115, 136, 171, 176, 186, 187, 210, 263, 266,-268
Colorado State Fair 27
Colorado (state of) 6, 24-28, 31, 32, 38, 64-65, 76, 79, 114-115, 136, 171, 175-176, 179, 186-188, 203, 210, 255, 263, 266,-268, 293
Colorado State University 64, 255
Colorado State University Rodeo Association 64
Columbia River Circuit 119
Comanche, Okla. 181
Comanche (tribe) 1
Combs, Benny 62
Combs, Connie 28, 81, 216, 225-229
Combs, Sherry 60, 62, 67, 69-70, 111, 136, 171, 216, 218-223, 233, 252, 272
Combs, Willard 183
Come Apart 116
Connecticut (state of) 64
Conrado, Ivy 54-55, 113, 126, 147, 153, 155, 244-245
Coolidge, Texas 14
Cooper, Betty Rose 208
Cooper, Tuffy 208
Coors 107
Copperas Cove, Texas 201
Cordovan Corp. 61
Corey, Steve 119-120, 259, 269
Corpus Christi, Texas 26, 31
Corsicana, Texas 14
Costa, Marcos 126
Cotton, Blanche 192
Cotton, Mildren (Farris) 4, 182
Cotton, W.B. 192
Cottonwood, Calif. 54-55, 132, 153, 155, 165, 182, 217
Cotulla, Texas 54-55, 149, 153, 155, 160, 162, 165, 168, 172, 199, 217
Coughlin, Mary Lee 32
Covid 98, 147, 158, 160
Cowan, Lillian 13
Cowboy Channel 159
Cowboy Christmas Trade Show 159

Cowboy Country Museum 2, 260
Cowboys Protective Association 52
Cowboys Regional Rodeo Association 104
Cowboys' Turtle Association 9, 43
Cowden, Walter Fay 10
Cowey, Lucyle 34
Cowgirls Barrel Racing and Rodeo Association 51
Cowgirls Barrel Racing Association 51
Cowgirls of the Rodeo 48, 261-262, 264
Cow Palace 75
Cowtown Coliseum 159
Cowtown, N.J. 62-64
Cox, Fannie Mae 25-26, 58
Craig, Colo. 72
Crawford, Jackie 74, 161
Cremer, Leo 26-27
Crooked Nose 116
Crosby, Jo Ann 66, 69, 218-219
Cross 6 Ranch 186
Crossley, Callahan 53-55, 154, 256
Crossroads, N.M. 17
Crowell, Texas 10
Crow, Joe Jr. 66
Crowther, Margo 168-169, 246
Cummings, Barbara 36, 71
Curtis, Jean 107
Custer 177-178, 203, 271
Cutter 128
Cyclone 144
Cypress, Texas 61

D

Dalhart, Texas 54, 56
Dallas, Texas 36, 44, 66, 69, 180, 197-198, 210, 220-221
Dasher 146
Dash for Cash 83
Davidson, Bruce 111
Davis, Hilda 36
Davis, Kay 107, 229, 258
Day, Jeana 73, 75, 80, 216, 223-225
Days of '47 126
Days of 76, A Deadwood Tradition 28
Deadwood Rodeo Museum 28
Deadwood, S.D. 27
Dear, Barbara 61
Decker, Tater 13
Dee Gee 83, 137, 188
Denver, Colo. 33, 38, 108

Denver National Western Stock Show and Rodeo 60
Depression, The Great 6, 152
Descent 116
Devenport, Destin 154
Dinero 83, 122, 179, 184, 192
DM Sissy Hayday 149, 199, 251
Doc Bar 176, 213
Dodge 107
Doom, Becky Jo Smith 39
Dora, N.M. 143
Draper, Stanley 70-71, 205
Driggers, Howard 179
Driggers, Joannie 179
Dr. Nicks Cash 172
Dryden, Texas 35
Duce, Jerri 52, 192, 224, 226-227, 259
Dudley, Janet 60, 62, 66, 68, 218-220
Duncan, Okla. 65, 197, 200
Dunn, Matt 164
Dunn, Vendi 164
Durant, Okla. 186
Dusek, Betty 20
Dust Bowl 6
Dutch 179-180
Dutch Watch 179
Dutton, Bertie 71
Dyna 172

E

Eastern Barrel Racing Association 64
Eastern New Mexico University 42, 208, 213, 255
Easy Jet 83, 176
Edwards, Anna Belle 10
Edwards, Billie 62, 220
Edwards, Mary Nell 10
Eggleston, Edith 71
Elko, Nev. 37
Elliott, Justine 56
Ellis, Cecil 132, 134
Ellis Glass Company 134
Ellis, Tina 132, 133, 270
Ellis, Wanie 132, 134, 270
El Monte, Calif. 61
Emmett, Idaho 46
Ennis, Texas 56
Ensure Plus 135
Epperson, Dorothy 25
Escondido, Calif. 154

Eustace, Texas 154, 160, 163, 165, 168
Evans, Billie Ann 60, 67, 218-219
Evans, Dale 48
Evant, Texas 144
Evetts, Alma 196
Evetts, Hoke 57, 196

F

Fairground Arena 103
Fallon, Nev. 37
Fame Fire Rocks 171
Famous Ladies Man 167, 251
Farmingdale, N.J. 64
Farquhar, Nancy 69
Farris, John 78, 182, 193, 259, 266, 271
Farris, Mildred 37, 60, 62, 65-67, 69-70, 182, 191-192, 218-223, 258-259, 265, 271
Farr, Thena Mae 4, 15, 26, 31, 257-258
Federal, Wyo. 32
Feller, Tom 96
Fell, Harrison 28
Felts, Jeana Day 80, 216, 225
Ferguson, Sharon 103
Ferrell, Vicky Lynn 32
Fields, Judi 74
Fiery Miss West 150, 172
Finger, Hank 38
Firewater Flit 81, 271
First Down Dash 180
Fischer, Tammy 126, 147, 241-242, 245
Five Minutes to Midnight 116
Flit Bar 3, 82-83, 126, 162, 179-180, 183, 251
Flomot, Texas 186
Florida (state of) 27
Fluvanna, Texas 10
Flying V Rodeos 12
Forney, Joe 38
Fort Collins, Colo. 64
Fort Klamath, Ore. 42
Fort Smith, Ark. 22, 59, 99, 130, 142
Fort Stockton, Texas 25, 31
Fort Worth Convention Center 159
Fort Worth Livestock Show and Rodeo 7, 11, 49
Fort Worth Stockyards 159
Fort Worth, Texas 1, 7,-9, 11, 17, 22, 35-36, 39, 48-50, 111, 159, 170, 193, 206, 214, 217, 221, 259, 261

Franks, Jess 103, 143
Franks, Mary Jo Pope 142
Fredericksburg, Texas 135
Freeman, Roxy 57
French Flash Hawk 137, 175, 206
Fresno, Calif. 57
Frosty 132

G

Gallino, Kaylee 54
Gamblin, Billie 35
Ganter, Angela 56
Garbe's Inde 40
Gartner, Kacey 167
Gatesville, Texas 133
Gaylor, Allene 70, 91
Gee, Sgt. Nicole 165
Geigle, Jane 28
Gentry, Kathleen, D.V.M. 109
Gibbs, Rollie 95, 259
Gillette, Wyo. 165
Gills Bay Boy 83
Girls Rodeo Association 3-4, 17,-25, 27-37, 42-44, 46-48, 51, 57-65, 69, 71-72, 74-75, 78-80, 83, 92, 101, 103-107, 111, 117, 121, 123, 129-130, 139, 144, 150, 168, 170-171, 183, 186-189, 193, 197-199, 201, 203, 205-207, 210, 213-214, 216-218, 257-258, 262-265, 269
Globe Life Field 98, 159
Gobble, Ruby 34
Goodspeed, Dottye Kraus 58, 59
Goostree, Carol 77, 81, 216, 227-228, 248
Gottsch, Patrick 159
GRA (see Girls Rodeo Assn.) 3, 17-18, 20-25, 27-29, 31, 33-37, 42-44, 46-47, 57-65, 69, 71-72, 74, 78-80, 83, 92, 101, 104-107, 117, 121, 123, 129-130, 139, 144, 150, 168, 171, 183, 186-189, 193, 197-199, 201, 203, 205-207, 210, 213-214, 216-218, 257, 263-265, 269
Graves, Lance 104
Gray, Steve 116, 195
Green, Maggie 130
Greenough, Karen 75, 223-224
Gregory, Bern 59, 96, 99
Griffith, Snookie 13
Grimes, Kathy 154, 244

Guthrie, Okla. 145
Guyman, Okla. 181
Guy Weadick Award 53

H

Hack, Jodi 120
Halls, Brandie 123, 238-240
Hamm, Millie 58
Hanes, Fay 61
Hanna, Alta. 51
Haraga, Isabella 193
Hardin-Simmons Cowboy Band 3
Hardin-Simmons University 39
Harms, Mary Ann 32
Harper, Wanda (Bush) 25, 26, 30, 34-35, 43, 100, 188, 216, 218, 250, 252
Harris, Howard Sr 63
Harrison, Donna 36
Harris, Stoney 63
Hastings, Vern Jr. 28
Hatchell, Steve 117, 268
Havana, Cuba 28
Hawk 115, 137, 175, 192, 206
Hays, Judy 20
Heaton, Buddy 28
Helfrich, Devere 68
Helldorado Days 181
Helldorado Rodeo 95
Hell On The Red 181, 251
Hell's Angel 116
Henderson, Norita 62, 220-221
Hendrick, Opal 36
Hepper, Mollie McAuliffe 42
Hermiston, Ore. 54-55, 154
Herring, Earline 104
Herrmann, Shannon 42
Hewitt, Ingrid 51
Hickman, Tom 2
Hico, Texas 172
Hillcrest Hospital 133
Hillman, Stevi 147, 153-156, 160, 162-166, 168-169, 171-173, 244-247, 250
Hines, Alleen 26
Hinson, Donna Faye 25, 26
Hobbs, N.M. 13
Hobby Horse 41
Hodge, Tina Sikes 131, 194
Hofstetter, Brittany 123, 240
Holeman, June 124, 239, 250, 268-269
Hoofs and Horns 30, 40, 43-44, 60-61, 63-64, 72, 84, 97, 131, 210, 261-267, 270-272
Hope, Ark. 129, 200
Hopkins, 'Ma' 43
Hopper, L.C. 49
Horton, Fay Ann 66, 69, 171, 218-221, 252, 257
Hot Shot 74-75
Hot Springs, Mont. 61
Houston Health Department 158
Houston Livestock Show & Rodeo 61
Houston, Texas 14, 23, 29, 47, 61, 107, 116, 128, 134, 158, 167, 170, 182-184, 189, 197, 199-200, 204, 206, 255-256
Howard College 186
HR FamesKissNTell 169
Hubbard, Sue Ann 61, 265
Hubbell, Dan 122, 260
Hudson Bay, S.K. 56
Hudson, Colo. 54, 55, 147
Hugos Diamond 128
Huntsville, Texas 78
Hurley, Jimmie 40, 84, 87, 97, 267
Hurley, Libby 91
Hurst, Ivy 154
Hurst, Joleen (see Jolene Steiner) 74-75, 94, 223, 248, 266-267
Hybarger, wilma 201

I

Idaho (state of) 40, 46, 147, 179, 256
I Got Bugs 176, 181, 209, 271
Inglewood, Calif. 92
Inman, Hoss 28
Iowa Park, Texas 60

J

Jacksboro, Texas 17, 35
James, Charlie 184
James, Charmayne 95- 96, 101, 103, 115, 118, 123, 125, 136-138, 161, 175, 194, 202, 204, 216-217, 230-238, 248, 250, 252-253, 272
Jensen, Shirley 37
Jespersen, Charlene 57, 167, 219, 221, 259, 272
Jimbo 144

Jim Norick Arena 69
JLo 147, 165
John Deere 97
Johnson, Col. W.T. 5, 8-9, 13
Johnson, Janeen 103, 232
Johnson, Sherry Combs 70, 111, 136, 171, 197, 216, 233, 252, 272
Johnson, Sherrylynn 123, 240-241
Johnson, Sherry Price 138
Johnson, Wenda 160-161, 163-166, 168-169, 172-173, 246-247
Joliet, Mont. 154
Jones, Bob 97
Jones, Ethel 104
Jones, Paige 161, 171-173, 247, 248
Jones, Phyllis 104
Jordan, Dottie 103
Jordan, Jolee 83
Josey, Martha 64, 91, 164, 177, 191, 195, 198, 216, 222-223, 227-229, 231-233, 236, 250, 252, 259, 271-272
Josey, R.E. 64, 91
Junction, Texas 24
Junior National Finals 159
Justin Best Footing Awards 96
Justin Boots 96

K

Kabul, Afghanistan 165
Kalland, B. 46, 264
Kamloops, BC 56
Kansas (state of) 6, 194, 198, 264, 267
Karnack, Texas 91, 164
Kernick, Joyce 118
Kerrville, Texas 24
Kesler, Liz 103, 259, 263
Kesler, Reg 41, 103
Kilgore, Anita 73, 223
Killeen, Texas 25, 43
Kimzey, Sage 126, 149
King 131
Kingsbery, Evelyn Bruce 38
Kinsel, Dan 149, 178
Kinsel, Hailey 54-56, 126, 147-149, 153-156, 160, 162-163, 165-166, 168-169, 172-173, 178-179, 199, 204, 217, 244-247, 250-251, 256, 265, 270, 272
Kinsel, Leslie 149, 178
Kirkpatrick, Dena 91, 209

Kirkwood, Fay 11, 261-262
Klamath Falls, Ore. 58
Knoefel, Louise 97, 259, 267
Knox, Jo Gregory 39
Knox, Kathlyn Younger 39, 255
Kosel, Summer 172-173, 247, 251
Kraus, Benny 58
Kraus, Dottye 58
Kraus, Norita 58, 218-219
Krieg, Vaughn 11, 12
Krum, Texas 160, 163
Kruse, Cassidy 161, 243

L

Lacey, Sadie 71
Lacy, NaDell 36
Ladies of Rodeo Luncheon 160
Lady Kaweah Cash 175
Lageschaar, Lisa 138
Lake Charles, La. 24, 39
Lamar, Colo. 28, 153, 155
Lamar, Neb. 32
Lamb, Betty 43
Lamb, Ted 22, 43, 257
Lamesa, Texas 182
Lancombe, AB 56
Las Vegas Events 159, 165
Las Vegas, Nev. 57, 69, 95, 98, 108, 117-119, 125, 147-148, 153, 156, 159, 164-165, 173, 179, 181, 187, 197, 204-205, 208, 230-247, 256
Lazy E Arena 145
LeCompte, Mary Lou 48, 261-262, 264
Legacy 90
Lemon Drop 164
Lena's Bar 83
Leo 83
LeRoy 161
Lewis, Ann 76, 129, 199, 216, 222, 248, 250, 253
Lewis, Bob 130
Lewis, Jan 130
Lewis, Mrs. 129
Lewis, Randy 130
Lewis, Yvonne 26
Ligon, Peggy 36
Linderman, Bill 36, 187
Lindley, Buster 38
Little Joe (ital) 29, 31
Little Rock, Ark. 62, 129, 200, 210

Llano, Texas, 26, 172
Lockhart, Lisa 53- 55, 123, 127, 147, 153-155, 160, 163, 165-169, 172-175, 200, 211, 240-247, 250, 253, 265, 269, 270, 272
Lohn, Texas 59
London, England 2
Long, Missy 65, 200, 216, 223
Long, Peggy 9
Longview, Alb., Canada 54
Lord, Shali 153, 155-156, 239, 245
Los Lunas, N.M. 154
Lotta Dollar 57, 197
Louie 128, 175, 200
Lovington, N.M. 13
Lubbock, Texas 1, 58, 293
Lucas, Tad 11, 17, 25, 48, 190, 199, 206, 257
Lucky 182
Lufkin, Texas 172
Lutich, Jewell 29
Lyons, Tommy 111

M

Mabton, Wash. 121
Mack, Patty 70
Madison Square Garden 7-10, 12, 48, 112, 261
Madison Square Garden Rodeo 9-10, 261
Magnolia Missile 99
Mahoney, Sylvia 40, 42, 259, 263
Manning, Taylor 56
Manual, Loretta 62, 70, 73, 216, 220-224, 266
Marana, Ariz. 125
Marburger, Faye 10, 29
Markham Ranch 49
Marr, Patt 69, 219, 221, 253
Marshall, Judy 57, 70, 219, 221-222
Mason, Texas 43, 59, 188
Massey, Janae Ward 93
Matador, Texas 15, 186
Matale, Lee 130
Mattern, Gail 165
Matthews, Taycie 171-173, 247, 256
Mattson, Jon 28, 259, 262
Mayberry, Dean 51
Mayo, Jane 27, 60-61, 63, 66-67, 69, 84, 118, 144, 161, 185, 189, 203, 216, 218-219, 250, 253, 267, 271
Mays, Brenda 123, 240-242

McAlester, Okla. 13, 44, 104
McBride, Billie 6, 36, 62, 66, 118, 137, 161, 204, 216, 218, 250, 252, 258-259, 269, 272
McCall, Kalli 172, 248
McClain, Pat 26
McDade, Texas 54, 154, 160, 162
McDougall, Gina 52, 202
McDougall, Ruth 52, 202
McEntire, Alice 142
McEntire, Clark 66
McEntire, Jackie 141
McEntire, John 141
McEntire, Pake 141
McEntire, Reba 141-142
McEntire, Susie 141
McFarland, Roxy 70, 222
McGilvray, Amy 22, 26, 216
McGilvray, Jeanelle 22
McHood, NaRay 36
McJunkin, Gene 49, 71, 264
McKenzie, Lynn 77, 81, 99, 216, 227-229, 250, 253
McNeese State University 39, 255
McNulty, Karin 87
McRae, Marlene 180, 202, 237, 259, 272
McEntire, Clark 141
McSpadden, Barbara Jo 14
McSpadden, Clem 71, 81, 141
Medford. Ore. 131
Medical Lake, Wash. 154
Mel Clark, Inc. 98
Merrick, Lana 162, 231-232, 248, 251
Merritt, Ramona 32
Messerly, Judy 57
Midland, Texas 10, 14, 186
Midnight 116
Millarville, Alb. 56
Miller, Debby 57
Miller, Elizabeth 10
Miller, Emily 54-55, 153-155, 160, 162-166, 245-246
Miller, Isabella 51-52, 193
Miller, Nellie 54-55, 132, 147, 153-156, 165-166, 182, 204, 217, 244-246, 250, 270-272
Milo 81, 180-181, 209
Minco, Okla. 153, 155, 160, 163, 165
Minnick, Peggy 10
Mission Ranch LLC 172

Missoula, Mont. 61, 103
Missouri (state of) 58-59, 71, 188, 194, 205
Miss Rodeo America 40, 53, 73, 138, 212
Miss Rodeo Texas 40, 199, 212
Misty Dawn 193
Mitchell, Manuelita 59, 67, 218, 257
Mohawk 172
Mo 126, 198, 205
Molly's Honor 121
Montana, Monte 103
Montana (state of) 26, 42, 61, 103, 200, 207, 213, 253, 255-256
Montana State University 42, 256
Montgomery, Janice 57
Montgomery, Margaret 13, 17, 24-26, 29-30, 48, 257
Montgomery, Robert 28
Moody, Jill 123, 240-242
Moore, Amberleigh 54-55, 126, 147, 153, 155, 244-245, 250
Moore, Diane 131
Moore, Lacinda 153
Moore, Lydia 58-59, 71, 78, 205, 259, 265-267, 272
Moore, Percy 58
Moore, Percyna 58, 205
Morgan, Shelley 154, 160, 163, 165-166, 168, 169, 241, 245-246
Moroni, Utah 145
Morris, Man. 52
Mullins, Donna 62, 220
Munns, Randy 103
Munroe, Jimmie Gibbs 73, 78-82, 101, 105, 108-109, 111, 118, 139, 176, 189, 195, 205, 216, 229-231, 255, 258-259, 261, 266-269, 271-272
Myllymaki, Rachael 178, 232-234, 236, 250
Myriad Convention Center 69

N

Nanton, Alb. 124
Natchez, Miss. 31
National American University 150, 256
National Anthem 141
National Barrel Horse Association 143, 197
National Barrel Racing Clinic 63
National Circuit Finals 128, 137, 200, 207, 212, 253
National Cowgirl Hall of Fame 40, 186, 189, 190, 193, 196, 199, 202-203, 206, 209, 215
National Finals Rodeo 23
National Finals Rodeo Commission 108
National Intercollegiate Rodeo Association 38, 40, 43, 206
National Little Britches Rodeo Association 145
National Reined Cow Horse Association 179
Natonal Cowboy & Western Heritage Museum 68
Nebraska Cowgirls Association 124
Nebraska (state of) 22, 27, 124, 262
Nelson, Erica 153, 155-156, 245
Nesbitt, tom 103
Nettleton, Ruth 104
Neugebauer, Gerry 103
New Jersey (state of) 63-64, 76, 130
New Mexico A&M 39, 255
New Mexico (state of) 6, 10, 15, 24, 36, 39, 40, 42, 67, 143, 184, 208, 213, 255, 256
New York City, N.Y. 2, 8, 10, 112
New York (state of) 2, 8, 10, 48, 64, 112, 210, 264
NIRA Alumni Association 40
NIRA (see National Intercollegiate Rodeo Assn.) 38, 39-42, 139, 172, 201, 204, 206, 208, 212-213, 263
Norman, Okla. 76, 207
North Fort Myers, Fla. 168
Nowata, Okla 147, 153
Nowlin, Tracy 147, 245

O

Ocala, Fla. 154
Odessa Junior Chamber of Commerce 129
Odessa, Texas 129
Oelrichs, S.D. 54-55, 153, 155, 160, 163, 165, 172
Ogden Pioneer Days 126
Oglesby, Faye 4, 36
Oglesby, Hay 36
Ohio Girls Barrel Racing Association 61
Okemah, Okla. 27, 63, 203
Oklahoma City Chamber of Commerce

70, 103
Oklahoma City, Okla. 31, 52, 69- 71, 75, 103, 107, 139, 193, 197, 205-207, 214-215, 222-230
Oklahoma Star Jr. 83
Oklahoma (state of) 6, 12-13, 24, 31-32, 36, 42, 52, 69-71, 73, 75, 83, 103, 107, 139, 150, 185-186, 193, 197-198, 202, 205-208, 214-215, 222-230, 255, 256, 265, 270-272
Oklahoma State University 42, 150, 186, 208, 255-256
Olafson, Bertina 56
Old Fort Days 92, 130, 180
Old Fort Days Futurity 92, 130
Old Spec 116
Olson, Susan 103
Olympia, Wash. 154
Omni Hotel 159
Ontario (province of) 64
O'Quinn, Sabra 154
Oregon Barrel Racing Association 58
Oregon (state of) 10, 40, 58, 132, 255, 269
O'Reilly, Jenna 56
Otto, Molly 165-166, 246, 251
Overland Trail Rodeo 28
Owens, Margaret 13, 17, 20, 34, 48, 216, 257-258
Owens, Sug 17, 257
Ozona, Texas 17

P

Paris, Texas 12
Parker, Ariz. 177
Patterson, Donna 75, 216, 223
Pauls Valley, Okla. 123
PC Frenchmans Hayday 83, 178-179, 184
Peanuts 116
Pearson, Katherine 17, 257
Pearson, Mrs. Sid 17
Pecos Pete 144
Pecos, Texas 129
Pedone, Ryann 160-161, 163, 246
Pendleton, Ore. 5-6, 119-121, 167, 171, 259, 269
Pendleton Round-Up 5, 119-121, 167, 171, 269
Performance Horsemanship Program 88
Perrin, Jackie Jo 81, 216, 226-228, 248, 250

Perryton, Texas 60
Peterson, Kristie 106, 114, 137, 161, 166, 175, 179, 206, 217, 234-237, 250, 253
Petska, Cory 179, 192
Petska, Gail 73, 76, 207, 216, 224-227, 250, 266, 272
Petska, Paul 207
Phoenix, Ariz 103
Phoenix Jaycees 80, 266
Pierce, Lewis 107
Pikes Peak or Bust Rodeo 25, 26, 262
Pikes Peak or Bust Rodeo: The First Fifty Years 26
Pilesgrove, N.J. 62
Pluemer, Leia 154
Poco Excuse 80
Poker Chip 116
Poppino, Tana 123, 239, 240, 241
Pop Rocks 171
Porter, Willard 60, 63, 272
Potter, Mel 76, 179, 266
Potter Ranch 104, 179, 184
Potter, Wendy 76, 104, 112, 190, 223-224
Powder Puffs & Spurs 22, 24
Power 90
Powers, Mrs. Ted 22, 257
Pozzobon, Carman 54, 148, 208, 244, 272
Prairie Circuit 97, 124
PRCA (see Professional Rodeo Cowboys assn.) 9, 51, 54, 80-81, 97, 103-109, 112, 117-118, 120, 123-125, 136, 138, 142, 148, 156-157, 159, 171, 179-180-181, 186, 190, 193, 200, 228, 240, 259, 266, 269-270, 272
Prescott Frontier Days 37, 263, 265
Price, Combs-Johnson 4, 138, 197
Price, Florence (Youree) 4, 59, 183, 214
Prime Diamond 128
Prime Talent 128
Probst, June 22, 26, 30, 257
PROCOM 81, 157
Professional Bull Riders (PBR) 54
Professional Women's Barrel Race 123, 240

ProRodeo Hall of Fame 3, 115-116, 136-139, 159, 164, 167, 170-171, 184, 187, 189, 193, 195-196, 198, 202, 206, 211, 252, 259, 262, 270

ProRodeo Hall of Fame & Museum of the American Cowboy 116, 259
Pruett, Gene 63
Prunty Brothers Diamond A Rodeo Company 37
Pueblo, Colo. 27, 65
Purina 107

Q

Quarter Horse 3, 57, 61, 65, 82, 125, 137, 143-144, 171, 176, 198, 201, 203, 265, 269, 271
Quarter Horse Journal 61, 203, 265, 269
Quinn, Ruth 56, 259, 264-265, 269, 271, 272

R

Ram National Circuit Finals 128, 200, 253
Ram Top Gun Award 161
Rankin, Charlie 38
Rapid City, S.D. 28, 124, 150
Rare Fred 123
Rasco, Leta 104
Ratliff, Betty Gail Cooper 208
Ray, Betty 67, 218
Ray, Celie Whitcomb 91, 176, 180-181, 261
RCA (see Rodeo Cowboys Assn.) 3, 20, 22-23, 25, 27-28, 31, 36, 43, 44, 46-47, 58-61, 66, 144, 187, 201, 205
Reba's Smokey Joe 132
Red Deer, Alb. 56
Reddy 181
Red 47, 56, 62, 116, 136-138, 141, 171, 181, 183-184, 188, 198, 204, 251-252, 270-271
Red Rock 116
Reed 130
Reeves, Sharron 71
Reger, Dixie 17, 25, 195, 257, 259, 271
Reg Kesler Rodeo 41
Reichert, Maegan 123, 240
Reiners, Dennis 103
Reliant Stadium 158
Renger, Deb 123, 239-240
Reno, Nev. 57, 108, 126
Resistol 148, 172, 269
Reynolds, Benny 103

Reynolds, C.B. 177, 198
Reynolds, Karen 58
RFD-TV 126-127, 159
Rhode Island (state of) 64
Rice University 40
Richards, Texas 54-55
Riley, Ilyssa 172-173, 247
Ripp 148, 208
Rippiteau, Jerry 32
Robin Flit Bar 183
Robinson, Jade 120
Robinson, Rayel 52, 233-234
Rocket Bar 83
Rodeo Association of America 43
Rodeo Cowboys Association 3, 9, 20, 22-23, 25, 27-28, 31, 36, 43-44, 46-47, 58-61, 66, 105, 117, 123, 144, 170, 187, 201, 205, 265-270
RodeoHouston 158
Rodeo Man of the Year 159
Rodeo News 40, 47, 88, 145, 267-270, 272
Rodeo Ranch Girls 10
Rodeo Sports News Annual 46, 264
Rodewald, Nancy 72
Rogers, Roy 29, 48
Rollo 165, 167, 170
Rosemary, Alb. 103
Rossen, Ronnie 103
Rosser, Cindy 107, 167, 252
Round Top, Texas 54
Routier, Jessica 54-55, 147, 149, 153-155, 160, 163, 165-166, 168-169, 172-173, 200, 244-247, 270
Routier, Payton 150
Routier, Riley 150
Rowell, Harry 43
Rowell Rodeo 44
Ruizicka, Stacey 56
Rule, Dona 153
Running to Win, How to Win at Barrel Racing Both Inside and Out 91
Run to Win with Me in Barrel Racing 91

S

Sadiesfamouslastwords 126
Sagers, Kendra 146
Salem County Fair 63
Salem, Ore. 54-55, 147, 153, 155
Salinas, Calif. 25, 108, 180, 197
Salt Lake City, Utah 126

San Angelo Roping Fiesta 36, 37
San Angelo Stock Show and Rodeo 36
San Angelo, Texas 17, 144, 171, 201, 257
San Angelus Hotel 17
San Antonio All-Girl Rodeo 31, 35
San Antonio Police Welfare Fund 31
San Antonio Stock Show & Rodeo 107
San Antonio, Texas 7, 31-32, 35, 58, 107, 130, 207, 212, 263, 270
Sanders, Peggy 36
San Francisco, Calif. 75
San Luis Obispo, Calif. 190
San Saba, Texas 24, 144
Santa Fe, N.M. 142
Santa Maria, Calif. 69, 197
Sargent, Betty 36
Savona, B.C., Canada 54
Sawtelle Government Hospital 15
Sawyer, Fern 10, 15, 17, 257
Scamper 83, 95-96, 101, 103, 115-116, 123, 137, 175, 184, 196, 204, 252
Schuster, Tiany 160, 163, 171, 244-245
Scoti Flit Bar Star Rising Award 126
Scottsdale, Ariz. 68
Seale, Miss Curley 3
Searle, Stan 27, 77
Sears, Lindsay 53, 123-124, 189, 217, 239-242, 250
Seligman, Ariz. 37, 57
Selman, Vickie 28
Sewalt, LaTonne 22, 25, 29-30, 35, 118, 195, 216, 218, 250, 263
Sewalt, Royce 29, 31, 210
Seymour, Texas 31
Shadwick, Bill 131
Shanahan, Gail 130
Shanahan, Teza 130
Sharp, Jean Libby 57, 219
Sharp, Jennifer 54-56, 153-156, 245
Shaw, Jack 120-121, 259, 269
Sheffield, Texas 13
Sheppard, Chuck 66
Shreveport, La. 78, 198-199
Sidney, Iowa 22, 24, 44, 262
Sikes, Joe 131
Simms, Mont. 61
Simon, Della 33
Simon, Frances 33
Sister 126, 132, 149, 161-162, 165, 169, 178-179, 182-183, 199, 204-205

Skitook, Okla. 168
Skocdopole, Dianne 54
Slash J Harletta 176, 180, 209
Smalygo, Leslie 168-169, 246
Smith, Barbara 14, 71, 259, 261, 263
Smith, Blanche Altizer 20, 257
Smith, Dale 66
Smith, Dude 23, 63
Smith, Frances 14, 63, 64, 70, 222-223, 261-262
Smith, Jimmie 54, 154, 160-163, 245, 248
Smith, Sue 172-173, 241-242, 247
Smith, Velda 36
Snow, Dorothy 62, 221
Snow, John 76
Snyder, Amberley 90, 146, 267
Snyder, Texas 154, 160, 162
Soden, Victoria 64
Solmonsen, Vickie 123, 251
Solt, Betty Sims 39, 40, 255, 263
Son Frost 176
Sonny Bit O'Both 164
Southeastern Oklahoma State University 186, 208
Southwest Exposition and Livestock Show 49
Southwest Texas Junior College 42
Sparky 124
Spearfish, S.D. 28
Spence, Dub 25
Spielman, Shelby 54, 56
Spratt, Pat 103
Springer, Kenneth 73, 77, 79, 95, 99-100, 106, 115, 118, 127, 142, 149, 154, 162, 177, 181, 260
Springer, Okla. 154
Stamford, Texas 1-5, 14, 16, 50, 152, 174
Standard, Wilma 15, 261
Star Plaudit 83, 136, 137, 183, 252
State Fair of Texas 180
Steagall, Red 141
Steal Money 164
Steamboat 116
Steeper, Jean 26
Steiner, Beverly 78

Steiner, Joleen Hurst 67, 74, 94, 191, 248, 259, 266-267
Steiner Rodeo Company 78
Steiner, Tommy 59, 78

Stephen F. Austin State College 78
Stephenville, Texas 41, 153, 156, 160-161, 163, 165, 208
Sterling, Colo. 8, 28, 181, 209
Sterling, Ohio 61
Stetson 148
Stewart, Lila Mae 61, 224-225
St. Louis Fireman's Rodeo 59
St. Louis, Mo. 58-59, 205
Stockdale, Texas 130
Stokes, John 144
Stokes, Lynn Kirby 144
Stover, Janet 121-122, 217, 230-231, 233, 236-237, 239, 250
Stressman, Karl 138
Strobele, Rosanne 119
Stryker, John A. 27
Sturgis, S.D. 28, 61
Sugar Bars 83
Sulphur, Okla. 129, 199
Sul Ross College 39
Sul Ross Rodeo Association 38
Sul Ross State Teachers College 38
Sunset, Texas 160, 163
Sutherland Springs, Texas 186
Symons, Martha Ann 67, 218

T

Tags of Honor 165
Tallman, Bob 160
Tarleton State University 41, 213, 255-256
Taylor, Berva Dawn 59
Taylor, Carly 154, 248
Taylor, Fallon 125, 210, 217, 235-236, 242-243, 250, 269, 272
Taylor, Sally 34, 257
Teague, Texas 14
Telford, Jessica 147, 154, 156, 245
Telford, Jessie 54-55, 160, 163, 246
Texas A&M University 38, 199, 212, 255-256
Texas Barrel Racing Association 36-37, 58
Texas Circuit 107
Texas Cowboy Reunion 1-3, 261
Texas Cowboy Reunion Old-Timers Association 1
Texas Rangers (baseball) 159
Texas Rodeo Cowboy Hall of Fame 187, 189, 193, 194, 198, 202
Texas (state of) 1-3, 5-7, 9-18, 20, 24,-27, 29, 31, 33, 35-43, 54-56, 58-61, 66, 71, 78, 82, 91, 98, 100, 106-107, 129-133, 144, 147, 149, 152, 159-161, 164, 171-172, 174, 180, 182-183, 186-189, 192-194, 198-199, 201-202, 205, 208, 210-213, 220, 221, 245, 253, 255-257, 261, 263-264, 270, 272, 293
Tharp, Mary Cecelia 114, 181, 259, 264, 268, 271
Thate, Edna 32
The American 126
The Ketch Pen 107, 267, 268
This Month in San Antonio the Official Hotel Greeters Guide 31
Thomas & Mack Center 98, 119, 148, 159, 160
Thomas, Viola 52, 211
Thompson, Claire 11
Thompson, Jackie 71
Three Bars 83, 143, 179
Thunder Stones 149
Thurman, Doug 130
Thurman, Karen 130
Thurman, Sammy 61, 63, 68-70, 84, 87, 97, 139, 219-223, 252-253, 259, 267
Thurman, Sissy 37, 62, 66, 69-70, 76, 129, 200, 218-222, 253
Thurman, Vanessa 130
Tibbs, Casey 15
Tina Junior 133
Tinkleman, Murray 77
Tiny Circus 176, 179
Tiny Watch 175, 176, 179, 180, 271
Tipperary 116
Tito 167
Titus, Bonnie 27
Toalson, Dixie 26
Tommy Star 40
Tompkins, Harry 41, 213
Tompkins, Martha 41, 76, 213, 223-224, 248, 255, 260, 263, 272
Tompkins, Rosemary Colborn 41

Tonozzi, Brittany Pozzi 54, 147, 153, 155-156, 160, 162-163, 165-174, 185, 244-246, 250, 272
Tony Lama 111

Tornado 116
Townsend, Dr. Charles "Bud" 12, 14, 259
Triangle Bell Ranch 25
Triple Chicks 143
Tripp, Dawn 71
Tri-State All-Girl Rodeo 15, 20
Troubles 115
Tucker, Boots 58, 219-220
Tulare, Calif. 57
Tulsa, Okla. 29-31, 185
Turnage, Phyllis 37, 57, 69
Turquoise Circuit 107
Tycoon 170
Tyler, Rebecca 82-83, 183
Tyler, Texas 132

U

Ukiah, Calif. 154
Underdown, Gloria 57
United States 7, 36, 43, 51-54, 158, 164, 170
University of Las Vegas 95
University of Nevada, Las Vegas 98, 159
Utah Barrel Racing Association 107
Utah (state of) 90, 107, 126, 145, 171, 255
Uvalde, Texas 82, 183

V

Valley Mount Ranch 58, 205
Van Allen, Betty 57
Vancouver Island 52
Van Cronkhite, John 66
Victoria, Texas 54, 211
Vietor, Carolynn 112, 119, 211-212, 258-259, 268, 272
Volz Fisher, Martha 58
Volz Packing Company 58
V's Sandy 83-84, 185, 203, 267, 271

W

Waco, Texas 129, 205
Waguespack, Sarah Rose 54
Walker, Byron 105
Walker, Mary 56, 113, 168, 217, 242-244, 250
Walker, Yvonne 36
Walling, Jo 71
Waltrip, Robin 109
Ward, James 93

Ward, Janae 42, 93, 121-122, 150, 215, 217, 237-238, 256
Ward, Renee 93
Ward, Rita Jo 14
Warner, Julie 42
Washington, D.C. 92
Washington (state of) 92, 108, 211, 215
Wasta, S.D. 54
Watt, Billy Bob 48
Watt, Elaine 52
Watts, Jim 38
Wayne, Okla. 161, 172, 205
Weast, Kylie 93, 147, 150, 181, 215, 245, 251
Weatherford, Okla. 54-55
Weatherford, Texas 147
Webbers Falls, Okla. 130
Weeg, Frances 33
Welsh, Amanda 164-165, 166, 246
Welsh, Jill 177, 271
Westergren, Gary 150, 172
Westergren Quarter Horses 150
Western Horseman 25, 44, 75, 87, 90, 262, 264, 266-267
West, Mary Nana 107
West Monroe, La. 31
West of the Pecos Rodeo 13-14, 17, 261, 263
West Plains, Colo. 33
West, Texas 131
West Texas Barrel Racing Association 58
Wheaton, Dixie 145
Wheaton, Lee 145
Whitaker, Kay 70, 222
Whitcomb, Celie 76, 91-92, 114, 176, 180-181, 209, 223, 230-232, 261
Whitcomb-Ray, Celie 114, 209, 231-232
White, Dennis J. 109
Whiteside, Kylie 54
White, Tana 69, 219
White, Vivian 11
Whitfield, Fred 118
Whyte, Maury 76
Wichita Falls, Texas 12
Wickenburg, Ariz. 57, 213
Wildorado, Texas 17
Willard, Mo. 153, 156
Williams, Alice 40
Williams, Beth 40
Williams, Sue 14

Wills, Brooke 56
Wills, Nelda 14
Wilson, Jill 154, 160-163, 245
Wilson, Monica 52-53
Wimberley, Cheyenne 153, 155-156, 160, 163-166, 236, 245-246
Winn, Sissy 168-169, 172-173, 246, 247
Wintermute, Doreen 157, 258, 260
Winter Olympic Games 164, 192
Womack, Andy 103
Women's Professional Rodeo Assn. (WPRA) 3, 28, 52, 54, 58-59, 71, 80-81, 83, 93, 96-97, 102-104, 106-110, 112-114, 117-120, 122,-126, 128, 132, 137, 139, 147, 149-150, 156-157, 163-165, 167, 170-171, 175-180, 182, 186-187, 190, 193, 201, 203-204, 206-208, 211-213, 215-217, 249-250, 253-254, 261-262, 264-272
Women's Professional Rodeo Association News 83, 110, 262, 264-272
Woodstown, N.J. 62
Woodward, Okla. 17, 24, 80
World Championship Rodeo 5, 7, 9, 13
World of Rodeo Luncheon 160
World's Championship All-Girl Rodeo 29
World War I 63
World War II 3, 11, 12, 43
Worthington, Jackie 17, 20, 26, 29, 34, 35, 36, 257-258
WPRA Barrel Racing Rookie of the Year 126
WPRA Media Guide 122
WPRA News 83, 110, 262, 264-272
WPRA Star Celebration Luncheon 97
Wrangler 3, 109, 111-112, 114, 117-119, 122-124, 126-127, 139, 145, 147-153, 155-157, 159-161, 164, 167-170, 172,-174, 193, 200, 209, 253-254, 265-266, 268-270
Wrangler Bonus Program 109
Wrangler National Finals Rodeo 3, 112, 117, 119, 122, 124, 126, 147-149, 151-153, 155, 157, 160-161, 168-170, 172-174, 193, 200, 270
Wright, Ed 213
Wright, Martha Tompkins 213, 260, 272
Wright, Mikal 120
Wyoming Girls Barrel Racing Association 58

Y

Year Tibbie 126
Yellowhead County, Alb. 56
Yokley, Sydna 9, 10
Young, D'Ann 44
Young, Mrs. I.W. 22
Youree, Dale 92, 139, 150, 183, 215
Youree, Florence 42, 59, 67, 69-70, 92, 103, 121, 138-139, 145, 150, 171, 183, 213-214, 218-222, 252, 258-259, 266-267, 270
Youren, Jan 46, 260, 263

Z

Zia Barrel Racing Association 143
Zombie 137, 201, 202, 204

Author Bio

Gail Woerner was born and raised on a ranch in northeastern Colorado and worked with cattle and broke horses with her grandfather. She has written several books on the history of rodeo, a children's book on rodeo and numerous articles in various western-related magazines and periodicals including magazines in France, Canada and Australia. She also reviews other writer's books several times a year, and continually answers questions about rodeo from e-mail queries from around the globe.

Gail is the Chairman of the Rodeo Clown Reunion which is held at various rodeos across the nation and generally has forty retired laugh-getters, bullfighters and barrelmen attend. They don their familiar make-up and costumes and sign autographs and entertain the fans. She also writes a newsletter to numerous retired rodeo clowns and their widows monthly.

She received the Academy of Western Artists Will Rogers Medallion Award for Western Nonfiction for her book entitled, "Rope to Win, The History of Steer, Calf and Team Roping" in 2008. She received the American Cowboy Culture Award for Western Writing at the National Cowboy Symposium held in Lubbock, TX, in 2009. Gail lives in Austin, Texas, with her husband, Cliff.

More Books
By Gail Woerner

A Belly Full of Bedsprings: The History of Bronc Riding
ISBN 9781571682093 • Paperback • 260 pages • 6x9 • Retail $19.99
ISBN 9781571682536 • Hardback • 260 pages • 6x9 • Retail $29.99

The Cowboys' Turtle Association: The Birth of Professional Rodeo
ISBN 9780981490366 • Paperback • 358 pages • 6x9 • Retail Price $26.99

Cowboy Up! The History of Bull Riding
ISBN 9781571685315 • Paperback • 322 pages • 6x9 • Retail $26.99

Fearless Funnymen: The History of the Rodeo Clown
ISBN 9781571682826 • Paperback • 240 pages • 6x9 • Retail $19.99

Rope to Win: The History of Steer, Calf, and Team Roping
ISBN 9780978915025 • Paperback • 294 pages • 6x9 • Retail $24.99

Western Women Who Dared to Be Different
ISBN 9781940130347 • Paperback • 262 pages • 6x9 • Retail $19.99

For the Little Buckaroos
Charley & Amanda
Meet Rusty the Rodeo Clown
ISBN 9781681792224 • Paperback • 34 pages • 8.5x11
Retail $12.99

Eakin Press
P.O. Box 331779 • Fort Worth, Texas 76163 • 817-344-7036
www.EakinPress.com

www.ingramcontent.com/pod-product-compliance
Lightning Source LLC
Chambersburg PA
CBHW031423150426
43191CB00006B/367